Investing in

Stocks & Shares

Investing in
Stocks &
Shares

*A step-by-step guide to making
money on the stock market*

6th edition

Dr John White

howtobooks

Dedication

For my father, Donald White, who (among many other kindnesses too numerous to mention) bravely introduced me to trading in shares through his own stockbroker and also taught me about investment trusts.

Published by How To Books Ltd,
Spring Hill House, Spring Hill Road,
Begbroke, Oxford OX5 1RX. United Kingdom.
Tel: (01865) 375794. Fax: (01865) 379162.
email: info@howtobooks.co.uk
www.howtobooks.co.uk

Fifth edition 2000
Reprinted 2000
Reprinted 2001
Sixth edition 2003
Reprinted 2004 (twice)
Reprinted with amendments 2006 (twice)

British Library Cataloguing in Publication Data
A catalogue record for this book is available from the British Library

ISBN 10: 1-85703-847-9
ISBN 13: 978-1-85703-847-7

Produced for How To Books by Deer Park Productions, Tavistock
Typeset by PDQ Typesetting, Newcastle-under-Lyme, Staffs
Cover design by Baseline Arts Ltd, Oxford
Printed and bound by The Cromwell Press, Trowbridge, Wiltshire

NOTE: The material contained in this book is set out in good faith for general guidance and no liability can be accepted for loss or expense incurred as a result of relying in particular circumstances on statements made in the book. Laws and regulations are complex and liable to change, and readers should check the current position with the relevant authorities before making personal arrangements.

NOTE 2: Use of the pronouns 'him' and 'he' in this book implies a person of either sex.

Contents

Appendices

List of Illustrations

Preface
to Sixth Edition

Investing in Stocks and Shares has proved to be one of the most enduring of guides to investment in stockmarkets since it was first published in 1992. This may be because it is maintained by a professional long-term investor and not by a financial journalist or a salesman peddling a 'get-rich-quick' book; or it may be due to the book's advocacy from the first edition of the importance of seeking dividend growth from investments in shares, and not buckling to the latest investment fashion.

The beliefs expressed in the first edition, that share prices would rise more than alternative investments and that the 'Logical Investment Strategy' would have a long term application, have been fulfilled despite the general decline in stockmarkets across the world since the last (5th) edition was published. Much of the decline was due to the bursting of the 'dot-com' bubble and the belated realisation by investors that mobile phone companies would struggle to grow once everyone had a mobile phone. Readers of earlier editions should have largely avoided both disasters.

However, the decline in global inflation has lowered expectations of returns from all types of investment. Gilts and house prices have enjoyed a good run in the last three years, but this cannot continue unless inflation (and thence interest rates) falls even further. Indeed, it is economically impossible for stockmarkets and house prices to move in opposite directions for any length of time, since both are ultimately driven by company profits via dividends or wages.

Tables and figures have been updated for this new edition. Unfortunately, taxation rules change so quickly, and so unpredictably, that only a general outline can be given here and the reader is advised not to depend upon tax information given in this book.

Although expectations of future returns from the stockmarket must be lower than those garnered from the past two decades, there is every reason to suppose that investment in company shares will continue to out-perform other investments in the next few years. Current stockmarket levels are assuming an economic climate similar to that prevailing in the depression of the 1930s. This seems to be much too harsh.

John White, January 2003

Stop press: Charles Schwab (Europe), often mentioned in this book, was taken over by Barclays Stockbrokers at the end of January 2003.

Update for January 2006
Between 2003 and 2006 the average share price rose by about 60%, far exceeding housing, cash and bonds.

Introduction

A STRATEGY FOR INVESTMENT ON THE UK STOCKMARKET

This book was compiled to demonstrate that it is possible to invest in the shares of UK-quoted companies in a sensible and logical manner that requires no special expertise; also, that the results will, in the long term, be better than those of more than half of the highly-paid professional fund managers.

It is directed at readers who may be considering investment on the Stockmarket as part of a balanced portfolio of investments. The early sections review features of the Stockmarket in a manner which is illustrative rather than definitive, showing the reasons underlying a '**logical investment strategy**'.

The first chapter provides an overview of the whole book, and should be read first. Subsequent chapters look more closely at the features of share investment and examine various strategies for investment on the Stockmarket with special emphasis on the 'logical investment strategy'.

The closing chapters deal with additional areas for investment likely to appeal to the more experienced private investor, such as traded options, gilts and bonds.

It is hoped that this book will serve the reader not only as a general investment guide but also as a handy reference manual to be kept on the bookshelf. Numerous technical terms are explained at length and a substantial glossary has also been provided.

It is most important for the reader to remember one central tenet – past performance is no guide to future performance. That means that the logical investment strategy cannot be guaranteed to work in the future.

ABSOLUTE BEGINNERS

This book has been written on the assumption that the reader is familiar at least with the concept of trading in shares. If you have no previous experience at all of dealing in shares, then the London Stock Exchange (see Useful Addresses) provides some excellent beginner's booklets at no charge.

SOURCES

Data used in the tables presented in this book have mostly been calculated from my private database.

Long-term tables of inflation, building society interest rates and share price indices were obtained from the London firm Barclays Capital Ltd. Permission to use these tables and charts is gratefully acknowledged and the appropriate addresses are given at the end of this book. The Stock Transfer Form shown in Chapter 5 is reproduced by kind permission of the Solicitors' Law Stationery Society Ltd.

ACKNOWLEDGEMENTS

Several investors, experienced and novice, read early and later drafts of this book. It is a pleasure to acknowledge particularly the valuable criticism, suggestions and contributions made by Ian Laurenson, former financial analyst at County NatWest. My wife laboured through many evenings to point out any areas which might need clarification for less experienced investors. Any errors which remain are my own.

DISCLAIMER

This is a book about one of several stockmarket investment strategies. In order to illustrate the reasons for creating the strategy, I have inevitably had to resort to using current charges, taxation levels, exemptions from tax and other variable figures. These were believed to be correct at the time of publication, but are certain to change in succeeding years.

The use of real companies to illustrate points made in the text should not be regarded as a recommendation to buy their shares. All of the companies illustrated in documents, such as share certificates, are fictitious and will not be found in the *Financial Times*.

Similarly, different investors have different objectives, priorities and financial standing. It is essential that they each seek qualified professional advice before making important financial decisions.

1

Why Buy Shares?

THE BENEFITS

The purchase of a company share gives the buyer a stake in the company and the entitlement to be paid a proportion of its profits known as the dividend. The value of shares in ordinary companies has, on aggregate, outperformed all other forms of investment over a reasonable period of time (say, most ten-year spans).

Figures given by the London stockbrokers, Barclays Capital Ltd (summarised by the author), show that in only six of the 71 consecutive rolling ten-year periods between 1920 and 2003 did the performance of government gilts (fixed interest bonds) exceed that of shares and most of these periods were in the dark days of the 1930s depression. Of 76 consecutive rolling five-year periods between 1920 and 2003, only 12 showed underperformance by shares, relative to gilts.

The following figures show relative performance between 1993 and 2003 and may come as a shock to those conditioned to believe that houses are the best investment.

Table 1. Relative performance, 1993–2003

	% Growth
Typical investment trust (with net dividends reinvested)	+ 128
Typical house	+ 97
Building Society (Halifax Higher Rate: net interest reinvested)	+ 71
Gilts (> 15 years to expiry with net interest reinvested)	+ 221
Inflation index	+ 28
(*Source:* author's data and Halifax Building Society. All figures given in this table are consistent with those published elsewhere.)	

It must be recognised that the 1990s were an exceptional period of share price performance. However, the same factors which raised company profits, dividends and then share prices, also served to raise salaries and hence house prices. It has long been known that house

3

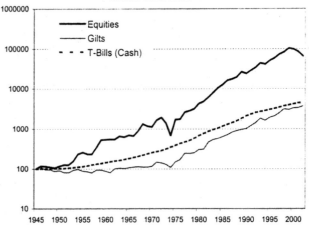

Barclays Total Return Indices: Nominal Terms, Gross Income Reinvested

Fig. 1. The Barclays Capital indices for equities, gilts and cash from 1945 to the present. The equity index clearly shows the crash in share prices in the 1970s. The graph shows the compounding benefit that reinvestment of gross (untaxed) income provides.

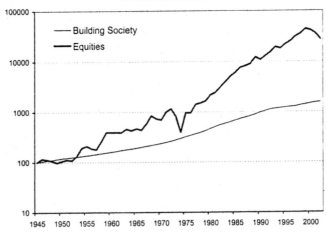

Barclays Total Return Indices: Nominal Terms, Net Income Reinvested

Fig. 2. This compares the relative performance of equities and building society investments assuming all net (taxed) income has been invested. The return on shares has been more volatile, but certainly greater than that on building society accounts. Note the difference between the final returns on equities with reinvestment of gross income (Figure 1) and net income (Figure 2).

4

prices are ultimately linked to family disposable income. Moreover, it is much easier to borrow money to invest in a house than it is to borrow to invest in shares. This phenomenon, known as 'gearing', will be dealt with in Chapter 3. It is particularly important to realise that the house price rise does **not** take into account maintenance costs, including rates, which substantially reduce the real increase in value of the house. Standard financial advice for many years has been to buy as large a house as you need but not an inch bigger.

The availability of bonds linked to the inflation index and backed by the government has now provided investors with a clear target to beat. It is possible to buy index-linked bonds which additionally pay up to 2.5 per cent extra in interest. Since these bonds form one of the safest of all investments, it follows that any investment which is more risky must return a better yield than these bonds in the long run. The performance of shares has handsomely outperformed this target.

Figures 1 and 2 provide an illustration of the long-term outperformance of shares relative to gilts, building society funds and the Retail Price Index. The 'Equity Index' measures share price performance with the dividends received from the shares. Shares are often referred to as 'the equity' or as 'equities'. Indices will be described more fully in the following chapter. The 'Gilt Index' similarly measures the performance of government gilts, also considering the interest which they pay to their owners. Figure 2 takes into account the effect of using the net (after-tax) income which shares and building societies provide, to buy more shares or to reinvest the money in the building society.

The ethicality of shares

The days when a wealthy enthusiast could back a good idea have now largely gone. Henry Ford started his car company between the two World Wars with capital borrowed from friends and made them millionaires, but that is no longer practical on a large scale.

The cost of installing a new blast furnace for British Steel would have made even Paul Getty blench. The only way to fund such costly developments is by the mobilisation of the savings of large numbers of ordinary people, by bank loans (using bank deposits) and by selling shares.

Current wisdom is that it is vitally important to put people's savings into productive industry, rather than into unproductive housing. Unlike the inhabitants of Kipling's island, the people of Britain cannot continue to eke out a precarious living by selling houses to each other.

Encouragement of the private investor

The decline in recent years in the number of private investors has caused unease among the boardrooms of British companies and among *laissez-faire* politicians, albeit for different reasons.

Private investors were traditionally loyal to the company management, while institutions have, with a few honourable exceptions, acquired a reputation for passing large blocks of a company's shares around like so many sacks of potatoes. This has meant that managers now have to keep an eye on their share register for the sudden appearance of potential predators. This may be no bad thing in itself, if it concentrates their minds on improving the performance of their companies.

In recent years a number of British companies have taken positive steps to encourage the growth of private share ownership. Some now offer their products to shareholders at reduced prices. However, they have to be careful about the pricing of such goods or the Inland Revenue may tax the benefit. Typically a discount of up to 20 per cent is offered to shareholders in food, brewing, hotel and other service industries. A number of stockbrokers publish lists of shareholders' perks.

Other companies encourage close contact with shareholders, while an increasing number now provide shareholders with a very cheap means of buying and selling their shares. For example, Abbey National bank customers can buy and sell its shares at a discounted commission by sending a simple form, obtained from their branches, through the post to an approved broker.

Privatisations

The government has also recognised the value of promoting private share ownership. Tax concessions are now available to those who own shares in the company for which they work and Personal Equity Plans (PEPs) have provided an increasingly valuable tax shelter for funds invested in British companies. All long-term investors should take out new-style PEPs (ISAs), and these are more fully described later in this book.

However, the main plank of the government's determination to raise private share ownership has been its privatisation programme. After the half-hearted, partial denationalisation of the oil company BP (in the late 1970s by Labour), the succeeding Conservative government sold off all the easily saleable nationalised industries such as British Telecom, British Aerospace and Amersham International. Some public utilities (water, gas, electricity) were also privatised, a step regarded in many quarters as being ethically dubious.

It soon became apparent that the shares of these companies were being sold cheaply and all later privatisation issues were massively over-subscribed by certain investors who sell shares immediately after purchase with a view to making a quick financial killing ('stags'). As a result, it became impossible to acquire a worthwhile holding in any privatisation issue and the number of long-term investors remained low. In addition, few of the new breed of privatisation investors went on to buy shares in other companies.

The Central Statistics Office reported in 1994 that there were 7.5 million private investors in the UK (up from three million in 1979, before privatisations began in earnest), of which only one and a half million owned shares in more than four companies. The underlying trend of private share ownership was still down.

What is the effect of inflation?

Inflation is the name given to the creeping process by which the price of everything moves slowly upwards. It is widely believed to be due to the circulation of too much money. It erodes the value of savings, since they can purchase less and less and most governments adhere to an avowed policy of reducing its rate of progress. Salaries and wages tend to be greatly influenced by inflation, in that inflation serves as the basis for the minimum demand for a wage increase.

Inflation is measured as an average percentage increase in the cost of everyday purchases and is estimated in the UK by the Retail Price Index (RPI), statistics compiled officially by the government. Every form of investment needs to grow at a rate at least equal to inflation, or the value of the investment is reduced.

Since most manufacturers try to improve their products, and thereby charge a higher price for the new item, there is an inbuilt element of inflation in ordinary technological progress.

Because shares provide a stake in a company they should, all other things being equal, prove to be comparatively immune to inflation. As inflation rises, so will the face value of the company's assets – its land, factory and stocks – and so will the prices which it can charge for its finished products.

The same phenomenon is seen for all asset-backed commodities, whether soya beans, Rembrandt paintings – or land. Gold is discussed in Appendix 5.

British inflation was negligible during the periods 1200–1550 and 1700–1900AD.

Barclays Total Return Indices: Real Terms, Gross Income Reinvested

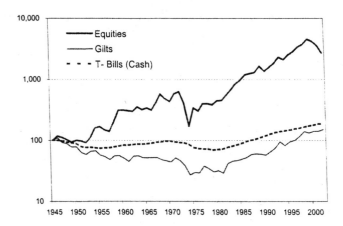

Fig. 3. This shows equity and gilt prices adjusted for inflation. It reveals very clearly the ravages of inflation on fixed interest investments, ie gilts.

Barclays Total Return Indices: Real Terms, Net Income Reinvested

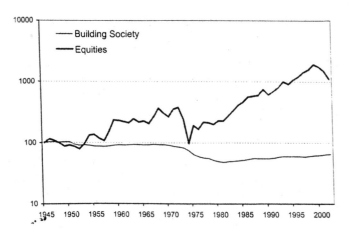

Fig. 4. This shows the data in Figure 2 adjusted for inflation.

WHY DO SHARES RISE IN VALUE?

Over any long period, shares in companies have always, hitherto, outperformed all other investments and the reasons are given below.

Inflation

As we have seen, a company can raise its prices and thereby its profits, in line with rising inflation, all other things being equal and provided there is no government intervention. However, it should be noted that this simple relationship breaks down in times of high inflation, when a government intervenes. The company has to pay high prices for its raw materials, but may be restrained by government edict (a 'prices policy') from raising its prices sufficiently to compensate.

The ability to raise dividends and capital values in line with inflation is not shared by bonds or gilts (unless index-linked), but is shared by property, paintings and related forms of investment. However, governments may impose periods of restraint on dividend growth as part of a general prices and incomes policy. This was last seen in the late 1970s under a Labour government.

The exceptionally high levels of inflation which British investors have to endure, much higher than those seen in the USA, Germany, Japan or other principal stockmarkets, mean that there is always a strong upwards pull on share prices. When inflation averages ten per cent per annum, share prices have to rise ten per cent just to stand still in real terms. This means that long-term investors in this country should always base their investment decisions on the premise that the stockmarket will rise in value.

It is possible to make a profit from a falling stockmarket by a variety of means. For example, buying 'put options' (see Chapter 7) or 'selling stock short', which means that you sell shares today in the expectation of buying them back cheaper at a later date. However, the upwards drag of inflation makes this a very risky pastime for any but the shortest of periods.

Figures 3 and 4 show the effects of inflation on the performance of shares, gilts and building society funds, and should be compared with corresponding Figures 1 and 2. Only shares have withstood the effect of inflation, while the performance of gilts (which do not in these tables include the index-linked types) has been disastrous in **real** terms.

Table 2. Net income paid per year on £100 invested

	Building Society (Higher Rate)	Alliance IT* Dividends
1/1/94	7.5	2.9
1/1/95	7.9	3.0
1/1/96	6.5	3.25
1/1/97	5.8	3.45
1/1/98	6.7	3.6
1/1/99	5.6	4.0
1/1/00	4.7	4.1
1/1/01	4.6	4.25
1/1/02	3.1	4.35
1/1/03	3.0	4.45
Capital:	£100	£148

(Value of original capital on 1/1/03)

Table 3. Total returns (all net income reinvested)
(Based to 1993 = 100)

	Building Society (Higher Rate)	Alliance IT*
1/1/94	107	165
1/1/95	116	150
1/1/96	123	180
1/1/97	131	198
1/1/98	139	232
1/1/99	147	267
1/1/00	154	312
1/1/01	161	304
1/1/02	166	278
1/1/03	171	228

(*Data from Alliance Investment Trust)

The employees care

The directors and workforce of a company have as much, or more, interest in the well-being of the company as the investor. They will strain every sinew to raise the profitability of their company (and thereby improve salaries and job security), thus working indirectly for the investors' benefit. Strictly speaking, the directors are supposed to work directly for the investors' benefit anyway, but it has been observed by industry analysts that many are more interested in empire building. However, manufacturing improvements, economies of scale and the like will all be working in the investors' favour.

In the long term

In the long term, companies may reasonably be expected to pay increasing dividends to their shareholders and the share price should continue to rise to reflect this increase. Pension funds and insurance companies calculate their returns to policy holders on the basis that long-term benefits from shares will exceed increases in wages by at least two per cent. Also that long-term growth of the share value will be of the order of 6–8 per cent per year.

It is particularly instructive to compare the gains made from a building society higher-rate interest account and the growth in income from an 'average company' (actually an investment trust, see page 78). See Table 2. The income derived from the building society wanders up and down, depending on current interest rates, while the underlying capital remains the same if the income is spent. By contrast, the income from the 'average share' starts from a lower figure than the building society but soon exceeds the income from the safer investment. Moreover, the capital value of the share has increased in value.

Tables 3 and 4 also serve to emphasise the long-term gain which, hopefully, accrues from investment in an 'average share'. Table 4 shows purely mathematical calculations. Table 5 shows recent inflation rates, which serve to devalue the performance shown in the earlier tables.

ARE SHARES RIGHT FOR YOU?

Buying shares means that the investor has taken a stake in the company. Companies can, unfortunately, go bankrupt, in which case the investor will lose all or part of the money he put into the

Table 4. Compound growth assuming fixed rates of increase.

Year	Dividend growth* (5% per year)
0	4.0 (initial net dividend)
1	4.2
2	4.4
3	4.6
4	4.9
5	5.1
6	5.4
7	5.6
8	5.9
9	6.2
10	6.5

(*Net dividend per £100 of stock)

Compound growth assuming £10,000 invested per year.

Growth rate (%)	Total after 10 years*
0	100,000
5	125,778
10	159,374
15	203,037
20	259,586

(*excluding dividends)

Table 5. Average inflation rates (AIR)
(Rebased to 1993 = 100)

Year	AIR (%)	Cumulative
1/1/94	1.4	101.4
1/1/95	2.9	104.3
1/1/96	3.2	107.7
1/1/97	2.5	110.4
1/1/98	3.6	114.3
1/1/99	2.7	117.4
1/1/00	1.9	119.6
1/1/01	2.9	123.1
1/1/02	0.7	124.0
1/1/03	2.9	127.6

shares. He will not, however, be personally liable for any part of the company's debt, provided that it is either a 'limited liability' (Ltd) or a 'Public Limited Company' (plc).

This means that shares can be a comparatively risky form of investment. You do not expect to lose money placed in a building society or in most gilts, but you could lose part of any money invested in housing (as was discovered by the unfortunates who bought at the top of the housing market in 1988) or in paintings or other collectables.

It follows, therefore, that the prudent investor should only buy shares with money that he, or she, can afford to lose. Diversification of risk is essential with money spread among many companies rather than concentrated in one or two. This means that out-performance of many shares will compensate for the occasional disaster when a company goes bankrupt (and this can happen to the most prudent investor, as the author can testify from personal experience). In short, the investor must be prepared for, or resigned to, the fact that part of his total investment – a small part, one hopes – is virtually certain to be lost in an investment career spanning several decades.

There is a widely held belief that only wealthy people can afford to own shares. Like many myths, this has some basis in fact. If it is necessary to invest only money which you can afford to lose (at any rate, lose in part) it follows that you must already have enough money for other commitments.

Commitments vary with age (especially) and with individual inclination. When one is younger, money is spent on rent, mortgage and/or children. But as the years unfold these commitments become less onerous. A 25-year mortgage would have seemed to require very high repayments when it was first taken out in 1988, but 15 years later they may only represent a small portion of the owner's salary.

Everyone requires an adequate financial cushion. Is your pension arrangement sufficient for your likely needs after retirement? Pensions are arranged with financial institutions and rely quite heavily on shares to provide long-term growth.

Indeed, insurance companies are now among the biggest owners of companies in the UK stockmarket, so virtually everybody who has, or is saving for, a pension is an indirect investor in the stockmarket.

Pensions are a complex subject in their own right and many employees will take out a stakeholder pension or else make additional voluntary contributions (AVCs) to top-up an existing company pension. Stakeholder pensions have been encouraged by the government, with tax incentives and a maximum 1% administration charge by the pensions company. Savers can also invest in Self Invested Personal Pensions (SIPPs), but these often require expensive administration by the provider even though the investor makes all the investment decisions. SIPPs are of most interest to those running their own businesses, when the business premises can, with tax advantage, be made part of the pension arrangement. In all cases, insurance companies will normally offer a variety of schemes, of which most will be based, at least in part, on investment in shares in the stockmarkets of the world. Increasingly, the pension saver has the choice of deciding which investments to make.

Individual Savings Accounts (ISAs, mentioned earlier) provide a form of savings used extensively for pensions or mortgages, as well as for more personal investments. While a financial institution is usually involved in the selection of companies for an ISA for the above purposes, the private investor will sometimes be able to make his own decisions.

Do you have sufficient insurance? Everyone of working age requires life (term) insurance, house insurance and, probably, car insurance. Would your wife and children be able to carry on after your death? If not, an urgent demand for your money exists before you even consider buying shares.

Do you have 'rainy day' money? What will you do if the roof falls in, the house subsides, you need to buy a new car (or repair the old)? It is essential to have 'safe' money available in savings to meet unexpected contingencies. This money must be readily accessible and will normally be kept in a bank or building society. One of the fundamental axioms of investment in shares is that the investor must **never** allow himself to become a forced seller of shares, when it may become necessary to sell at an unfavourable price. It is necessary to maintain a contingency reserve sufficient to avoid enforced sales of shares.

If, after making provision for all the contingencies mentioned above, you still have enough residual cash, or income, then you have enough spare money to consider investment in shares.

Shares are part of a range of investments

A holding of shares is only one of the many different types of investment and is one of the more risky.

Alternatives include investments in property (typically your own home), building society accounts, National Savings and fixed-interest bonds such as gilts (bonds guaranteed to pay a fixed rate of interest on the sum invested). The 'fixed' element may be relative to a moving index such as occurs with index-linked gilts, 'granny bonds' and the like. More arcane investments include the purchase of paintings, stamps or even toy soldiers.

Nevertheless, statistics show that over long periods an investment in shares outperforms all other investments, including property.

It is very important to remember that investments in shares should form part of a **balanced** portfolio. What is meant by balanced? A portfolio is said to be balanced if it is spread across many different types of investment so that a fall in value of one part of the portfolio is balanced by a compensating rise in another part.

Thus it is likely that a balanced portfolio will contain investments in a building society or on deposit with a bank (these investments are called 'cash') in addition to the contingency fund previously mentioned. Excessive economic growth (overheating) will cause share prices to surge. If the government takes corrective action by raising interest rates, then share prices are likely to fall but the amount of interest received on deposit will rise in compensation.

Professional investors, such as pension institutions, seek to diversify risk among property, foreign shares and government bonds (gilts) as well as with shares and cash.

Table 6. Typical pension fund asset distribution in 2002

Asset	%
UK shares (equities)	56
Overseas shares	8
Property	2
Bonds (UK and overseas)	29
Index-linked bonds	1
Cash	4

Modern economic theory has provided much information about the management of risk and this is discussed in more detail later in this book. A professional (institutional) investor would add convertibles and traded options to his portfolio in order to get the right blend of long-term growth of capital and income with the desired degree of security. Private investors cannot so readily mimic the professionals' practice, owing to the high cost of dealing in these so-called 'derivative' instruments.

It is axiomatic that high risk investments must carry higher rewards than low risk equivalents, or else no one would take the greater risk.

Greater Reward = Greater Risk

Where to buy and sell shares

Shares are traditionally traded through a stockbroker, who may offer a simple dealing service, advice or portfolio management. Charges will vary according to the amount of service provided. Banks also offer dealing facilities. The 'touch-screen' operation of National Westminster Bank, whereby transactions are handled at a computer screen in the bank branch, provides an especially convenient service. It seems likely that retail outlets, such as bank and building society branches, will provide increasing competition for the more traditional methods of dealing and this development is being encouraged by the government.

The various share trading options are discussed in much greater detail later in this book.

Independent advisers

How often have you seen the phrase 'Consult your Independent Financial Adviser'? In recent years, the role of the so-called 'financial adviser' has become closely defined. All advisers must be members of one or other of the regulatory authorities and must state whether they are entitled to sell all financial products (independent adviser), products from a short-list of companies (multi-tied), or only those of one company (tied adviser).

Independent advisers live mostly off the commission which they earn by selling financial products. Although required by the Financial Services Act to give 'best advice', in practice some of them may advise the purchase of those products which provide the highest commission. There have been many complaints from financial professionals that some 'independent' advisers invest in one way for themselves and in another (more profitable in terms of their commissions) for their clients.

The levels of commission can be surprisingly high. For instance, arranging a typical pension will earn the independent adviser something like a thousand pounds.

The alternative is to use a fee-based adviser. He or she will charge perhaps £85 per hour, so that a typical consultation for a pension will cost you £340. The fee-based adviser ought also to return any commission he receives from the insurance company whose pension he recommends. However, the returned commission is subject to income tax.

A good stockbroker should provide an excellent source of information about shares at no charge to the investor, although the broker's commission structure for share dealing with advice is likely to be higher than that of a 'dealing only' service.

The addresses of local stockbrokers and financial advisers, of all types, can be found in your telephone book. Unfortunately, crooked, or fraudulent, advisers do still exist and a number of their ploys are described later in this book.

A HISTORY OF SHARES

Ancient history

The ability of individuals to take stakes in companies has long been known. The Romans used to fund expeditions to India for silks. Indeed, there were contemporary fears that the export of solid silver in exchange for perishable silks would ultimately bankrupt the Empire, a prediction not fulfilled. Many merchants became rich as a result of this trade while the Empire exacted a tax on it.

Nevertheless, many of the aristocracy were debarred from taking part in commercial ventures, while the real mark of wealth was to own land. The larger the estate the better and this would provide the primary source of income for the 'old rich'. As a result, the Romans never really sorted out the principles of modern lending (banking), accountancy (they lacked the security of double entry systems) or companies with multiple shareholders who could trade their holdings.

After the collapse of the western Roman Empire in 476 AD, there was a long period of stagnation in Europe. European financiers in medieval times, particularly those of the maritime trading cities such as Venice, invented and developed many of the modern accounting systems that today we take for granted. For example, paper money and transactions between distant banks, and double accounting and the use of black and red inks for positive and negative value entries. However, the Reformation and the spread of British sea power created a new class of entrepreneurs who sought their fortunes in overseas goods.

In the sixteenth to eighteenth centuries a typical method of trading was to create a company by borrowing from wealthy backers. The money would be used to buy a ship and finance an expedition to one of the colonies or further afield. When, or if, the ship returned, the cargo would be sold, the crew paid off, the ship sold and the money so obtained divided between the original backers. Profits had to be very high to compensate for the risk that the ship might not return.

The first record of such early companies was 'The Mysterie and Companie of the Merchant Adventurers for the Discoverie of Regions, Dominions, Islands and Places Unknowen' (1553), which subsequently became known as the 'Muscovy Company' for rather obvious reasons! Other famous companies which began in this way included the East India Company, trading primarily with the new 'jewel in the crown' of India, and the Hudson's Bay Company.

Developments

By now it had become recognised that to create and disband companies after every venture was inefficient. Instead, it was much better for everyone if the company could continue. This was achieved by issuing 'shares' in the company. Instead of breaking up the company at the conclusion of its original purpose, a new venture (typically a new journey overseas) was arranged. The original investors could retain their 'shares' or they could sell them on to someone else who wanted to take a stake in the company.

From here it was but a short step to creating a 'market' in which investors would meet to buy and sell their shares. The Royal Exchange in London was an important venue for banking. Trading of shares continued informally here until the disturbance was such that the traders were ejected. The surrounding coffee houses (coffee being a new imported luxury), especially those in Threadneedle Street, subsequently became popular as meeting places for the exchange of shares. In 1773, the coffee shop 'New Jonathan's' became known as the world's first 'Stock Exchange'.

The trading of commodities was already much better established than the trading of shares and the trading empires of the continent had already experienced spectacular ups and downs. Holland had been importing tulips from Turkey since the 1560s and had created a strong local demand. This demand became so high that by 1634 there was a huge market dealing in the supply of tulip bulbs as speculative items.

Demand outstripped supply and the price of bulbs rose to fantastic heights with whole estates changing hands for a single bulb! In 1636 the authorities advised against further purchases of tulips, a panic set in, no one would buy the bulbs and by 1637 the market was almost dead with many people still clutching the now worthless tulip bulbs.

A similar period of crazed speculation led to the 'South Sea Bubble'. In 1711 the Chancellor of the Exchequer persuaded many of the government's creditors to accept shares in a new company rather than take interest payments raised through taxation. The new company was called 'The Governor and Company of Merchants of Great Britain Trading to the South Seas and Other Parts of America' and was granted a monopoly of trade to Spanish America (principally South America).

The company proved to be extremely popular with speculators, notwithstanding the fact that there was a war continuing with Spain. The directors of the company felt able to sell more and more of the government's debts to eager investors, using the money the investors handed over to pay fat initial dividends to those investors. The whole merry-go-round collapsed in 1720 when no new investors could be found to purchase further stocks. Variants of this confidence trick (using the investors' own money to pay them their dividends, until the money runs out or the company folds) are still with us today.

By the end of the eighteenth century most companies comprised partnerships with unlimited financial liability for the partners in the event that their companies went bankrupt. This promoted extreme care in trading by the partners.

At the beginning of the nineteenth century, it became recognised that further progress of the Industrial Revolution required the raising of capital on a grand scale. This led to a number of more-or-less unrelated developments, some legislated by Parliament.

In 1802, the Stock Exchange was formally constituted with 550 subscribers and 100 clerks. Other regional exchanges opened throughout the century. Finally there were over 30 exchanges, the seven regional survivors of which were incorporated into the London Stock Exchange as recently as 1973.

Subsequent legislation created the concept of 'limited liability' (Ltd). It meant that the owners of a limited company were not liable for its debts, beyond the money which they had already sunk into the venture. This greatly reduced the risk to the investor of buying shares in a company, and thus had the effect of encouraging investment. Another very important development was the separation of ownership and management. The owners of a company could appoint managers to run the business while the owners stayed in the background.

The unregulated stock markets of the nineteenth century saw investment on a huge scale at home and abroad, and in all the corners of the British Empire. A particular favourite was investment in the new railroads, which first appeared in Britain but which subsequently spread their tentacles all over the USA and then Latin America.

The great difficulty was in knowing where to invest since communications were, by modern standards, poor and fraud was rife. Wealthy individuals could make many investments and thereby spread their risk, but this option was not open to the smaller investor.

The 1822–1825 bond bubble exploited the stocks of Latin American governments. The bubble burst when several countries defaulted on interest payments.

The first investment trust, 'Foreign and Colonial', was created in 1868. Its stated objective was 'to give the investor of moderate means the same advantage as the large capitalist, in diminishing the risk of investing in foreign and colonial government stocks, by spreading the investment over a number of different stocks'.

The early investment trusts were immensely popular. They were set up as real trusts, but a court decision (subsequently overturned) declared that they were not legally trusts. Consequently the first trusts were turned into limited liability companies. By 1900 over one hundred investment trusts had been formed.

The First World War began in August 1914. The Stock Exchange closed its doors on the first day of the war, fearing a massive wave of selling, and no trading was permitted for the remainder of the year. Post-war saw the merging of several British companies into forms which are still recognisable today, for example Imperial Chemical Industries (ICI) formed in 1926. The oil companies began their rise to prominence and shares began to move into favour with institutional investors.

Up until the First World War, inflation in Britain had been negligible and rates of interest were low. This was the period of the government bonds known as 'Consols', which paid either a 2.5 percent or 4 percent interest per annum. Consols were 'safe', while shares were more risky and therefore gave a higher yield to their owners. Advice given to Harley Street doctors of this era was to 'put your first £100,000 into Consols, then buy shares'. However, the aftermath of the war saw a surge in inflation (still low by today's standards) which made shares, with their asset backing, more attractive.

The value of shares rose steeply in the 1920s, led by the USA. This led to the same speculative excesses seen in earlier times. The Great Crash came in 1929 and the depression followed. The Great Crash is vividly associated in the public's mind with financiers throwing themselves out of the windows of skyscrapers. The reason was that so many investors had borrowed heavily to fund share purchases. When the market collapsed their holdings became worthless and they could not afford to repay the borrowings.

In some cases, bank staff had 'borrowed' illicitly from their banks to buy shares. They were certain to lose their jobs and receive jail sentences when they could not repay their unauthorised loans. Others had mortgaged their homes or estates.

But what of those who bought shares with their own money? In the popular TV series *Upstairs, Downstairs*, the servant girl Rose is advised at the height of the 1929 boom to put her inherited money into an investment trust – a wise scheme, even if the timing was wrong. The story ends with the market crash, the adviser dead by suicide (he had borrowed heavily) and Rose penniless – but is she? She still has the holding in her investment trust and owes no one any money. In years to come, Rose would find that her share certificate would refund all her money and more.

The rise and fall of stockmarkets is a cyclical phenomenon, with the markets rising and falling in cycles of several years. Periodically investors forget that shares are tied to underlying companies, the 'tulip phenomenon' sets in until the market crashes and investors are taught a sharp lesson. Economic processes also play their part in causing the values of shares to rise and fall, usually with a cycle of roughly four to five years in the UK (see Figure 1). Some commentators have claimed to see a very slow underlying cycle, or wave, with a time span of around fifty years. This presupposes that nothing changes in human or economic terms over several cycles, each of nearly two generations.

Fraud was an increasing problem during the boom years of the 1920s, and the Stock Exchange became known as the 'thieves' kitchen'. Some financial magazines had acquired a reputation for touting worthless shares, particularly in new issues, and this and other abuses needed to be cleaned up. The authorities imposed restrictions in 1930 on new issues of shares.

The boom period of the 1920s created a demand for monitoring the performance of shares. Hitherto, individual stockbrokers or magazines had attempted to monitor selections of shares, and the 'old' *Financial Times* started an index in 1926. On 1 July 1935, the

Financial News – which was subsequently to acquire the *Financial Times* and change its own name to the 'new' *Financial Times* – created the celebrated FT-30 share index, measuring the performance of thirty of the top publicly-quoted companies in Britain.

1931 saw the launch of the first true public trust. Municipal & General, still one of the most respected names in the field, created its first 'unit trust' with trustees to watch over the fund. Unlike the investment trusts, which were real companies owned by shareholders, the unit trusts were severely restricted in their range of investments. Purchase of 'units' gave the investor a stake in a wide range of companies. In 1936 control of unit trusts was transferred from the Stock Exchange to the Board of Trade.

The outbreak of the Second World War in September 1939 reversed what had been a steadily rising stock market into a slow decline. This steepened rapidly in 1940 when it was feared that the Germans would invade Britain. By 1941 the market was rising again. Inflation became a serious anxiety in Britain throughout the Second World War.

Modern times

In 1950 it was still possible to buy shares with borrowed money, repaying the interest from dividend income. This situation rapidly changed as inflation took hold in the post-war years. It became apparent that asset-backed shares could survive inflation much better than low-interest gilts. This resulted in a reversal of gilt and share yields. Previously gilts, such as Consols, paid a lower yield than shares to reflect the latter's greater risk. Now prices of shares rose, causing a lower percentage dividend yield from the shares, in recognition of their ability to show long-term growth and to withstand inflation.

Social factors created another major change. With the increasing role of the State in an individual's affairs, the number of private investors began to decline. There were two principal reasons for this:

- The provision of State health care, social security and pensions reduced the need for individuals to save.

- The increased burden of taxation required to finance the benefits of the Welfare State reduced the ability of individuals to save.

In the place of the private investor came a whole series of financial institutions, such as life funds, insurance companies and unit trusts.

Their faceless managers handled the pooled savings of large sections of the population and charged heavily for the service.

Changes in taxation by successive governments favoured the channelling of savings into tax-sheltered institutions, quickening the transfer of share ownership from private investors. A number of scandals rocked the investment trust industry. The old investment trusts found that their original base of private investors was falling and the institutions took their place on the trusts' share registers. But then the institutions assembled their own share management teams and sold out of the investment trusts, whose share prices fell heavily. Many investment trusts were swallowed up by predators, others entered specialist areas in which the institutions as yet lacked expertise. It is only in recent years that investment trusts have managed to encourage the private investor back again.

The process of transfer of shares from private investors to institutions was greatly accelerated by the terrible market crash of 1973–1974. This was caused by high inflation, a quadrupling of the oil price, ruinous taxation of inflation-induced gains and a subsequent dividend freeze imposed by the Labour government. Nearly 70 per cent of the peak market value (of 1972) was lost. The market largely recovered in 1975 and 1976, but the shock had been even more severe to investors in this country than that of 1929.

In 1979 a new Conservative government was elected to power with the avowed intention of rolling back state intervention. A rocky start in 1980, brought about by a recession induced in an attempt to lower inflation, caused share prices to fall, but they rose steadily thereafter all through the 1980s.

London was by now the largest stockmarket in the world, in terms of shares traded. The Office of Fair Trading criticised the Stock Exchange's cosy cartel which kept commissions high. In order to protect the Exchange's position and its 'invisible earnings' for the country, a number of changes were announced to be brought into simultaneous operation on one day in October 1986. That day came to be known as 'Big Bang'. The Big Bang meant primarily that fixed commissions for handling shares would go and outside (mostly foreign) competitors would be allowed in. Another innovation was the amalgamation of brokers (who acted for investors as agents) and jobbers (who made the markets at the Stock Exchange) into one function – the 'market maker'.

These changes had a variety of effects, some probably unintended. Commissions fell steeply for the large institutions (from around 1.5 per cent to 0.2 per cent), but were raised for private clients who had previously been subsidised by the institutions' fees. The introduction of competition meant that the new market makers had to become bigger to survive. There were numerous mergers of the old stockbrokers with outside firms. City salaries rose steeply.

Another difficulty was that of the abuse of 'inside information', which had newly been made illegal. The new market makers were not allowed to use privileged information (for example, that they had just been wrong-footed into buying a load of expensive rubbish) in order to gain an advantage (for example, to dump the rubbish onto their private clients as a 'good long-term investment'). So-called 'Chinese Walls' were supposed to prevent the passage of privileged information from one department of the market maker to another. Several subsequent prosecutions showed that the Chinese Walls were as flimsy as the paper originals.

In 1987, a Conservative government having just been re-elected, share prices exploded upwards out of control again. In October, coincidentally after two days of the fiercest storms of the century which caused widespread damage around Britain, markets plunged in panic, losing a third of their value in just three days. The fastest crash in history. It is, however, noteworthy that the UK stockmarket indices ended the year still slightly higher than when they began. As usual, recovery occurred and a new stockmarket peak was reached in 1990.

The 1987 crash was initiated by the selling of unit trusts in the USA (known there as 'mutual funds'). The situation was exacerbated by 'program trading', the programming of idiot computers by human idiots to force-sell shares at any price once a certain fall in share prices had occurred. There was subsequently a widespread outcry against program trading, and so-called 'circuit-breakers' are now in operation in the USA designed to break the vicious circle of selling causing further programmed selling of shares.

A new Labour government, appropriately entitled 'New Labour', was elected in May 1997, the first in 18 years. Its first budgets contained some major tax changes for private investors, the significance of which were perhaps not properly appreciated at the time.

Tax credits on dividends could no longer be reclaimed by those who paid no tax; thus those on low incomes, charities and, especially, pension funds immediately lost 20 per cent of their income from shares. For private investors, the tax credit was maintained for five years (until year 2004) at the reduced level of ten per cent; however, the government promised that changes in personal taxation rates would ensure that neither higher- nor lower-rate taxpayers would pay more income tax in consequence, before or after 2004. However, the critical link between the standard income tax rate and the dividend tax rate has been broken with unpredictable long-term consequences.

Advance Corporation Tax (ACT), whereby companies paid tax at the same time as their dividends as an advance against their year-end tax bills, was subsequently abolished from April 1999. It was this tax pre-payment that had provided the dividend tax credit to the recipient of the dividend in the first place. Foreign Income Dividends (FIDs), derived from companies that did not have to pay ACT on large overseas earnings, were also abolished from April 1999.

These changes to dividend payments have had the long-term effect that many companies are now more willing to return excess capital to their shareholders and to buy back their own shares for cancellation than was hitherto the case. Although such changes give rise to capital gains tax (CGT), pension funds and many other large institutions are exempt from CGT. Ironically, the new Chancellor had attacked 'short-termism' in the holding of company shares by predominantly these institutions, yet he now proceeded to make changes to CGT, in the name of encouraging long-term share holding, that would affect only non-institutional shareholders, such as private individuals.

Previously CGT had been based on capital gains made after the initial acquisition costs of an asset had been indexed for inflation. The new 'tapering' tax system for individuals ended indexation, but reduced capital gains on a sliding scale according to how long the asset had been held. The same Budget ended the practice of 'bed-and-breakfasting' – the sale and repurchase of the same shares so as to establish a capital gain on the sale date and rebase the cost to the new purchase date. Finally, the new Labour government ended the ten-year-old Personal Equity Plan (PEP) and TESSA schemes and introduced an inferior replacement called 'Individual Savings Accounts' (ISAs).

The new government had assumed as a matter of belief that payment of dividends was a Bad Thing, taking money out of businesses which should have been re-invested. Instead, capital gains (rise in share price) were to be the investors' reward. This strategy worked briefly, but by early 2000 the stockmarket had temporarily peaked with the TMT (technology, media, telephones) boom. Share valuations had completely exceeded reality, and with the widespread failure of the so-called 'Dot-coms' (companies created to make money from the Internet) it was now downhill all the way. Accounting scandals in the USA also left their mark on British companies (although they were not directly implicated), and the market had declined by almost 50% in value by the low point.

The three-year decline caused severe financial stress to many pension funds. Some commentators observed that the amount taken out of dividends by the abolition of the tax credit (£5 billion per annum for five years) closely matched the new shortfalls in the pension funds (£27 billion in 2002). By the end of 2002, three-quarters of the popular Final Salary Pension schemes had closed to new entrants. Those individuals seduced into taking up first the replacement Personal Pensions and later the Stakeholder Pension found their pensions savings greatly reduced. These fiascos occurred despite the government's avowed aim of inducing individuals to save more for their retirement.

All these new changes are explained within this book, mostly in the Appendices. But the complication for private investors of holding shares personally in individual companies has increased under the new rules. Many readers will prefer to invest through collective savings vehicles, such as investment trusts, rather than have to deal with the new tax rules directly.

THE DIFFICULTY OF SELECTING SHARES

Someone once asked me, 'How do you select the shares which you buy?' This simple question at first mystified me. I purchase shares which I have long been wanting to buy, but for which I have only just acquired the money by saving out of income.

This response, however, only serves to set the question one remove back. How did I decide which shares I wanted to buy? It occurred to me that this is a matter of no small significance to the private investor without access to expert information, and may explain the perennial popularity of tip sheets. However, as a former Chancellor of the Exchequer once drily observed, 'In rising markets, all tips are good. In falling markets, all tips are bad.'

This book will describe 'The Logical Investment Strategy', one of the many possible strategies for buying shares. It is the strategy which I use myself. But first it will be necessary to examine the background of investments in shares available to the person with a few thousand pounds to spare.

2

An Explanation of Shares

BASIC INFORMATION

A share in a company gives the investor, most importantly, a share in its dividend which is declared once or twice a year. Also a stake in the company's assets and property and a vote, proportional to the size of the investor's holding, in the company's business at its annual general meeting (AGM).

The assets

The assets of the company comprise its cash-in-hand, property (land, buildings, fittings) and the company's stock of raw materials and work-in-hand, less its liabilities in the form of borrowings or payments to creditors.

Nominal share value

Most shares have a nominal value (typically 25p, but often more or less), which originally represented the asset value of the company. The shares were once sold at a **market value** which represented both the worth of the assets and their ability to make money. A 25p nominal share might once have been sold for one pound, reflecting the earnings potential of the company. The total of the nominal sum of all the issued shares is the **issued share capital** of the company. The shares of a company are also known as its **equity** or **stock**.

There are in existence some non-voting shares for certain companies, the shares usually being designated by the suffix 'A'. These shares normally enjoy most of the benefits of other shares, but the holder has no vote in the company's strategy. The original idea of these shares was to enable control of the company to be retained in the hands of the founding family (controlling the voting stock). However, these non-voting shares are unpopular with major investors, trade at a lower price than the voting stock and are going out of fashion with a gradual conversion from non-voting to voting status. The holders of the original voting stock are usually rewarded by an increased allocation of stock.

MEGASTORES plc

FORM OF PROXY

For use by Members at the Annual General Meeting to be held on 1st January, 200X, and at any adjournment thereof.

I/We being a member(s) of MEGASTORES plc hereby appoint the Chairman of the meeting, or*
as my/our proxy to vote for my/our behalf at the Annual General Meeting of the Company to be held on 1st January, 200X, and at any adjournment thereof.

The manner in which the proxy is to vote shall be indicated by inserting X in the space provided. Where no X is inserted the proxy will abstain or vote as he thinks fit.

Ordinary Resolution	For	Against
1. Adoption of the Directors' Report and Statement of Accounts and Declaration of a Dividend		
2. Re-election of Mr. R. Peabody as director		
3. Re-appointment of auditors		
4. Amendment to Savings Related Share Option Scheme		
Special Resolutions		
5. Authority for Directors to allot unissued share capital in accordance with Section 80 of the Companies Act 1985		

Signature or Common Seal .... Date 200X

12345
Mr. Anthony Investor
Of No Fixed
Abode
London AB1 9ZY

Notes
1. To be effective this form of proxy, duly signed, together with the power of attorney (if any) under which it is signed, must be deposited at the Company's registrars not later than 48 hours before the time appointed for the meeting or adjourned meeting at which the person named in the form is to vote.
2. If this form of proxy is given by a Company it must be given under its Common Seal, or as prescribed by Law, or signed by an attorney or duly authorised officer of the Company.
3. *If you wish to appoint a proxy other than as specified above, please make the necessary alteration and initial it. A proxy, who need not be a member of the Company, must attend the meeting to represent you.
4. Completion of a form of proxy will not prevent members from attending the meeting and voting in person should they so wish.

Fig. 5. Example of a proxy form for voting at a shareholders' meeting.

An example of a company which, at the time of writing, still possesses non-voting shares is Young, the brewers.

Companies which have non-voting shares find it hard to raise money by rights issues (page 55).

The dividend and its cover

The dividend of the company is that proportion of its profits paid to its owners, the shareholders. Normally a company will pay only part of its profits as a dividend. The remainder is retained to fund internal growth of the company. It may also serve as a store of 'fat' with which to maintain dividends in lean years, when the profit is falling.

The number of times that a company could have paid its net dividend is the **cover** of the dividend. If a company makes a profit of one million pounds, but pays only a quarter of a million in dividends, then the dividend is said to be 'covered' four times.

On one day in January 2003, the price and dividend for Great Universal Stores (GUS) was:

	Price	**Yield (%)**
Great Universal	571	3.9

The cover for the dividend of Great Universal was 1.9. This was discovered from the appropriate entries in the Financial Times and is explained in more detail below.

P/E ratio

The company's profits are known as its earnings. When the earnings are divided by the number of shares in existence, we get the 'earnings per share' (eps). The P/E (price to earnings) ratio measures how many years of earnings per share at the current share price would be needed to pay for the share. A P/E of 10 means that ten years of earnings will pay for the price of the share.

Not all of the earnings are paid as dividend (see 'cover' above), so further years will be needed to repay the share price out of dividends. Against this, however, it is hoped that the earnings and dividends will rise each year, reducing the repayment time of the share price and thereafter all dividends will be pure profit.

Of course the stock does not have to be held forever, and can be sold at the current going rate, the 'market price'.

MEGASTORES plc

ORDINARY SHARES

Reference No. 00123456/123	Date of payment 1st January 200X	Security Code 0–123–456

Final dividend of 9.00p per 25p ordinary share for year ended 30th September, 200X, to shareholders registered on 1st December 200X.

Number of Shares	Tax Credit	Dividend Payable
1000	£10.00	£90.00

Mr. ANTHONY INVESTOR
OF NO FIXED
ABODE
LONDON AB1 9ZY

This voucher should be kept. It will be accepted by the Inland Revenue as evidence of a tax credit.

Megastores plc, Secretary

Fig. 6. Example of a dividend payment certificate. Note that tax has been credited at a rate of 10% (April 1998 budget).

We can discover from the *Financial Times* that the P/E ratio is:

Great Universal   P/E = 13.7

The yield

Another important measure of a company's performance is its **yield**. The yield is typically expressed as a net percentage (*ie*, after income tax) of the current share price. The long term average yield in the UK is around 3.6 per cent net. In other countries the average yield may be different, for example 2.8 per cent in the USA or 1.0 per cent in Japan.

The yields in each country are usually lower than the interest which could be more safely obtained by investment in local bonds, or in the local equivalent of a building society. This is despite the fact that, in general, acceptance of risk entitles the risk taker to a higher return than from a 'safe' investment. The lower return from shares reflects the growth potential of dividend payouts, not usually (and certainly not consistently) seen with 'safe' investments.

Trading shares

The market
The buying and selling of shares in a company can be done privately. This entails registering the change of ownership with the company registrar and avoids all charges (except, where applicable, stamp duty). It is, however, more commonly and more conveniently done through a stock exchange, an authorised central clearing house which matches buyers and sellers. The price at which buyer and seller agree to trade is known as the **market price** of the share, and usually moves up and down over a trading day, reflecting supply and demand. The closing price, *ie,* the price agreed when the exchange closed, is printed in various financial newspapers, such as the Financial Times, and can also be found on Teletext.

Until very recently, the market was principally the floor of the London Stock Exchange (there are also regional stock exchanges in Belfast, Birmingham, Glasgow and Manchester) where brokers met jobbers (the latter now known as market makers) to buy and sell shares. Today, virtually all trading is conducted on computer screens and telephones and the floor of the Stock Exchange is deserted. This change has meant that a market maker does not have to answer his telephone when the going gets tough. In the three days of the great market crash of October 1987, there were numerous complaints from investors that they could not get through to their brokers, nor brokers to the market makers.

There is a constant struggle between the **bulls**, those who think share prices are too cheap and who want to buy stock, and the **bears**, those who think share prices are too high and who want to sell their shares. Professional traders may change their position, buy or sell, within a few days, or even within a few hours.

The constant struggle between the bulls and the bears is marked by the age-old human emotions of fear and greed. This means that it is possible, as will be shown later, to apply mob psychology to stock market behaviour.

Bankruptcy
If a company goes bankrupt, its remaining assets will be sold to pay off its creditors, particularly the banks. Ordinary shareholders come last in the queue and quite often get nothing back at all (preference shareholders may be luckier).

On the other hand, the principle of limited liability ensures that shareholders cannot lose more than the value of their shareholdings.

Despite being the owners of the business, they are not liable personally for the company's debts.

The Financial Times

Cover, net yield, P/E ratios and share prices for almost all companies (and many foreign ones) can be found in the pages of the *Financial Times* and other financial newspapers. In addition many current share prices can be monitored on *Ceefax* or *Teletext*. There are also a number of telephone dialling systems which furnish share prices and market reports, usually at elevated charge rates (typically 45p/min cheap rate and 60p/min at peak times).

Here is a typical example taken from the *Financial Times* for Great Universal Stores:

	Notes	Price	+ or −	2002/3 high low	Vol 000's	Yield	P/E
Great Universal	♣†	571	−14	714 429	3,068	3.9	13.7

Note: the net dividend (pence) and cover of Great Universal Stores (and other shares) are given only in the **Monday** edition of the *Financial Times*.

The high (714 pence) and low (429 pence) figures show the limits between which the share price of GUS has fluctuated in 2002. Its middle price when the market closed yesterday was 571 pence (so the investor will have to pay something like 573 pence per share to buy them; or receive about 569 pence per share if he sells them at that middle price). The stock comprises GUS Ordinary shares (since no qualifier is stated; other types of shares or convertibles will be stated explicitly in this entry).

The '♣' symbol indicates that the company will send a free report by phoning the *Financial Times*.

' + or − ' means that the price has fallen by 14 pence since the closing price of the day before yesterday.

The 'volume' (3,068,000) is the number of shares traded.

The net dividend is 22.2 pence (Monday, FT; not shown above). This is the total sum that will be paid on each share in dividends after tax has been deducted.

The yield net is 3.9 per cent. The total sum that will be paid on each share in dividends = 3.9 per cent of 571 pence, roughly 22.3 pence per share. [This is roughly correct, see previous paragraph.]

Other information can be given in the form of a special symbol in any column and is explained in the key given on the inside back

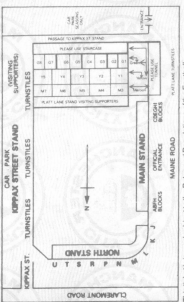

This ticket is issued subject to the Rules and Regulations of the Football Association and the Football League, and is valid for the date shown on the face hereof or for any other date to which the match may be transferred, but the price of this Ticket will not be returned to the holder in any circumstances if the Match has to be abandoned.

The Club accepts no responsibility whatsoever if the seat to which this ticket refers is affected by adverse weather conditions (Seats on Rows A to E in blocks A D E F G) or if the view therefrom is affected by pylons or other structural apparatus and the acceptance of this ticket implies full recognition of this condition by the holder.

IT IS AN OFFENCE TO BRING ALCOHOL INTO THE GROUND. OFFENDERS WILL BE PROSECUTED.

Maine Road, Moss Side, Manchester

F.A. Premier League

MANCHESTER CITY

v

MANCHESTER UNITED

Saturday, 20th March, 1993

Kick-off 3.00 pm

at Maine Road, Manchester

You are advised to take up your position 5 minutes before the kick-off

KIPPAX STREET STAND £8.00

Turnstiles 29 to 40 and 50 to 51 ADULT

General Secretary

Season 1992/93

MANCHESTER CITY F.C.

1000₢

cover of the *Financial Times*. The dagger (†) means that the dividend has just been increased. Another example would be a diamond, meaning that a bid or reorganisation is in progress.

The C'vr (cover) is 1.9 (Monday FT, not shown above) indicating that payment of the dividend is covered 1.9 times by the company's profits. The cover can be computed by the standard formula, cover = 100/(PE x Net Yield percent). The price-earnings (P/E) ratio (13.7) tells the number of times the current share price exceeds the company's profits (earnings) per share which can be distributed as dividend.

WHY COME TO MARKET?

Companies seek a listing on the Stock Exchange, ie, come to market, when they need to raise money. A new company may be seeking start-up capital, an older company may seek additional funds for expansion. An established family firm may want to let its owners sell out their stake, or part of it, to other investors.

Companies come to market through four major routes:

- **An Offer-for-Sale**. A prospectus is published in the newspapers and anyone can apply for shares at a fixed price. Most government privatisations have been of this type.

- **An Offer by Tender**. Would-be investors make an offer to buy stock at a price they think the company is worth (usually subject to a minimum price). The highest bidders get the stock at the **striking price**, the highest price which will enable all the shares to be sold. On rare occasions, the highest bidder has to settle at his full tender offer – see the terms of the prospectus.

- **A Placing**. New shares are placed with the large institutions by the company's broker or agent at an agreed price. Some placings may now be made to financial intermediaries, such as brokers.

- **An Introduction**. No new shares are issued. Instead old, privately held shares are sold primarily to institutions.

Most issues of new stock are guaranteed by the **underwriters**, ie investors, normally large institutions, who undertake to buy any unsold shares in the issuing company at a fixed price. For this they receive a fee. Several underwriters were seriously caught out by the great offer of BP in October 1987, which coincided with the market crash. Few investors bought stock and the underwriters had to purchase the unsold shares then offload them at a very poor price, taking heavy losses.

MORE ABOUT SHARES

The yield gap
The difference between average share yields and bond yields is known as the **yield gap**. This usually remains quite steady for any one country over many years. Thus, a rise in the prices of bonds such as gilts (lowering of bond yields) is normally followed by a rise in share prices (lowering of share yield), while a fall in share prices follows a fall in bond values.

The yield gap reflects the balance between the growth potential of dividends and the safety of a bond. The yield gap in the UK is typically 4 to 5 per cent (depending in part upon whether all companies or only larger companies are considered). At end-2002 the yield gap was only 1.0 per cent. The effects of a long-term widening of this gap can be very serious, resulting in a sudden fall of share prices to restore the long-term norm.

The yield gap is sometimes known as the 'Reverse Yield Gap', reflecting the fact that share yields, which once were higher than those from gilts, are now generally lower.

The business cycle
Economic rises and falls tend to follow well-defined cycles, with an average turn of about four to five years. This effect can be seen, indirectly, in Figure 1.

First the economy does well, interest rates fall, gilts (with fixed high interest rates) rise, share prices rise and, as the effect feeds into personal pockets, house prices rise and spending increases. Taxes may even fall!

Then the economy overheats, the government raises taxes, interest rates rise, personal disposable income falls, sales of goods fall, company profits fall, share prices fall and finally house prices fall (at least in real terms).

So the government tries to stoke up demand by lowering interest rates and the economy returns to where we came in two paragraphs ago.

Short-term ownership of shares is risky

Although the ownership of shares has proved to be a profitable investment over the long-term for the past two centuries, there is no guarantee that this will always be the case (no guarantee that it will not, either!).

In particular, shares may show abrupt falls in the short-term for the reasons stated above – the drastic 'crash' of October 1987 was the steepest one-day fall ever recorded – and there may be occasional years of 'bear market' to endure.

Bull and bear markets

Fear and greed are the two principal emotions which drive a stock market, leading to two types of investor: the **bulls** and the **bears**. Bulls expect prices to rise. Bears expect them to fall.

A **bear** market is one in which the bears prevail, ie, share prices consistently fall to new low levels, and has been defined as any period of falling share prices which exceeds six months. The worst bear market of the last 100 years was that of 1972–4 when shares lost 70 per cent of their peak value in a panic.

Shares are normally reckoned to lose a maximum of one third of their peak value during a bear market, although the decline is punctuated by frequent **rallies** in which the shares attempt to recover their lost ground. Rallies tend to recover briefly about two thirds of the lost ground. The typical UK bear market lasts an average of two years before share prices start to rise again from their lowest levels. However, two bear markets this century (those of 1929–1932 and 1937–1940) were significantly longer.

A **bull** market is one in which the bulls prevail, ie share prices consistently rise to touch new high levels. Share prices normally rise slowly, then gain momentum, reaching a frenzied climax after which a 'hangover' sets in and a new bear market begins.

The long term

The trouble with investing for the long term is that the investor must be able to avoid urgent calls on the money tied up in shares. In addition, in the long term we are all dead, so that short-term considerations may also become important.

It is essential that the investor retains sufficient cash in easily accessible form so as to be able to meet any sudden emergencies without having to be a forced seller of shares. It would be particularly distressing to have to sell shares just as they reach their lowest point!

The 1973–1974 Stockmarket crash

There have been many ups and downs in the roller-coaster called the Stockmarket. However, one appalling crash sticks out on every chart of average share price plotted versus time and that is the great crash of 1973–4.

Most bear markets retrace about one-third of their previous gains, an event seen almost overnight in the panic of October 1987. After reaching a peak in 1972, share prices fell steadily in a typical bear market for over a year, declining to about 80 per cent of their previous high levels. The fall levelled off and analysts spoke hopefully about the return of a new bull market.

Then three disasters hit the market. In 1973 there was the great oil shock when oil prices quadrupled almost overnight; the Conservative Prime Minister, Edward Heath, had endured a long miners' strike, culminating in a three-day working week to save power; and inflation roared ahead. Heath called an election to ask 'Who rules the country? The government or the miners?'. The electorate decided for the miners and put in a Labour government which imposed a freeze on dividend increases.

This caused a 'crisis of capitalism'. Was there any future in private industry? Shares fell steadily for the next 13 months, bottoming at a level of just 29 per cent of their peak 1972 value.

Yet the sequel is worthy of note. A consortium of institutions conspired together to buy shares simultaneously to force prices up. They succeeded, and the average share price doubled in a fortnight. This led to an almost unbroken rise to new heights for the next 12 years, culminating in the 1987 reversal.

The great 1973–4 crash was probably a once-in-a-century event. In this country it was far worse than the notorious 1929 collapse in share prices. But one can never be sure...

CAPITAL VERSUS INCOME

The private investor in shares must decide whether he is aiming for capital growth, income growth, or a combination of the two.

Capital growth involves an increase in the value of your assets, most simply expressed as a rise in share prices (or in other investments). It is generally reckoned to be best suited to younger investors, seeking to raise their level of funds.

Income growth is believed to be better for retired investors, seeking to eke out their pensions. It involves an increase in the amount of income earned from the investment – from the dividend in the case of shares.

Balanced growth is presumably for the middle-aged, but gives a rising dividend stream to younger investors as the years roll by.

Capital growth

Capital growth used to be especially favoured by high rate tax payers, since its tax treatment was favourable, attracting a lower tax rate on capital gains than tax on dividends.

Capital gains are made when shares are sold at a profit. If 10,000 shares were bought at one pound in 1994 (cost = £10,000) and sold for three pounds in 2002, the capital gain is £30,000 – £10,000 = £20,000, before adjusting for inflation!

Capital Gains Tax (CGT)

Capital Gains Tax (CGT) has to be paid on all capital gains that exceed the year's tax-free allowance. Recent changes in the tax laws and tax rates (maximum rate currently being 40 per cent for capital and income tax) have greatly reduced the appeal of a policy of capital growth. At the time of writing up to £8,800 (for tax year 2006–7) per year of capital gains are permitted free of tax. Other capital gains and income are taxed at the same rate for the individual as his current rate of tax. However, many institutions pay no tax at all on capital or income gains, with implications for the private investor as we shall see in Chapter 4 (Pooled funds).

CGT has become terribly complicated in recent years, and the present situation is summarised in Appendix 16.

It should be recognised that pursuit of income growth frequently results in high capital growth as well. Indeed, one well-known investment strategy involves simply picking the twenty highest-yielding stocks whose share prices stand at a higher level than they did twelve months previously. This strategy has apparently brought good results and is supported and monitored in the *Investors' Chronicle* magazine.

Individual Savings Schemes (ISAs)

A further attraction of high-yielding stocks was that they were particularly suited to use in a Personal Equity Plan (PEP). Introduced in 1986 by the then Chancellor, Nigel Lawson, funds were invested in a PEP through an authorised plan manager. Income and capital gains from the PEP were all tax-free.

The new Labour government ended the PEP scheme in 1998, allegedly on the grounds of high cost, and replaced it with the Individual Savings Account (ISA) which gave similar tax shelters for shares and cash (maxima respectively £7,000 and £1,000 per annum). Unfortunately, the new Chancellor also abolished the repayment of tax credits on dividends to those who paid no tax, although a tax credit of ten per cent will be made available for the first five years of the ISA scheme.

The rub is that the ISA must be administered by an authorised plan manager. You cannot do it on your own behalf, unlike some continental plans, and in the early years of the old PEPs the manager's charge was likely to be so high as virtually to defeat the tax-avoidance element of the scheme, see Table 7 below. It is worth emphasising that, if the manager makes a flat one per cent annual charge on the value of the scheme, then the scheme needs to provide an annual gross yield of five per cent per annum in order for the 20 per cent tax payer to break even. If the manager's charge did not include VAT, the break-even yield will be higher. Government reductions in the standard rate of income tax will also reduce the ISA scheme benefits and, in recent years, management charges have fallen to reflect this reality. However, the ISA continues to provide a real benefit to higher rate tax payers, and all investors will gain from the protection from Capital Gains Tax, particularly now that the latter has become so complicated (see Appendix 16).

An example of a series of typical ISA transactions (Figure 7) is given on page 40.

Table 7. Management charges – PEPs in 1987

Initial investment of £2,400; time taken for tax benefits to compensate initial management charges of typical PEP scheme, assuming 29% tax rates.		
Growth Rate (annual)	**Time (years)**	**Cash benefit (£) after 10 years**
5%	7	60
10%	6	94
15%	6	131

Does tax avoidance pay?

It is particularly important that the investor should recognise that no investment should ever be bought, sold or retained purely for reasons of tax avoidance. It frequently occurs that shares are retained for too long, while the company involved performs badly, in order to avoid Capital Gains Tax. This strategy is held by many experts to be incorrect. Sell up, pay the tax and reinvest the proceeds in something more profitable, if you can identify the opportunity!

Investment Income Tax
From April 1991, most investment income is liable to tax at the investor's normal rate of tax; currently (2006) dividends at 10 per cent and interest at 20 per cent, or either at a higher rate.

Separate taxation for husbands and wives
April 1991 saw the complete separation of taxation for husband and wife. Previously, all investment income was taxed as though the husband had received it, even if the partners concerned had expressly requested separate taxation (in which case the husband lost his married man's personal allowance).

In practice, this now means that the investments of a husband and wife should be so distributed as to minimise the tax burden. For example, if the wife has no paid job it would be prudent to make her the owner of most, or all, of the investments which are providing income; at any rate as long as the total investment income is less than that of the husband's earned income. This assumes that earned and unearned income are taxed at the same rate, as is currently the case. However, in previous years unearned income has often been taxed at a higher rate than earned income.

All the above presupposes that the two spouses are not contemplating divorce, which might make the separation of incomes permanent in a way which had not originally been intended.

THE STOCKMARKET INDICES

The average performance of world stockmarkets is measured by a number of indices. There are indices for all the world, for major and for minor stockmarkets and for major and lesser stocks.

The oldest index in the UK is the FT30 (or FT-ordinary) index, created in 1935 by the *Financial Times*. Previously, only estimates of stockmarket performance were available. The index was based at 100 in 1935, and currently exceeds 1700. This index takes no account of dividends paid and considers equally the share prices of thirty of the largest industrial UK companies chosen to represent the market

BRITISH AND GLOBAL INVESTMENT TRUST

ISA STATEMENT AND VALUATION
FOR PERIOD 06 OCT 200X TO 05 APR 200Y

Account No: 12345   Client: A. N. Investor
                                  Of No Fixed
                                  Abode
                                  London AB1 9ZY

STATEMENT OF TRANSACTIONS:

Date	Ref	Description	Amount	Balance
06-10-0X	0001	Cash Deposit	2,400.00	2,400.00
07-10-0X	0002	Purchase of shares 2350 @ 100.00p	2,350.00–	50.00
07-10-0X	0003	commission	23.50–	26.50
07-10-0X	0004	stamp duty	12.00–	14.50
20-11-0X	0005	Dividend	45.00	59.50
20-11-0X	0006	Tax credit reclaimed	5.00	64.50
20-11-0X	0007	Annual Plan charge	12.00–	52.50
02-04-0Y	0008	Purchase of shares 39 @ 105.13p	41.00–	11.50
02-04-0Y	0009	commission	0.41–	11.09
02-04-0Y	0010	stamp duty	0.21–	10.88

The times of the transactions will be supplied on request.

VALUATION AS AT 05 APR 200Y

Holding	Mid-price	Value
2389 Shares in British & Global	1.06	2,532.34
Uninvested cash		10.88
TOTAL:		2,543.22

Fig. 7. ISA transactions: what a typical statement of such transactions would look like.

as a whole. The companies are changed occasionally to reflect changes in company size or takeovers.

The FT-Actuaries (FT-A) All Share index was introduced in 1962 and the **FTSE 100** in November 1983. These later indices measure representative samples respectively of the top 800 and top 100 companies in the UK, and their performance is supposed to track the movement of the market as a whole. Whereas the older FT30 index gives equal value to the shares of each company, and is now primarily of historical value, the FTSE 100 index is weighted so that larger companies have a larger effect on movements in the index. The FTSE 100 index is now plotted every minute by the Stock Exchange and has been designed to mimic closely the larger FT-A index. The FTSE MID250 index (1993) deals with the 250 next biggest companies after the FTSE 100.

There are many indices for foreign stock markets. The USA equivalent of the FT30 index is the **DOW** index, monitoring leading US stocks. The equivalent of the FTSE is the **Standard & Poors** index, following 500 American stocks. For Japan, the most-quoted index is the **Nikkei-Dow**. The **Morgan-Stanley** index assesses the weighted average performance of the world's stockmarkets, and is measured in dollars. The **FTSE-Eurotrack 100** is a composite index of various large European companies but does not include companies based in the UK.

MARKETABILITY OF SHARES

There are about 2000 stocks traded on the London Stock Exchange (the UK Stock Exchange, sometimes known as the International Stock Exchange). Of these, about 1000 stocks are traded actively. **Quoted** companies are those registered with the Stock Exchange and can normally (although not always) be traded reasonably easily. **Unquoted** companies are normally dealt with only on a matched-bargain basis (see below).

The stocks of different companies are now divided into several different classes according to their marketability. Marketability is an important concept for the private investor. There is no point in buying shares if you cannot then sell them at a later date.

Types of market
Several different UK markets also need to be distinguished.

The **main** (or senior) market contains all the companies which have received a full quotation, meeting stringent criteria of financial control before admission.

The much newer **USM** (Unlisted Securities Market; the junior market (founded in 1980)) contained companies which met less stringent financial criteria, possibly because they were too young to have acquired a long track record. EEC rules required a relaxation of admission rules to the Main Market and the USM was ended in 1996.

The replacement junior market known as '**AIM**' (**Alternative Investment Market**) is described in Appendix 12. The new Stock Exchange Alternative Trading System (SEATS) is described in Appendix 9.

Many companies will switch from the junior market to the main market as they become better established. The advantage to these companies is that they will find it easier to raise money to fund expansion on the senior market. Inevitably, the junior market contains a high proportion of the less-easily traded stocks.

Leading stocks on the Stock Exchange are distinguished by the number of market makers who are prepared to deal in the stock in question.

The spread (touch)

The **spread or touch** of a stock is the difference between the price which the market maker will pay to buy the stock (the **bid** price) and the price he will require to sell it to you. The buying price for the investor – the **offer** price at which the market maker sells – will always be the higher of the two figures. The spread represents the market maker's profit and will tend to be larger when stocks are difficult to trade, eg for many small companies or even for all companies in a bear market.

Technically, the spread refers to the difference between the market maker's bid and offer prices, and the touch to the difference between the best bid and offer prices. However, the two expressions will be used interconvertibly in this book.

Alpha, beta, gamma, delta stocks

Prior to 1991, shares were divided into groups of marketability based on the number of market makers who traded the shares. **Alpha** stocks represented the most-traded companies, usually the largest. **Beta** stocks were also readily traded. **Gamma** stocks formed the bulk of the market in terms of numbers (about 1,500), and could sometimes be difficult to sell. **Delta** stocks made up the remainder of the market. Trading of these stocks could be very difficult and the dealing spread frequently exceeded ten per cent.

This system was criticised since it did not reveal how easy it was actually to trade stocks. There might be a very poor market for some companies and the dealing spread could be as high as 50 per cent. Moreover, in the difficult years of 1988–1991, there were few market makers for many of the smaller companies. Indeed, for some there was only one specialist market maker, Winterflood Securities, which charged these companies for providing a market for their shares at all.

Not surprisingly, a number of the smaller companies elected to give up their Stock Exchange listing, arguing that the cost was too high and there was no real market in their shares anyway.

In January 1991, a new system of designating marketability was introduced by the Stock Exchange, known as Normal Market Size.

Normal Market Size (NMS)

Normal Market Size (NMS) bands are based on a percentage of the average daily turnover of the shares in a company (in cash over 12 months), with quarterly reviews.

The bands go from 500 to 200,000 shares (or units in the case of some multi-share packages). Companies newly listed on the Stock Exchange are initially assigned a band estimated from the bands of similar companies. Companies in which dealings have been suspended are assumed to have performed during suspension in the same way as they performed after their return from suspension.

Market makers must now deal at quoted prices for all transactions of a scale fitting in the NMS bands. Very large transactions can be negotiated.

FT classification

The *Financial Times* newspaper now classifies share price listings solely on the basis of market capitalisation.

Suspended shares

Dealing in shares on the London (International) Stockmarket can be suspended at any time. This occurs for two reasons:

- **The Company Requests Suspension**
  Dealing in company shares is supposed to be on the basis that the entire investment community has access to equal information. A

company may ask for its shares to be suspended because of an impending announcement of material significance to investors and where a 'disorderly market' may occur as word leaks out. The most common reason for a company to ask that dealings in its shares be suspended is that it is about to participate in a bid for, or by, another company. However, numerous other reasons may be given; for example, the company is about to announce unusually bad news (the managing director has just fled to Brazil). The Stock Exchange frowns on long, voluntary suspensions. It is generally reckoned to be desirable that investors should always be able to sell unwanted stock, even if at very bad prices.

- **The Stock Exchange Suspends Trading**
  This usually heralds very bad news, although suspension can also be the Exchange's only effective sanction against a listed company which persists in breaking the Exchange's rules.

Shares suspended by the Stock Exchange find it hard to return to a full listing. Sometimes the company in question has gone bankrupt. Investors locked into their investments in this way have very little in the way of options. They can grit their teeth and hope that the company will one day again be traded on one of the Stock Exchanges. It may be possible to trade shares on the Bulletin Board (see Appendix 9) or, just occasionally, to sell the shares 'off-market' to another investor. Sometimes it happens that a wealthy investor will want to try to take control of the company by picking up unwanted shares cheaply, even contacting individual investors directly—see Chapter 5.

Matched bargains and Rule 2.1 (a) (v)

A number of companies are traded so infrequently that trades are done on a **matched-bargain** basis. Before you buy or sell, the broker needs to find someone prepared to trade with you. This may take a long time (weeks or even months).

Some foreign stocks which are not quoted on the Stock Exchange may also be traded in this way under the Stock Exchange's Rule 2.1 (a) (v) which permits such transactions. Companies so traded are usually marked in the share price listings of the *Financial Times* with a heart symbol. Many Australian and South African shares are traded in this way on the London Stock Exchange.

See Appendix 9 for a description of the 'Bulletin Board'.

Overseas investments

Direct investment overseas can be very slow and very expensive, in terms of commissions. Some countries require the purchase of blocks of stock in fixed-size bundles. A few overseas stocks, especially those from Australia and South Africa, can be traded under Rule 2.1 (a) (v) (see previous section).

Some overseas companies also have normal quotations on the London Stockmarket. This is usually to enable an international company to have its stock freely traded in a market other than its native one. The company can also raise money on any market on which it has a stock exchange listing.

OTC stocks

'**Over-the-counter**' (OTC) stocks are traded primarily through a licensed dealer who may also be the sponsor of the stock, ie the agent who originally sold the stock. This could result in an obvious conflict of interest, since the dealer may be more interested in offloading the stock than in buying it back again. OTC stocks are therefore potentially difficult to market, since the only market maker may be the principal seller. Also, they are likely to be inherently very risky, as only very small companies are expected to be traded in this way. OTC stocks are now becoming very rare under new government legislation and the activities of various City 'watchdogs'. They can, however, be purchased overseas.

OFEX

The company PLUS Markets Group is currently authorised by the Financial Services Authority (another City watchdog) to trade in many small companies. Many trades are on a matched basis, but the market is intended primarily for professional investors. Again, marketability of OFEX stocks may be poor. Prices of OFEX stocks are often quoted in *Investors Chronicle* and the *Financial Times*.

BES/EIS companies

The **Business Expansion Scheme** (BES) was a new idea from a Conservative Chancellor permitting full tax relief on investments in unquoted new companies. That is, investments in such companies could be allowed against income tax. The scheme was intended to encourage investment in new companies just starting up and was, therefore, attended by a high degree of risk. Investment in companies involved in letting homes to tenants was later encouraged. The rules for tax relief on BES schemes were periodically altered, but the shares had to be held for five years to qualify for the tax benefit.

The BES was replaced by the **Enterprise Investment Scheme** (EIS) in November 1993, returning to the original objective of the BES scheme.

During the qualifying period, marketability of these shares is likely to be very poor indeed. Thereafter, most BES/EIS companies hope to obtain a quotation on one of the markets of the Stock Exchange, which will enable the investors to trade their shares freely.

The main attraction of the BES/EIS scheme was always to high rate tax payers. Recent reductions in the highest rate of income tax, however, make these very high risk investments less attractive. Inevitably, some BES/EIS companies will have been bankrupted before the five years are up.

For the current rules, see Appendix 7.

MARKET SUBDIVISIONS

Companies quoted on the Stockmarket are grouped together to form five major subdivisions:

- **Capital goods:** This comprises investment in heavy manufacturing, such as building materials, engineering or ship building.

- **Consumer goods:** Investment in consumables, such as food and drink.

- **Financials**: Companies involved with financial management, such as banks or unit trust managers (yes, you can buy shares in the profits of the managers of unit trusts).

- **Commodities**: Companies involved in commodities such as cereals, gold, mining, gas and oil.

- **Property**: Companies involved in the ownership, development or management of commercial property. Very recently, a few BES companies became involved in the private rented market, leasing out buildings to private tenants (the expansion of the private rented sector is a stated government objective).

SHARE SECTORS

Companies are allocated to different stock sectors by a number of arbitrary processes. Many newspapers provide lists of current share prices for stocks under the papers' own sector headings. Typical headings may, for example, include 'industrials', 'leisure, entertainment and hotels, 'textiles', 'construction' and 'retailers'.

The companies pay for their listings (over £1,900 per year for a daily listing in the *Financial Times*) and can pick their own sector in some papers. However, the *Financial Times*, *Times* and *Daily Telegraph* now list companies according to their classification in the FT-A index. Thus the company Grand Metropolitan Hotels, which did appear under 'Hotels' in the *Financial Times*, and was then listed under 'Brewers & Distillers' in the same paper, now appears under 'Beverages' with its new name 'Diageo'.

The FT-Actuaries index (see Stockmarket Indices, above) also lists some 800 of the most-traded stocks under its own sector types, and indices of performance by each sector are regularly published (eg in the *Financial Times*).

It is particularly important, when comparing P/E ratios and yields of companies, to compare them with their own sector average, and not with the market as a whole. Thus 'retailers' are frequently regarded as property companies, since the value of a prime site can be very high. Their assets may be dominated by the property valuation and the yield will appear to be low, reflecting the high preponderance of capital backing for the share price.

Conversely, engineering stocks tend to have much weaker asset backing since their materials arrive from outside contractors just in time to be used, so that the engineers do not keep large stocks hanging around on the premises. Hence average yields of engineering firms tend to be higher than for 'retailers', while P/E ratios are generally lower.

It is also important to bear in mind that at any moment one market sector may be 'fashionable'. This tends to result in an over-rating of that sector, prices are high, P/E ratios are high and yields are low. The usual consequence is that one day the fashion changes, and all share prices within the formerly favoured sector suddenly show an abrupt fall.

TYPES OF SHARE

The last sections examined the marketability and sector types of company shares. This section examines the types of share which can be found within any market and its sectors.

Blue chips

Some of the largest and most-traded companies on the Stock Exchange are known as **blue chip** companies. These are generally reckoned to be reasonably 'safe' investments in the sense that although their share prices may fall and rise like the rest of the market, they are unlikely suddenly to go bankrupt.

A disappointing exception in recent years was the blue chip company Dunlop. When this tyre manufacturer ran into financial trouble some years ago, a rescue package was immediately put together by other companies and the institutions. Its aim was to protect the 'widows and orphans' involved in the company, and to maintain the Stock Exchange's image as a safe(-ish) place for investment. Dunlop was finally taken over by the conglomerate BTR. There is no guarantee that this bale-out would be repeated for another blue chip company. British and Commonwealth was not so lucky in 1990. Nor Marconi in 2002.

Privatisation issues

The Conservative and new Labour governments have, since 1982, indulged in a process of denationalisation of state-owned companies, starting with Amersham International (the first to be completely returned to the private sector).

These companies are nearly all very large and are more often sold for political reasons than for economic ones. One frequently stated reason is to increase the number of private shareholders in the UK. The number had previously declined dramatically under a succession of governments of both political persuasions who were more interested in social issues than in maintaining the manufacturing base of the UK.

Consequently, the shares of privatised companies are frequently sold at a genuine discount – read 'cheap'. This has made such share issues so popular, however, that it is difficult for prospective owners to obtain a worthwhile allocation of shares.

Once issued, most of the privatisation companies to date have been traded on the main market, mainly as alpha stocks. However, some of the companies concerned were sold directly into private hands (eg National Freight Corporation, which subsequently came to the Main Market after selling new shares). The full list of privatisation stocks is given in Appendix 1.

Growth stocks and recovery stocks

Growth stocks are companies from which a high rate of growth –

much higher than the sector average – is expected in the next few years. Growth stocks are characterised by high share prices, low yields and high P/E ratios.

The opposite phenomenon is seen with **recovery** stocks. Some companies that have fallen on hard times will be suffering from low share prices (making them a prey to bids from other companies), high yields (which are expected to fall as the dividend is reduced) and low P/E ratios. A few of these companies will ultimately go bankrupt.

However, some companies that look as though they were in trouble may now be ready to start climbing upwards again with their problems sorted out (eg rationalisation after a falling order book). Investment in such companies can provide spectacular gains, but there remains a high risk of bankruptcy. Perhaps the best way to take advantage of recovery stocks is through participation in a pooled fund (see Chapter 4), and M&G's Recovery Fund is often cited as the classic example of successful application of the principle of spreading risk by investing in many recovery stocks. The Fund is the best performing unit trust yet launched, considering its overall performance since it was founded in 1956.

An interesting feature of growth stocks is that, if the market's perception is correct about a high growth rate, the share will grow into an ordinarily rated one. If the market is wrong, the investor will be left with a high-priced failure.

The converse holds true for recovery stocks, where if the market is right the yield will tumble into an ordinarily rated one, while if it is wrong the investor will have a bargain.

Consequently, the author would always rather buy a stock for potential recovery than for potential growth, although to be sure the risk is higher with the recovery share.

Mature industries

After years of growth, some companies find that they have saturated their consumer market, so that growth in their number of customers is no longer possible. Examples of this kind of industry include most of the utilities such as electricity, water and gas, and certain other manufacturing sectors, such as the makers of refrigerators (clearly, no customer needs to keep buying fridges).

These industries are said to be mature. Their share prices are usually lower (with higher yields) than companies from which growth is still expected.

Nevertheless, mature industries can still show some improvement in profits, for example by controlling costs and sometimes by raising prices for 'improved' products – computer-operated refrigerators? – and their dividends can in any case be expected to keep pace with inflation.

Mature industries often serve as what are known as cash cows. With no need to worry about reinvestment in the latest machinery, they can give high yields to their share owners. There is room for one or more mature industry stocks in any balanced portfolio of shares.

Smaller companies

Although blue chip companies are reasonably safe, it is an observable fact that the riskier small companies give a better long-term performance. And this is as it should be, since greater risk should mean greater rewards.

In recent years, the FT-A (all share) index has frequently out-performed the FTSE index, even after the 1987 crash. Equally, unit trusts investing in smaller companies have a better long-term track record than those investing more widely.

Spreading risk is particularly important for investment in smaller companies. It is here that pooled funds (such as unit trusts) can be particularly beneficial, providing all of the benefit and little of the risk.

Small companies tend to be harder to trade than their larger counterparts. The Stock Exchange has taken steps to revitalise the market by making a market in the shares of smaller companies (see 'AIM', Appendix 12).

Technology stocks

It is a sad fact for a scientist to have to admit, but investment in shares in new technology has generally given poor returns, the pharmaceutical companies excepted. There was an unusual boom in 1998–2000, which ended with a sudden crash. At the forefront were the so-called TMT (technology, media, telephone) companies. Even pooled funds, such as unit trusts, have been poor performers relative to the market average.

Investment in technology requires acceptance of high risk and possibly being asked often to stump up new cash for rights issues (see Share Dilution, Chapter 3). In exchange, there can be very high returns – if you guess right.

Pharmaceutical companies have tended to do better, but again involve acceptance of high risk as compensation claims for a faulty drug can ruin the company financially. In return, they offer higher growth rates, typically seen as high P/E ratios and low yields. Companies like Glaxo-Wellcome and Astra-Zeneca offer a straight play on the pharmaceutical sector. Start-up pharmaceutical companies are usually referred to as 'Bio-Tech' companies. The largest in the UK is British Biotech.

Penny shares

A special subsection of the shares of lesser-traded small companies comprises the so-called **penny shares**, named because the price of one share is measured in a few pennies (usually less than 40). Penny shares can show great scope for large rises, since each penny increase on a 10p share represents a rise of ten per cent of the initial value. Conversely, losses can also be heavy. However, a 10p share cannot lose more than 10p from its value, while there is no limit to the potential gain. This provides the chief attraction in these high-risk stocks which are down on their luck.

Problems of marketability and a wide spread remain, but penny shares are often widely tipped for their recovery potential. The tip itself may cause a sharp rise in the value of a share as thousands of investors rush in together (far better to wait until the price falls again, if you must follow tips). The directors of these companies dread having their company tipped, since they have to devote excessive resources to registering and posting accounts and dividends to the vast army of newly-arrived small investors.

Penny shares tend to do very well in bull markets, but badly in bear markets. Only rarely is their popularity founded on fundamental strength. Usually investors rely on wishful thinking, which tends to be in short supply when the market goes down. Investors in penny shares must expect more than their fair share of bankruptcies.

It has been pointed out that some penny share companies will need to double in size just to cover the dealing costs of trading in their shares!

Shell stocks and reverse takeovers

It is an expensive business to get a stock market listing, and a company which has such a listing has an intrinsic value even if it has stopped trading. It sometimes happens that companies which had previously been doing well lose their markets for some reason. Perhaps the fashion for their product changes, or imports provide too much competition. The company reduces, or stops, its trading, but is still sitting on its assets, perhaps has a pile of cash and still has the expensive listing. Companies in this position are known as **shells.**

What usually happens is that outsiders move in to start the operation up in a completely different manner, retaining the old listing. The new company rarely bears any relation to the old, and must be assessed on its own merits.

Sometimes a small company backs itself into a shell company (*ie*, the shell issues shares to the owners of the new company in exchange for the latter's businesses), taking over just the old name and the listing. This saves the new company the trouble of applying for the listing. Occasionally parts of the old business may be retained, so that one sometimes sees the absurd combination of, say, a computer software distributor (the new) with a carpet manufacturer (the old).

Conglomerates and raiders

Some companies expand at a fast rate by taking over other companies, not only their competitors but also companies in any area where they think they can improve profitability by changing the management. The combination of many companies is known as a **conglomerate**, and smaller versions are known as **mini-conglomerates**.

Other companies are put together for the sole purpose of providing a suitable vehicle to mount a bid for a target company. The vehicle (the **raider**) provides a convenient means of separating the bid from the actions of the parent company. Sometimes companies which are taken over are revitalised by new management, but a common fate is for the victim to be sold off in portions to anyone who will pay enough. This is known as an asset strip, which has always, perhaps unfairly, received a bad press.

'Unbundling' was the term coined by Sir James Goldsmith in his attempt to take over the giant conglomerate BAT. It means breaking up and selling off the component parts of the conglomerate in the belief that the sum of the parts is worth more than the whole.

Market professionals today tend to agree with this view, which runs entirely opposite to the old principle of diversification by a company from mature markets into new ones. The professionals say that if they wanted to invest in new industries, they would do so directly, not through a conglomerate.

Companies which have split off subsidiaries (eg Courtaulds, Racal and, recently, BAT itself) and thereby obtained two market prices – one for the rump of the original company and one for the new split-off company – have nearly always found that the two companies are worth more than the original, combined operation.

Consequently, the current fashion is for streamlining once diverse companies into their core businesses.

Crime pays

Crime can pay in two ways for the investor. Firstly, there is not the slightest doubt that insider trading – the use of inside knowledge about a company – can produce good short-term profits. If you know for certain that company A is about to bid to take over company B, then you will almost certainly make money by buying the shares of company B.

The problem is that insider trading is now illegal in the UK. For a long time this was not the case and you could get early warning of an impending event at a company by watching the drift of its share price (up on good news, down on bad). Now the good or bad news affects the share price almost overnight for everyone, except...

...except that an awful lot of people seem to get away with insider trading, despite investigations by the Stock Exchange. The laws of libel prevent the exemplification of this remark, but the *Daily Telegraph* newspaper cynically recommended all inside traders to say 'not guilty' and expect not to be prosecuted. One sharetrader investigated by the Stock Exchange claimed that his purchase was a 'coincidence', and he was not charged. My calculation of the probability of this coincidence was that it was something like one in 750 million.

Secondly, it is very well known that the best growth rate in this country comes from crime. There is no good way of investing directly in the Mafia. For one thing, how would you demand your money back if the godfather decided to keep it? However, you can invest in companies such as Group 4 Securicor.

Property/capitalisation of interest/property yield gap

It is necessary to distinguish between property **traders** and property **investors**.

Companies which are traders build, or refurbish, property which is then sold. Companies which are investors retain property which is let, primarily to commercial tenants, for a rent.

It follows that the traders show greater scope for short-term profit, but the investors provide a more steady source of income, since rents can usually be raised.

Many property traders and supermarkets regard the payment of interest on loans to acquire a building site as part of the 'cost' of the site. The interest due to be paid is added together (capitalised) and deducted, with other costs, from the sale price of the building to give the supposed profit reported in the company accounts.

The problem comes when the building cannot be sold. The trader has no income, but the interest bills keep rolling in. Several property traders went bankrupt in the collapse of commercial property values in 1989–90. The capitalisation of interest is a ploy which has now become deeply unpopular with institutional investors. Learn from them and avoid companies which do it (the necessary information can be gleaned from published company accounts).

One of the factors studied by professional investors in rented property is the property yield gap. This is the ratio of the yield obtained from rented commercial property divided by the average yield from shares.

This ratio has varied widely over the years, rental income exceeding dividends during most of the 1970s and 1980s. The fall in property values in the period 1988–91 resulted in the property yield gap reaching its highest level for decades, rental income in 1991 being double that of average dividend income for the same size investment.

Most institutional investors agree that commercial property provides a better long-term investment than private property. Food for thought for those who 'invest' in their own homes, particularly as even commercial property frequently underperforms the rest of the stockmarket.

Property funds

Direct investment in commercial property is possible through the purchase of units or shares in property funds, although not all may be regulated and compensated by the Financial Services Authority. The regulations for unit trusts provide that investors must always be able to sell on demand. However, it is not practical to sell a large office block so promptly in order to repay them. In practice, then, there are very few property unit trusts and those that do exist are required by new regulations to keep at least 20% of the fund in liquid investments (typically cash, bonds or even property investment trusts). Since property investment trusts are closed-end companies, they suffer from no such regulation and can invest as they please. If too many investors try to sell together, the price of the investment trust drops instead.

3

Factors Affecting the Price of a Share

SHARE DILUTION

In this section various actions taken by companies are considered which may affect the number of their shares, and their shareholders' entitlement to dividends. Any increase in the number of shares in issue potentially has the ability to dilute the earnings per share and thence the dividend paid on each share.

Scrip issue

Scrip issues are made whenever a company feels that its share price is too high. Many small investors would rather own 1000 one pound shares than 100 ten pound shares, so that reducing the value of the shares improves their marketability.

If you already own 100 ten pound shares, you will be issued with 900 further new shares, each valued at one pound. The nominal value of each share, which may originally have been 50p, is now reduced to 5p, but the **issued share capital** effectively remains the same (see Chapter 2).

Each new share will earn one tenth of the dividend of the old shares, but the investor will still receive the same dividend entitlement as before. There has been no dilution of his holding in real terms.

Rights issue

Rights issues occur when the company wants to raise money. It offers to sell new shares at a stated value, usually cheaper than the current share price. The new shares are normally entitled to the same proportion of the dividend as the old, so the dividend is spread between more shares. Consequently, the value of the old shares falls in proportion.

If there is a 'one for nine' rights issue – ie, one share is offered for sale for each nine shares originally held by the investor – the dividend entitlement of each old share will fall to nine tenths of its original value.

ALLOTMENT LETTER No. DEF-123

This document is of value and is negotiable until 3pm on 25th April 200X. If you are in any doubt as to the action you should take or if prior to receiving it you have sold all or part of your holding of ordinary shares in the company, you should take personal financial advice from your stockbroker or other professional advisor immediately.

THIS OFFER EXPIRES AT 3PM ON 4TH APRIL 200X.

The Council of the Stock Exchange has agreed to admit to the Official List the new Ordinary Shares which are now being issued. It is expected that dealings will commence on 1st April 200X. Shareholders should consult the attached circular before deciding to take up their rights.

MEGASTORES plc

(Registered in England – No. 123456)

RIGHTS ISSUE OF UP TO TEN MILLION NEW
ORDINARY SHARES OF 25P EACH PAYABLE IN FULL ON
ACCEPTANCE NOT LATER THAN 3PM ON 4TH APRIL 200X.

PROVISIONAL ALLOTMENT LETTER

LAST DATES AT MEGABANK plc P O BOX 111 THREADNEEDLE STREET LONDON EC1 2CE TEL 0171 123 6789	Mr. ANTHONY INVESTOR OF NO FIXED ABODE LONDON AB1 9ZY

	Holding of Ordinary Shares at close of business on 1st March 200X	Number of new Ordinary Shares provisionally allotted	Amount payable on acceptance by 3pm on 4th April 200X
Latest time for splitting (Nil paid) 31st March 200X			
Latest time for acceptance and payment in full 4th April 200X			
Latest Time for Splitting (Fully paid) 25th April 200X	1000	500	£500
Latest Time for Registration of Renunciation 27th April 200X			
Definitive Certificates despatched 20th May 200X			

Dear Sir or Madam   15th March 200X

1. Details of terms of rights issue (in very small print).
2. Details of acceptance and payment (in very small print).
3. General information (in very small print).
4. Restrictions on applicants (mainly on those from North America; in very small print).
5. Instructions for renunciation and registration, splitting and consolidation (in very small print).

Yours sincerely
Chairman

Fig. 8. Example of a Provisional Allotment Letter for a rights issue of ordinary shares.

It used to be a legal requirement that rights issues be offered to the existing shareholders first, since their holding is being diluted. However, this legal requirement no longer exists, although it is still customary to favour the original shareholders.

It is not necessary to buy the offered rights issue, but failure to do so results in a dilution of the investor's holding. Standard advice to private investors is to sell enough of the rights entitlement to finance the purchase of the remainder. Since rights issues are usually underpriced to ensure that they are taken up, the rights document has some saleable, intrinsic value.

Convertibles

Another way in which companies can raise money is to issue **convertibles**. These assets are sold like bonds. A fixed price entitles the purchaser to a certain income every year until maturity, when repayment is made at **par**: a fixed, prearranged sum for repayment, normally £100.

However, convertibles can also be converted into ordinary shares at certain times each year before maturity. It is there that the element of dilution comes in. The precise conversion conditions vary from issue to issue, and can be very complicated, (eg seven pounds of convertible stock for nine ordinary shares). Convertibles can, therefore, offer some of the security of bonds with some of the growth potential of shares. They are quite popular during bear markets, when they may rank ahead of ordinary shares in the event of compensation after the liquidation of the company.

There is an old brokers' adage, 'Never buy for the conversion'. This means that convertibles should be purchased primarily for their value as fixed interest bonds. Any favourable opportunity to convert the bond into shares should be regarded as a bonus.

When companies spend the money that they raise by the issue of convertibles, they assume that the investors will turn the bonds into shares before the conversion date. Sometimes, however, the company performs so badly that no one wants to convert the bonds. They would rather have the loan repaid instead. The company is, therefore, forced to find a huge sum of money just when it can least afford to pay it. This 'Sword of Damocles' upset a number of companies after the 1987 market crash, Saatchi and Saatchi providing a good example.

Preference shares

It is necessary that a company should be able to generate enough

CERTIFICATE NUMBER	TRANSFER NUMBER	DATE OF REGISTRATION	NUMBER OF WARRANTS TO SUBSCRIBE FOR ORDINARY SHARES
WAR01009	W001234	21MAY0X	– – – 1000 – – –

WARRANTS TO SUBSCRIBE FOR ORDINARY SHARES

MEGASTORES plc

(Incorporated under the Companies Act 1948)

THIS IS TO CERTIFY that

Mr ANTHONY INVESTOR
OF NO FIXED
ABODE
LONDON AB1 9ZY

is/are the registered holders of **ONE THOUSAND**
ordinary warrants, each warrant entitling the Holder to subscribe for one new Ordinary Share of 25 pence, fully paid, in MEGASTORES plc subject to the memorandum and articles of association of the company, the Instrument dated 1st January 200X constituting the Warrants and the Particulars endorsed hereon.

Issued under the common seal of the company

S-E-A-L

NOTE: No transfer of any of the warrants comprised in this certificate will be registered until the certificate has been surrendered to the registrar's office: MegaBank plc, Registrar's Dept, PO Box 111, Threadneedle Street, London EC1 2CE.

Fig. 9. Example of a typical warrant certificate. Note: the dates and other details for the conversion of the warrants will be stated on the reverse side of the certificate in very small print.

cash to pay the interest on its bonds and convertibles. Different classes of company bond are discussed in Chapter 8, but **preference shares** may conveniently be described here.

This class of share receives preferential treatment over ordinary shares (and over some bonds) for dividend payments. In the event of the company going bankrupt, preference shareholders will be paid back from what remains of the company assets ahead of the ordinary shareholders.

In exchange for this greater security, preference shares usually have reduced, or zero, voting rights (unlike the ordinary shares) and provide lower returns than ordinary shares, at any rate over the long term.

Frequently the yield is fixed, as with a bond, while many preference shares are also convertibles (see above). The principal difference between convertible preference shares and convertible bonds is that the interest on the preference shares is usually shown net of standard rate tax.

Warrants and gearing

Warrants are also issued by some companies, usually in the form of a bonus to existing shareholders. They confer on the holder the right to convert the warrant to ordinary shares at a fixed price, at any future date until a deadline is reached (usually after many years). Until then, warrants have no right to dividends and no voting rights. Their primary attraction is for **gearing**. A small rise in the ordinary share price results in a large rise in the warrant price, while a fall in the share price has an equally dramatic downwards effect on the price of the warrant.

For example, if a warrant is issued conferring the right to buy shares at 100p each, and the current value of the shares is 150p, then the intrinsic value of the warrant is 50p. If the share price rises to 200p (a rise of 33 per cent), the warrant will rise to 100p, a rise of 100 per cent.

The first warrants were issued in 1969. They are definitely vehicles for bull markets only, since a fall in the underlying share price causes a drastic drop in the value of the warrant. In theory, a warrant could have a negative value. In practice, however, this never happens since there is no obligation to exercise the warrant.

'Covered Warrants' are issued by certain stockbrokers. They are often settled in cash, rather than with shares that the broker is unable to issue (see also Appendix 18).

Liquid yield option notes (LYONs)

These were issued by EuroDisney in June 1990, and correspond to warrants which can be converted into the cash equivalent of a stated number (19.651 [*sic*]) of EuroDisney shares on the stated date. They provide no yield and have a lifespan of 15 years from their date of issue.

Shares in lieu of dividends

In the days when income tax was not merely high but outrageous, some companies issued tax-free shares in lieu of dividends. This ploy was soon stopped by the Inland Revenue and the practice ceased. These early share issues were often known as 'B'-shares.

Recently, some companies have reintroduced the scheme of offering shares instead of dividends. There is no tax benefit but it is cheap for the company, which can retain one year's dividend payments. It can also be beneficial to the investor who volunteers to receive the extra shares, since there are no handling commissions to pay. The issue of these shares is, in effect, equivalent to a rights issue.

However, the investor should satisfy himself that he would be prepared to pay the current share price for the company issuing the new shares.

Those who do not pay income tax cannot reclaim the tax whether paid on shares received in lieu of dividends, or if they received the dividends in cash.

In the early 1990s, several companies offered 'enhanced scrip dividends' where extra shares, up to 150 per cent of the original entitlement, were offered as a bribe to take shares instead of cash. The shares could then be sold at a pre-fixed price by a broker on the day of issue. These 'rights issues' were unpopular with the institutions.

Many companies have opted to make scrip issues (see above) of their shares in connection with a scheme for paying shares in lieu of dividends. By lowering the share price, more of the dividend can be paid out in the form of shares.

For example, if a company's shares cost 100 pence each then a net dividend of £55.50 converts into 55 shares with only 50 pence remaining to be paid in cash. If the shares cost £12 each (before the scrip issue), only four shares could be purchased with £7.50 left over.

THE PERCEPTION OF SHARE VALUES

How much is a share worth? The usual, and unhelpful, answer is—as much as someone else is prepared to pay. So let's rephrase the question. How much should the small investor be prepared to pay?

This section describes some of the features which affect the market's perception of the value of a share, and looks at how important they are.

Reality

The reality of share investment in the UK is that share prices are underpinned by dividends. While new or recovering companies are not expected to pay a dividend immediately, they will rapidly go out of favour if they do not ever do so.

MEGASTORES PLC

PLEASE DETACH AND RETAIN THIS COUNTERFOIL TO ASSIST YOU IN THE PREPARATION OF YOUR TAX RETURN

Dear Shareholder,

The certificate attached represents the new Ordinary Shares allotted to you in place of the final cash dividend for the year ending 1st January 200Y. The basis of the allotment was one new ordinary share for every 77 ordinary shares on which you made a valid election.

The nominal cash dividend of 0.0013p per share on the ordinary shares on which a valid election was made, together with the full cash dividend of 1.4p per share on the balance of ordinary shares in respect of which no valid election was or could be made, is being forwarded separately, together with the appropriate tax voucher.

Yours faithfully,

Chairman   20th December, 200X.

No. of ordinary shares on which a valid election was made:	1848
No. of new ordinary shares allotted	24
Total cash corresponding to new ordinary shares	£25.85
Notional Tax	£2.87
No. of shares on which full cash dividend has been paid	0
Total number of ordinary shares held at 1st November 200X	1872

Fig. 10. A share dividend counterfoil.

Whilst the asset backing (capital value) of the business should be reflected in the share price, even if only to deter an asset stripper, rises and falls in UK share values also reflect market perceptions of the profitability of the company concerned. This relationship does not always hold in other countries. In continental Europe, and especially in Japan, it is traditional for a company to improve its capital strength (eg by increasing in size) rather than by paying out high dividends. This means that share prices in these countries tend to outstrip dividend growth.

All other things being equal in the UK, the share price should rise evenly as the dividend grows. In practice, this is not so straightforward in the short term as share prices tend to move to reflect anticipated company prospects.

Nevertheless, in the long term the dividend payments should continue to show a gradual increase, and the share price will normally follow the trend. In Table 8 it is possible to see how the 1987 market crash served to bring the share price of an investment trust back into line with its dividend growth.

Companies are normally very reluctant to cut dividends as this is seen as one of the most serious indicators of bad performance. Since

Table 8. How the 1987 Stockmarket crash brought dividends and share prices into line.

Year	Share Price	Dividends
1/1/78	100	100
1/1/79	108	112
1/1/80	100	140
1/1/81	119	147
1/1/82	147	158
1/1/83	217	173
1/1/84	261	190
1/1/85	315	242
1/1/86	342	292
1/1/87	465	352
1/1/88	393	387

(Data: Alliance Investment Trust, rebased to 1978 = 100)

they normally pay out only one quarter to one half of their profit, there is usually enough 'fat' to carry on paying a dividend in the odd bad year. However, consistent unprofitability will result in the loss of the dividend which can often take many years to be reinstated (the bank will want its interest paid off first). ICI's reputation was very badly tarnished when it reduced its dividend for a single year in the early 1980s, although the dividend was restored in the following year. ICI has repeated this trick again recently – but without restoring the dividend.

Fundamentals

The linkage of share price to dividend payment and asset backing represents the fundamental worth of a company's shares, taking into account projected future dividends.

The market tries to anticipate future events in a company's performance and it is usually said that share prices reflect the events of the next twelve to 18 months. Growth stocks, described in Chapter 2, are expected to show unusually high dividend growth and this is reflected in their high share prices. Other companies which are going through a difficult time tend to have low share prices.

The growth potential of companies is the subject of endless analysis by financial experts. They try to project what the companies' profits will be in the months and years ahead taking into account anticipated sales and profit margins. Studies have shown that the analysis is frequently incorrect.

A company's yearly profits must exceed six per cent of its capital, or it would be better advised to place its money in a building society. **Profit margins** can be the source of some confusion. A food retailer makes one per cent on every item of food sold. That doesn't sound very much, does it? But if the food is sold every day for a year, then the gross profit margin on the original capital employed is 365 per cent! This figure (return on capital employed) is the figure to watch for in company reports, not the profit on sales.

Sentiment

The price of shares on the stock market can be affected by the sentiment of the market, or rather of its investors. Sentiment depends entirely on investors' perceptions of how external events will affect the profitability of companies. A good example is the way the market rises every time a Conservative government is elected, and falls when a Socialist government is elected (the same reaction is seen in all Western countries).

Sentiment can be affected by many other factors, including some which appear to have little to do with external events. Shares in the ancient (1881) stock Channel Tunnel Investments rose steeply when the latest Channel Tunnel venture was announced, although the old company had nothing whatever to do with the new. The announcement of a £10 billion defence order from Saudi Arabia in 1988 caused the entire market to rise steeply, not just defence stocks.

However, a general malaise may also set in, forcing prices lower. This is commonly seen after an earlier market collapse or through a fear of high inflation or strikes.

Bids

Perceptions of a company's worth may alter radically after a bid to take control by a second company. The usual immediate result is a rapid rise in the share price of the target company (sometimes a fall in the share price of the bidder, if it is thought to be offering to pay too much), and often a rise in the shares of companies trading in the same sector.

A classic example of this came early in 1988 when Nestlé and Suchard both bid for the chocolate manufacturer Rowntree, saying that Rowntree's brands were of immense value. Suddenly the value of all companies with good brand names rose steeply, whether they sold chocolate, beers, washing powders or anything else to the public.

Directors' shares

Company directors are not allowed to use their inside information to buy or sell shares in their own companies at certain times of the year (eg just before the publication of their accounts).

If the directors are reported to be buying their own shares just after the annual general meeting, then that must count as a very favourable omen for buying the shares. If the directors are reported to be selling their stake, then so should you.

The Saturday edition of the *Financial Times* newspaper and the *Investors' Chronicle* magazine report selected directors' dealings weekly. More comprehensive information can be obtained from Hemmington-Scot (Tel: (020) 7496 0055).

Monday blues

The typical small investor spends all his time reading tips over the weekend, then phones his orders to his broker first thing on Monday morning. This doubtless annoys the broker, or at least fills him with contempt for people unable to make their own decisions. It also causes unnatural share price movements on Mondays which will always work against the investors concerned. Far, far better to wait until Tuesday.

Failure of new share issue

When a new share issue fails, as when a company comes to market and a lot of its shares are left with the underwriters, the **overhang** of unsold stock badly depresses the value of the share price for the stock.

Share buy in

A company with plenty of cash in its bank may decide, with the necessary shareholders' approval, to buy back some of its shares from the market.

The shares so purchased are not retained by the company for its own benefit. Instead, they are cancelled. This means that the available dividend payment is spread among fewer shares, so that the dividend per share is increased for the benefit of the remaining shareholders.

This form of 'corporate cannibalism' is sometimes seen as a measure of desperation by the directors of a company in a mature industry. It implies that they are unable to think of a better way of spending the money to expand the business and improve profitability.

The rules in the USA for companies to buy back their own shares are different – cancelled shares may be re-issued.

Follow the USA

Another major influence on the UK stockmarket's movement is the performance of the US market. When US market indices rise, so do those in the UK. When US indices decline, they are followed by the UK. At times, particularly in recent years, the dog-like devotion of the UK market to the lead given by the US has been quite marked.

Nevertheless, the UK market does not follow the US trend to the point of blind stupidity. If the US market falls very sharply for purely domestic reasons, there are enough canny buyers to ensure that the UK market does not follow suit. Strong UK shares will always come good in the long term, regardless of the machinations of the US market.

Ex-dividend (xd)

When a company's shares are marked 'ex-dividend' ('xd' in the *Financial Times*), it means that they are being sold without entitlement to the most recent dividend. Shares are marked ex-dividend a few weeks prior to the payment of the dividend in order to give the registrars a settled share ownership from which to assess the dividend entitlement. Shares declared ex-dividend usually undergo a sharp drop in value and this is particularly marked with shares which pay large dividends.

The market in general tends to show a fall in value at the end of the dividend season (March to May), when many companies pay their dividends at the end of their financial year.

Shares described as 'cum dividend' are those purchased with an entitlement to the dividend in the few hours before the shares go ex-dividend.

Stabilisation

Stabilisation is the name given to the process when a new company comes to the Stockmarket and the friends and colleagues of the company (or of its issuing agent) band together to buy its shares in the first few weeks, thereby stabilising the price in the early days of trading. This may create an artificially high share price for the new company, which can be expected to drop to its true value when the same people sell out again after a few weeks.

Stabilisation is a legal and accepted mechanism for supporting a new share issue in its first days of trading.

THE MOVEMENT OF MARKETS

The efficient market hypothesis (EMH)

This hypothesis, much beloved of academics trying to model the stockmarket, states essentially that, since all facts are known about all shares virtually instantly, the price of a share accurately reflects its fundamental value at that time. The corollary of this hypothesis is that it is impossible to beat the market, except by chance, so buying expensive investment advice or management is a waste of time and money.

There are a number of problems with this hypothesis:

- There is the logical problem, exemplified by the story of the professor of EMH walking in the university park with a student. 'Look', cried the student suddenly, pointing to a piece of paper fluttering in a shrub, 'a ten pound note!' The professor shook his head. 'It can't be', he opined, 'or else someone would have found it by now.'

- There is the practical problem in the extent of the analysis needed to keep up with all known facts for all companies. There are some 2000 stocks on the UK market alone, of which about 1000 are traded reasonably actively. The best known alpha stocks, such as ICI, are extensively analysed. There are numerous **analysts** employed in the City by stockbroking firms to assess different companies' performances. The larger the company, the more likely it is to be analysed, and there will be few surprises when one of the giant companies announces its results. However, smaller companies may be much more poorly analysed, and this creates openings for a private investor to find undervalued stocks.

- The EMH does not satisfactorily explain a sudden stockmarket collapse. How can shares be worth one pound each on the Friday and 70p each on the Monday? Academics are now revising their theoretical model to take account of the tardiness of perception of fundamental value by investors. 'Efficient Learning Markets' assume that investors learn from experience with new companies and/or asset classes; thereafter EMH applies to the share price. It does, however, remain true that share prices will adjust themselves to meet revised profit expectations from a company. This is particularly noticeable when a company announces unexpected profits in its annual report. Good results may still be met by a fall in share price, since the results were not so good as expected.

- If everyone believes in the EMH, so that no one bothers to carry out any research into the value of a company, then pockets of inefficiency (poor valuation) will inevitably arise.

- Surveys have shown that shares which used to do badly have a better than average chance of out-performing the market in the following years, while shares which have done consistently well tend to underperform a few years later.

Charts

Belief in the Efficient Market Hypothesis has an interesting side consequence. If share prices already discount all predicted news (ie, the prices fully reflect all known fundamental factors), then mob psychology may prove a potent factor for predicting share price movements in the short term. **Chartists**, or **technical analysts** as they prefer to be called, study plots of share prices over periods of time in the hope of discerning common patterns of behaviour.

Inevitably, this process requires the bulk of the market to pay no attention to charts, or the predictions would become self-defeating. Chartists were spectacularly unsuccessful at predicting the 1987 crash, and often disagree among themselves over the interpretation of their charts. At their most absurd, chartists tried to predict the course of the 1987–88 bear market by trying to retrace the pattern of the 1929–30 crash, as though nothing had changed in the intervening 60 years. The analogy soon broke down.

Another problem for chart followers is that they frequently cannot even agree about which parameters are the most significant to plot on their charts. Belief in some chartists' predictions requires a suspension of common sense, but there can still be some merit in studying charts. Naturally the investor wishes to buy stocks when they are at their lowest price and a chart of share prices gives a rapid assessment of whether the stock is near a recent high or low level. This feature can much more readily be observed from a chart than by studying tables of share price movements.

Further information about the use of charts to predict share movements is given on page 136.

The random walk

Share prices, then, move randomly in the short term, in a manner which cannot be predicted. And this must be so, or else any predictive method would rapidly become self-defeating as everyone tried to use it.

In the long term, there will normally be a tendency for share prices to rise, reflecting improving company profits and inflation.

Arbitrageurs

Arbitrageurs are the market professionals who trade on quite small differences between what a price should be and what it is (a computer helps). These differences are normally too minute to be profitably exploited by small private investors, even if they could spot them in time. An important exception occurs with a bid or takeover for another company, when the price of the shares of the target company may shoot up to exploit the difference between the bid price and the previous share price.

Hedge funds are expected to balance the risks in their portfolios ('hedging'), but some have acquired recent notoriety for acting as arbitrageurs, even borrowing huge sums of money, to exploit perceived minute differences between market values. A few of these have become bankrupt as a result of errors in their calculations, losing borrowed money which cannot then be repaid.

The small investor is too remote from the computer-mediated market of professional investors, and cannot hope to outperform the professionals in the short term. The private investor should therefore adopt a long term strategy of buying shares in companies which are perceived to have excellent long term prospects.

THE IMPORTANCE OF TIMING

Timing refers to the investor's ability to know when to buy stocks and when to sell them. Its importance can scarcely be overstated.

The long term

Correctly timing when to buy or sell shares is essential. Stockbrokers Barclay de Zoete Wedd showed that an investor who put £1,000 into a building society in 1945 would by 1996 have earned nearly

£10,400. If the same money had been put into the stockmarket, it would have made £218,000. However, inflation would have reduced this sum to a **real** increase of about £10,000, while the building society investor would have stood still in real terms.

If our investor had been clairvoyant, knowing on 1 January of each year which type of investment would do better during the calendar year and had switched accordingly, he would have made the colossal sum of over three million pounds. (My calculation.) Few people are clairvoyant, despite occasional claims to the contrary, and most must settle for the hope of buying a stock before it rises – with the risk of a fall – or after it has started to rise – with the risk of a sudden change of direction.

There is not, in my opinion, anything shameful in buying as the market falls, despite the danger of finding that your investment has quickly fallen further. If you wait until the market starts to rise before buying stock, the chance still remains that the market will fall again after the purchase has been made. There is also the other difficulty that everyone may be trying to pile in as the market starts to rise, causing an excessively rapid increase in share prices so that you may miss your chance to buy cheaply.

The short term

A short-term aspect of timing comes with recommendations of shares by newspapers, tipsheets and the like. If a writer tips a stock, it will immediately jump in value although normally the price will subside to its previous level in two to four weeks. Following recommendations is therefore worthwhile for they tell you what **not** to buy in the near future.

The trend is your friend – or is it?

This well known stockbrokers' saying has proved over the years to be generally true, but the reversal of a trend can be unexpected, sudden and painful.

One oft repeated trend is that share prices tend to fall in times of slack trading. Christmas and the August holidays are typical. In the latter case, there is the saying 'Sell in May and go away; come back again on St. Leger's Day' [September].

It is particularly important to remember, when share prices are manifestly overvalued and everyone is piling into share ownership, that the trend is in imminent danger of reversal. There is a finite pool of buyers. When everyone has bought, who will hold share prices up? Similarly, the best time to buy shares is when everyone else has lost interest in the stock market.

COMPANY BIDS AND TAKEOVERS

Takeovers occur when one company successfully bids for control of another, by buying a majority of the voting shares from the shareholders of the target company.

Agreed bids

Bids may be agreed or contested, but it is the shareholders of the target company who have the final say as to whether the bid succeeds. If the bid is an agreed one, then the directors of the target company have agreed that the bid is fair, and it will usually succeed at once.

A bid involves an offer by the bidder company to take over a target company. Such a bid must be made by one company for another if the first already owns more than 29.9 per cent of the second company's shares. The bidder will gain control if he can buy over 50 per cent of the available shares (in practice, 40 per cent is reckoned to be enough to give the bidder voting control). Bids will usually start as conditional, meaning they are conditional on enough shareholders accepting the offer. If the bidder secures a sufficient number of acceptances, his offer will go unconditional and the bidder will pay the same offered sum to all shareholders who sell their stake. If the bidder can secure 90 per cent of the total shareholding, he can compulsorily purchase the outstanding shares from the remaining shareholders.

A takeover bid is limited to 60 days unless another company bids. Day zero is the day the offer is posted to shareholders.

Contested bids

Any shareholder who holds a stake of more than three per cent in a quoted UK company is obliged to announce that fact and, if the shareholder is a well known predator of target companies, this will usually cause the price of the target company to rise steeply in anticipation of a bid. Consequently, attempts to take over target companies often begin with a 'dawn raid' where the bidder seeks to pick up as much stock as possible before having to disclose his intentions and see the share price rise. Only then will the predator announce that he is making a bid.

If the bid is contested it is nearly always necessary, in practice, for the bidding company to raise its offer for the target. Of course, it is not obliged to do so. Defences open to the directors of the target company include an appeal to its shareholders not to accept the bid, and the following:

Poison pills, Pac-man and white knights

Poison pills
A poison pill defence involves the target company performing some action, in the event of the bid succeeding, that is so objectionable the bidder is not willing to endure it. This defence is much more common in the USA than in the UK, and may typically involve the target company mortgaging itself to the hilt to take over another company itself.

Another favoured strategy is for the target company to award its directors outrageous 'redundancy' payments in the event of the bid succeeding. These strategies are becoming decreasingly successful in the USA owing to the willingness of other shareholders to take court action to stop the poison pill defence, so that they can benefit from the takeover price being paid.

A recent variant of this ploy seen in the UK is for the target company to say that it is in such a mess that no one ought to want to buy it!

Pac-man defence
Another form of defence, most commonly seen in the USA, occurs when the target company tries to turn on its predator by making an offer for it. It is known as the Pac-man defence, after the computer game of the same name where a hunted player can swallow an energy pill and turn on its attackers. This defence rarely seems to work in practice, although it does raise the interesting speculation of who would own whom if both bids succeeded.

White knights
A target company may accept that its days of independence are over, but still be unwilling to be taken over by the original bidder. In this case it may look for a white knight, another company which will buy part or all of its stock. The white knight may be prepared to keep the original business going as it was.

Acceptance of an offer
Since a contested bid usually results in higher offers from the same or a different bidder (another company may not want to see one of its competitors fall into the hands of a rival), it is generally good advice for the shareholder not to accept the first offer. Subsequent offers should be considered on their merits. Cash offers should normally be preferred to an offer to give the predator's shares in

exchange for the investor's holding in the target company. Before accepting the latter offer, the investor should always ask himself whether he would buy the predator's shares at the price the market is claiming they are worth when they are offered to him.

A further consideration is that accepting a cash offer may invoke a large bill for Capital Gains Tax. Accepting the bidder's shares avoids the tax charge.

Mergers and de-mergers

Sometimes two companies agree to merge, instead of one taking over the other. This will cause less animosity among senior managers than a takeover, while still creating opportunities for savings in duplicated administrative costs. Usually one company behaves as the senior and issues its own new shares for the shares of the junior partner. Thus shareholders in Junior may be issued one new share in Senior for (say) every three shares held in Junior.

A de-merger occurs when a company splits itself into two or more parts. Again new shares will be issued to existing shareholders for all the new companies.

Tracking stock

British companies are not allowed de-mergers until they are at least five years old. Instead of de-merging profitable subsidiaries in order to raise cash for their main business, fast-growing new companies may issue 'tracking stock': special shares whose value tracks the underlying business that might have been de-merged. Thus the main company still manages to raise the money that it needs.

Loan notes

Loan notes are interest-bearing bonds (technically 'unsecured loan stocks', see Chapter 8) that can be sold back to the issuing company before a stated date. They can only rarely be traded on a stockmarket. Loan notes may often be offered, as an alternative to cash, by a successful bidder to the target's shareholders.

The advantage to the investor is that some of the loan notes he has received from the bidder can be cashed in each year, so that each sale earns less than the CGT allowance for that year. Thus, a big CGT bill arising from the sale of shares to the bidder may be reduced or avoided altogether.

See Appendix 16 for details of Capital Gains Tax.

'C' shares

'C' shares have been issued by some existing investment trusts to new cash purchasers. If ordinary shares were issued, then for a while the original investors would find themselves in a fund that contained investments and a large amount of cash, when they wanted to be only in the underlying investments. The issue of C shares allows the original investors' holdings to remain undiluted with cash. The fund managers will slowly invest the cash from the C shares into other investments, and only then will the C shares be exchanged for ordinary shares in the original trust. Another advantage is that all the costs of the new issue of shares will fall exclusively to the new investors.

Treasury shares

Since December 2003, British companies have been permitted to repurchase their own shares into 'Treasury', instead of cancelling them. Shareholders' approval is required, and for investment trusts the maximum number of shares that can be held in treasury is one tenth of the entire issued share capital. Treasury shares may be re-issued to the stockmarket for cash when the company deems fit. However, institutions are unenthusiastic, citing pricing difficulties and possible price weakness caused by the potential overhang of shares waiting to be sold from the treasury. See also **Share buy in**, page 64.

4

Avoiding Undue Risk

AVOIDING LOCAL RISK

Investment in shares is inherently a risky business since the company may go bankrupt, rendering the shares worthless. More frequently, the company may go through a spell of poor profitability, reducing dividends and thence the share price.

There are two types of risk associated with investment in company shares, specific risk and market risk.

Specific risk/alpha risk

Also known as alpha risk, specific risk is associated with the individual risk inherent in holding shares in individual companies. There is absolutely no reason to endure specific risk, since it can be alleviated by buying a spread of companies across several market sectors. The usual rule given is to hold around 20 (at least ten) different stocks. It is not necessary for them to be in 20 different market sectors, but they should certainly be in ten or more sectors.

Mathematical calculations show that 90 per cent of the risk of holding individual shares can be lost by holding a portfolio of just ten shares; 95 per cent of risk with 20 shares.

A good example of the consequence of specific risk was seen in 1999 when the UK retail sector fell out of favour and share prices dropped heavily. A well-diversified portfolio would have been only slightly troubled by this, and shares held in other sectors might well have gained as money removed from the retail sector was reinvested (pushing up prices) in other sectors.

If you cannot afford to own ten or more shares, the same spread of risk can be obtained through investment in a pooled fund such as a unit trust (see Pooled Funds on page 77).

Market risk/beta risk

Market risk reflects the fact that all the market may drop together, as in a crash or a bear market. There is no way of avoiding this except by hoping that things will get better again in time. Or, if you were lucky, by selling everything before the fall became noticeable. The difficulty then is that you might sell up only to find that the fall was purely temporary.

A risk associated with a market fall is the so-called beta risk. When markets change direction, some shares traditionally change in the same direction to an exaggerated extent. Thus if the market falls by ten per cent, some individual stocks will fall by only five per cent, and others by 20 per cent. This difference relative to the market represents the beta risk of the share, and it is possible to buy large tables of beta risks for all shares. High beta risk stocks should be sold if you think the market is about to fall, or bought if the market is about to rise.

Penny shares have high beta risks, unit trusts have low beta risks. It is important to remember that the tables of beta risk were compiled on the basis of past experience, which may not recur in the future.

There has been some debate about the accuracy of beta values. A new model by Ross, 'Arbitrage Pricing Theory' (APT), seeks to subdivide beta risk into the following components:

- inflation
- industrial production
- investors' liking for risk
- interest rates.

Returns are assessed from the sensitivity of a share to each component.

Risk and marketability
Do not confuse alpha and beta risks with alpha and beta ratings of marketability (see page 42).

OVERSEAS INVESTMENTS

It is not necessary to restrict your investments only to the UK market and there are many foreign stock exchanges to choose from. Interestingly, the London Stock Exchange, sometimes known as the International Stock Exchange, is the world's largest single exchange in terms of turnover.

The world's biggest markets, in terms of capitalisation, are those of the USA and Japan. The UK is third and other large markets include West Germany, Italy, Australia, Hong Kong and Canada. After an agreement between the electronic trading arms of both stockmarkets, it is now much easier and cheaper to trade shares between Britain and the USA. A British investor pays no stamp duty or VAT on purchases, but a US levy of 0.03% on all sales (as well as broker's commission).

So-called 'emerging markets' form part of overseas investments, and are covered in Appendix 13.

Advantages

The advantages of investing overseas are principally centred on the spread of risk and reducing your exposure to the vagaries of your own economy and government. You may also be able to benefit from currency movements, which can also be listed under disadvantages!

Disadvantages

One big disadvantage is the expense of investing overseas as many brokers have high handling charges and require large minimum investments. However, it is easy enough to invest overseas through pooled funds such as unit trusts (see Pooled Funds on page 77).

Another serious problem is that of currency exposure. When you invest in the UK, all the profits come directly to you. If you invest overseas, then a rise in the value of the pound sterling against the local currency may completely offset a large profit in local terms. Conversely, a stationary foreign economy may still give you huge returns if the pound falls in value. The UK investor who places his money abroad is, in effect, betting that the pound will fall, or at worst hold steady, against the local currency. It is a sad but observable fact that the pound does show a steady downwards drift against other major currencies, as it has done throughout the last 100 years.

Finally, for the direct investor, there remains the problem of converting dividends received in foreign currencies into sterling. The minimum commission exacted by the converting bank is now around seven pounds, which may easily be more than the value of the dividend! However, foreign currency cash funds managed in the UK will often be pleased to take dividends in that foreign currency at no extra charge.

Nevertheless, in the short term, foreign investment involves a high degree of currency speculation by the investor, broadly expressed as a hope that the pound will fall against the foreign currency. From 1999 the effect of the new Euro has also to be considered.

Pressure selling

While on the subject of overseas markets, the reader's attention is drawn to the fraudulent activities of some foreign-based high-pressure share salesmen. These individuals, formerly operating largely from the Netherlands, but more recently for brief periods from any safe haven before the local police track them down, attempt to sell you 'bargains' in little known shares trading on the world's minor stock exchanges, often over the telephone. Never, ever buy shares over the telephone from a 'cold-caller'. Even when the shares exist at all, they have very poor marketability. Several international efforts are being made to crack down on these con-men.

A common trick is to send the investor a list of 'tips' on reliable companies, but with special emphasis on one dud company. This will be the one which is pushed as the con-man's 'star tip'.

POOLED FUNDS

One well established way of spreading specific risk is to invest in a pooled fund. The money of many small investors is pooled and invested in a sufficient spread of shares, each investor having a share of the total fund.

In the USA, it is quite common for groups, or clubs, of investors to join together to do this pooling of funds, and stocks are selected by mutual agreement or even with a pin! The great attraction of this method is that there are no management charges involved. Such schemes are rare in the UK, doubtless owing to the small percentage (relative to the USA) of the UK population which actively invests in shares. The ProShare organisation (address at back of book) will provide details on how to set up your own investors' club.

Pension funds, insurance groups and similar organisations also invest funds on a pooled scale for the benefit of their depositors. However, the performance and probity of different fund managers may vary, so it is **vitally important to spread investments in pooled funds among several different managers**.

There are two principal schemes for pooled investment open to the small investor in the UK. These are unit trusts/OEICS and investment trusts.

Unit trusts

Unit trusts (known as mutual funds in the USA) are true trusts, with trustees, and are regulated by a government department. The trusts are open-ended funds: units are created whenever an investor wants to buy some, and are destroyed when the investor sells them back. Thus the unit trust manager is forever having to buy and sell the component shares of the trust in the market to meet the demand of investors. There are limitations imposed by the trustees on the investments which a unit trust manager can make, and the investor has no say in what the manager does. Until very recent legislation, no unit trust was allowed to borrow money to invest in shares.

Unit trusts are freely and extensively advertised in the newspapers and elsewhere. Management charges vary, but are frequently quite high, typically a 5–6 per cent offer-to-bid spread and 1–1.5 per cent management fee. The offer-to-bid spread is the difference between the prices quoted to the investor to buy units (the trust's 'offer' price) and to sell units (the trust's 'bid' price); managers can now choose to abolish the spread. The management fee is levied on the total market value of the shares of the trust, and is therefore deducted from the trust's dividend income. What income remains is distributed to the unit holders.

It is apparent from the foregoing that in a bear market the unit trust managers' incomes will take a knock. Many managers have a nasty habit of raising their management rate (say from 1 per cent to 1.5 per cent) to compensate for this. The last person to suffer from a market collapse is always the trust manager. It is also believed that pure unit trust managers tend to show a better performance overall than unit trusts managed by, eg, life insurance companies, the reason being that the pure funds do not have to pay enormous commissions to door-to-door salesmen.

When too many investors sell units simultaneously, the managers must sell their best shares quickly to pay the investors. The residual investors are left with the unsaleable rubbish. For this reason, unit trusts are unpopular with professional investors.

Investment trusts (ITs)

Investment trusts are not really trusts at all and the oldest (Foreign & Colonial) predates the unit trust industry by many decades, having been founded in 1868.

They are companies which invest in other companies' shares. Like all companies, investment trusts are not permitted to advertise except in full-scale share prospectuses. However, they are permitted to advertise their savings schemes. The investor in an investment trust can vote on its strategy and can buy its shares on the stockmarket as for any other company, with the same charges.

Investment trusts are closed end funds. The funds under their control are not affected by the purchase or sale of investment trust shares. Instead the price of the shares of the investment trust rises to reflect their increased demand. Shares trade at a premium or, more commonly, at a discount, to the underlying value of the shares in which the trust is itself invested.

This offers the potential to an investor to buy a share in an investment trust for, let us say, £1 and thereby to own pooled shares worth £1.20, a common occurrence with ITs and a problem which makes them vulnerable to large predators. A large company may offer £1.10 to buy your own pound share, and sell the underlying assets for their full value of £1.20, although it is of course necessary for a majority of shareholders to agree to this.

The *Financial Times* newspaper now publishes daily the discount (or premium) for each investment trust, using data supplied by Fundamental Data Ltd. This information is computed from published dealings by the trusts, and has been shown to be usually very accurate (to within 1–2 per cent) when the trusts publish their own figures at six-monthly intervals.

Investment trusts are also able to buy any stock they want, subject to shareholders' approval, and can borrow money to invest in shares. If the new shares rise in value faster than the cost of the interest charges on the borrowings, then the trust gains considerably in value. This procedure is known as gearing (or, occasionally, as leverage). It is a practice indulged in at times by most investors in other contexts. Buying your own home with borrowed money represents gearing. You would not do it if you thought the value of the house in 25 years' time would be less than the money you had paid back in capital and interest.

Naturally, if the newly acquired shares do not rise fast enough in value to cover interest charges, then the trust will lose money at an unusually fast rate. An illustrative case of this was seen with the Govett Strategic Investment Trust after the 1987 crash, when the trust sold stock rapidly at a depressed price to repay its high borrowings as quickly as possible. Govett Strategic's share price tumbled to about 50 per cent of its pre-crash level, against an average market fall of 30 per cent.

The charges of investment trusts are quite modest relative to unit trusts. A broker's normal buying and selling charges will amount to around 5 per cent altogether, ie inclusive of both buying and selling, while management charges are normally less than one per cent of the total fund – often much less for the larger trusts.

Table 9. Total return from investment trusts and unit trusts.
(Net income reinvested)
Value in January 2003 of £100 invested for:

No. of Years	Investment Trust	Unit Trust
1	73	74
3	62	61
5	91	92
10	174	172

The great attraction of investment trusts is their savings schemes (available now for most of the larger ones). Here the investor can save a regular amount every month, re-invest dividends from the trust and make occasional lump sum purchases. The total buying charges in these schemes rarely exceed 0.5 per cent, and may be as low as 0.3 per cent of the value of the shares purchased. Selling the shares often needs to be done through a bank or broker and is therefore more expensive, but a few trusts offer very cheap selling arrangements too.

Investment trusts have a clear cost advantage over unit trusts through their savings schemes and lower annual charges. Moreover, their long term average performance is better than that of unit trusts, except after a steep market fall, see Table 9.

So why are investment trusts not better known? The answer is twofold. Like all quoted companies, investment trusts are not permitted to advertise themselves, and most of them pay no commission to 'independent' advisors. There was recently a major 'ITs' advertising campaign on television to improve the public's awareness of investment trusts.

The reader's attention is drawn to the variety of different shares available from certain types of so-called 'split capital' investment trusts. These fill special investment niches, are not applicable to the investment strategy described in this book, but are described in more detail in Appendix 6.

Open-ended investment companies (OEICs/ICVCs/UCITS)
OEICs are intermediate between unit trusts and investment trusts, and are much more popular in Europe than in the UK. They became eligible as PEP/ISA investments in 1995.

OEICs are open-ended funds but, like investment trusts, are covered by company law rather than trust law. Their tax regime is similar to that of unit trusts, but there can be many types of share. There is one price for buyers and sellers (no bid-offer spread), so management charges may be higher instead.

When investors sell units in open-ended funds (eg unit trusts and OEICs), the funds have to sell their underlying shares. If too many investors sell too much at once, the fund will be a forced seller of too many shares, obtaining poor prices. In order to protect the remaining investors in the fund, a **dilution levy** is charged to those selling out.

The many share types make for easy switching between funds. One OEIC can have, for example, shares in an equity fund, shares in a bond fund and shares in a cash fund.

Pooled funds overseas

Unit trusts and investment trusts provide ideal vehicles for investment overseas, although the warnings given previously about overseas investments and currency movements still apply. With luck, their fund managers, often based in the foreign market, will know what they are about and all the changes in investment will be made in the local currency.

One problem to consider is whether the trust should remain fully invested in a market which the manager expects will perform badly, or should the trust sell its shares and hold cash for a while until things improve (and if so, should the cash be held locally, or in sterling)? Different fund managers have different views on this, so it is necessary to check whether the fund's strategy fits in with your own views.

The small investor in a trust invested overseas must decide whether he will make the decisions about moving in and out of a fully-invested overseas fund, or stay permanently in a fund from which the managers are permitted to disinvest into cash as they think appropriate.

Management performance of pooled funds

Tables of management performance are widely available for both unit and investment trusts, the latter being mostly members of the Association of Investment Trust Companies (AITC), which publishes many tables of data, including monthly in their own publication.

Experience shows that few fund managers are consistently able to maintain a good performance in each and every year. It is certainly wiser to stick with the best and longest established names, who have reputations to protect.

Management charges may now be deducted from fund income (as was always the case) or from the fund's capital. Deduction from capital provides a higher yield to the investor at the expense of fund growth, and is not suited to long-term investors with no current need for income.

Tax advantages of pooled funds

Unit and investment trusts also have tax advantages over individual investments by a private investor. If the latter keeps buying and selling shares, he will soon run into the capital gains exemption limit on capital gains.

The trusts have no such problem and can buy or sell as often as they like without incurring Capital Gains Tax. The holder of the trusts only incurs his tax liability when he sells the units or investment trust shares, and he only incurs tax on his gain on the original investment, not on all the transactions carried out by the trust.

Fund of funds

The ultimate in pooled funds is the 'Fund of Funds', a class of unit trust which invests the money of its investors in other unit or investment trusts, usually on a global basis.

This provides the extreme in spread of risk for small investors, unless there is a world-wide collapse of shares (not unknown). However, not only do the original unit trust managers make a charge, but so do the Fund of Fund managers. This double imposition ensures below-average performance, since such a wide spread of shares is nearly certain to match the average performance of global share prices – before the charges. Indeed, it is possible that the managers of one of the subsidiary funds may be selling a stock while the managers of another subsidiary are buying it!

Not recommended, then, except for the very small investor who wants an exceptional spread of risk.

Off-shore funds

Off-shore funds, such as some unit trusts, do have certain tax advantages, especially to expatriates working overseas. UK residents will have to pay Capital Gains Tax after selling their units regardless of whether the fund is off-shore or UK based, unless they emigrate first. Moreover, switching between different off-shore funds, which was once possible free from UK tax, also became liable to Capital Gains Tax after April 1989. Favoured off-shore investment havens include Luxembourg, Liechtenstein, Bermuda and the Channel Islands.

One stated reason to use off-shore tax havens is to defer paying tax from a high rate today to a lower rate later.

The obvious disadvantage of the funds is their inaccessibility if something goes wrong – remember Barlow Clowes? If you must invest in this way, and there is little benefit if you are a permanent UK resident, be sure to use one of the large, well-respected fund management groups with an off-shore branch.

Ethical trusts

A number of unit trusts have been launched specialising in ethical investments only. These trusts, depending on their stated degree of ethicality, avoid investment in any or all of stocks associated with armaments, tobacco, whale products or anything else which offends liberal views.

These are new trusts and, during the great bull market of the 1980s, their general performance was acclaimed as being as good as those of the non-ethical unit trusts. Less is heard of the investment merits of ethical trusts today. It is likely that they will always underperform the ordinary trusts in the long term, since the latter can always make the same investments as the ethical trusts, while the ethical trusts will always miss out on booms in non-ethical sectors.

'Green' trusts invest exclusively in companies that are environmentally friendly.

Purchase of unit trusts

Unit trusts are widely advertised in newspapers, and if you clip out and fill in a form, then you have agreed to accept the contract of purchase.

If, however, you have bought a unit trust stake through a salesman who came to your home, then you currently have 7–14 days to 'cool off' before the contract is legally enforceable. There is no 'cooling off' period for purchases of unit trusts made in most other ways, nor for purchases of investment trusts. The exception is for purchases within an ISA scheme when the cooling off period is currently seven days.

Timing of unit trust purchases

One of the biggest problems for those who market unit trusts to investors is that they are always at their most popular just after a large market rise, ie at the top of a bull market when they are most likely to fall, rather than after a market crash or in a bear market when prices are probably cheap. There are whole generations of would-be investors who buy unit trusts just before a crash, then, disillusioned, sell out after the crash, thereby ending their chance of getting their money back when the markets rise again.

THE INSTITUTIONS

The institutions are those large companies which invest huge sums of money, usually pooled money, in the shares of the Stock Exchange, as well as in other investments. The institutions include pension funds, insurance funds and unit and investment trusts.

The buying and selling power of the institutions completely dominates the market. Private investment has been a declining force as a proportion of the market share throughout this century. This decline has quickened since 1945 as successive governments have made private investment decreasingly tax-efficient relative to ownership of housing, pensions and, until recently, life assurance. The recent huge privatisation issues by the Conservative government were intended to broaden the base of private share ownership. However, studies have shown that few of the buyers of such stocks have gone on to become active investors in other companies.

Today, private investors hold fewer than 20 per cent of the shares traded on the UK stockmarket. This may sound like a large voting block and so it would be if the shares were all in a few hands. But two pension fund managers can put their heads together to swing, say, ten per cent of a vote at the company's annual meeting. To achieve a counter-balancing vote in the opposite direction might require some 3000 private investors to collude together.

Because the dominance of the institutions is so great, there is no point in trying to buck their views. If all the institutions have decided to sell stock today, then it is simply futile to buy stock until the fall has been arrested no matter how wrong the institutions may be on fundamental grounds.

A good example of this occurred on the third day of the October 1987 stockmarket crash when, after two days of price falls, many private investors reckoned the market was oversold and plunged in.

They were probably right, but the institutions swamped the market with more selling of stock as prices rose, and down went the share prices to new lows again.

THE ZERO SUM GAME

A zero sum game is one in which there must always be as many equal winners as there are equal losers. Chess is a zero sum game, darts is not since here the ratio of winning margin of winner to loser may vary.

The dominance of the institutions on the stockmarket makes investment in stocks effectively a zero sum game for them. For every institution that performs well, another must do badly since the contribution of the private investor is negligible.

The consequence is that the institutions as a whole cannot perform better than the relevant indices of stock movement. In fact, on average they underperform the index by an amount equal to their costs of buying and selling shares.

It follows inevitably that anyone who can match the index perfectly will outperform more than 50 per cent of the institutions who, let it be remembered, include the unit and investment trusts.

It may be that some fund management groups can often outperform the FTSE or All-Share indices, but experience shows that very few do so on a consistent basis. Moreover, a good manager tends to move around from fund to fund, so that even a good trust may do badly after his departure.

To be sure, there are some good fund managers around with better records than most (M&G and Fidelity come to mind), but the zero sum game ensures that the average unit trust will slightly underperform the market and charge the investor a large fee for the privilege.

Fund managers like to run lots of unit trusts, partly because it offers lots of choice on the 'washing powder' principle (the more types of washing powders you sell, the greater the chance someone will pick your powder and not that of the competition), but also because, by the law of averages, some trusts are bound to perform better than average and can be heavily marketed. The less successful funds are kept hidden until, by a lucky chance, their turn at the head of the performance lists comes around.

The problem of consistent underperformance is well recognised by the unit trust industry, and one attempted solution has been the launch of index-linked funds. As the name suggests, these funds are designed purely to track the relevant indices of share movements, and their performance will always exactly equal the zero sum average performance in terms of unit price performance. Several trusts now compete on their low charges. Examples include those managed by Virgin and Legal & General.

However, once again the fund manager will take his cut, so that the income which the investor will receive is certain to be less than he would have received had he invested directly in the stocks of the index himself. Perhaps the primary attraction of the index-linked fund is to ensure average performance from money invested overseas. One or two investment trusts provide index-linked performance, for example the Edinburgh UK Tracker Trust.

The main problem with an investment in a tracker fund is that it must, by definition, follow a falling index all the way down. By contrast, an active fund manager can move some or all of the share holdings into cash. Thus index trackers tend to out-perform active fund managers when the market rises, and under-perform when the market falls.

5

Dealing in Shares

CERTIFICATES OR NOMINEE ACCOUNT?

All investors today have to make the decision whether they prefer to hold shares themselves in certificated form, or to let a broker or a fund manager hold the shares for them in 'nominee accounts'. By law, shares held in a nominee account are *actually owned* by the broker or fund manager, although the investor retains 'beneficial ownership'. The nominee investor is therefore entitled to the proceeds (eg dividends) from the investment, while the nominee operator receives the company accounts and any perks. The reader should note especially that whereas the Financial Services' Compensation Scheme pays out up to £48,000 compensation per shareholding if the stockbroker goes bankrupt while carrying out share-dealing transactions, the maximum **total** payout per investor is £48,000 for **all** the shareholdings together held in the same stockbroker's nominee account.

Some companies have been prevailed upon to make their perks (such as cheap shopping) and accounts available to nominee investors, but a few, most notably the shipping line P&O with its well-known ferry fare concessions on some types of stock, make the perk available only to direct investors.

The advantages of direct shareholding are therefore manifest. Less obvious are the advantages of being a nominee holder; typically, fewer worries about where to store the share certificate, often cheaper dealing and, allegedly, less paperwork (my experience is that the investor receives a deluge of statements instead).

Of course, an investor can choose to hold some shares directly and others in a nominee account. For example, in 2006 all ISAs must be held as nominee accounts.

A third option is to become a direct electronic shareholder through Crest, and this will be discussed below.

Many brokers put a limit on the total sum which can be owed to them within an account by private investors. Some even limit the maximum expenditure on any one transaction.

THE BROKER

Choosing a broker
There are several ways of buying shares.

- Directly from the company when it makes an Offer for Sale with a prospectus in the newspapers. This is particularly the case with government privatisations. If your offer is accepted, you will receive a Letter of Acceptance – see example on page 89.

- Directly from a unit trust group, who advertise extensively in the newspapers. Alternatively you can buy shares in an investment trust through the trust's savings scheme.

- Through a bank, accountant or solicitor. Unfortunately, all these parties may want their cut. Also they may have an infuriating habit of demanding cash from you instantly when you buy stock, while paying you much later.

- Through the stockbroker arm of your bank, if it has one (not to be confused with dealing through your bank manager).

- By becoming a client of Charles Schwab (formerly Sharelink), a telephone-based dealer with headquarters in Birmingham. Their charges are moderate and they have a large (in excess of 180,000) client base. Schwab now handles about ten per cent of all bargains transacted on the London Stock Exchange, and its address and telephone number are given at the end of this book. US shares can also be purchased directly through Schwab. You will not, however, be able to seek advice from Charles Schwab.

- By joining one of the number of cut-rate 'dealing only' services, such as those of 'Share-Dealing' (Halifax plc). Halifax uses nominee accounts to save paperwork so you do not receive the actual share certificate, which is held by Halifax on your behalf.

- The government is encouraging the introduction of Share Shops, retail outlets which deal in shares. There are very few of these at present, but a number of banks and building societies have expressed interest.

   A good example is the National Westminster Bank's 'touch-screen' dealing system installed in many of their larger branches. Sales and purchases of a selected range of shares can be made on the spot and settled for immediate cash, provided that you take the share certificate and identification in with you.

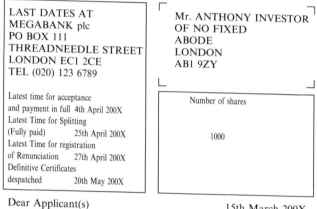

ALLOTMENT LETTER No. ABC-123

This document is of value and is negotiable until 3pm on 25th April 200X. If you are in any doubt as to the action you should take or if prior to receiving it you have sold all or part of your holding of ordinary shares in the company, you should take personal financial advice from your stockbroker or other professional advisor immediately.

The Council of the Stock Exchange has agreed to admit to the Official List the new Ordinary Shares which are now being issued. It is expected that dealings will commence on 1st April 200X.

NEWSTORES plc

(Registered in England – No. 345678)

LETTER OF ACCEPTANCE

LAST DATES AT MEGABANK plc PO BOX 111 THREADNEEDLE STREET LONDON EC1 2CE TEL (020) 123 6789	Mr. ANTHONY INVESTOR OF NO FIXED ABODE LONDON AB1 9ZY

Latest time for acceptance and payment in full 4th April 200X
Latest Time for Splitting (Fully paid) 25th April 200X
Latest Time for registration of Renunciation 27th April 200X
Definitive Certificates despatched 20th May 200X

Number of shares

1000

Dear Applicant(s)   15th March 200X

1. Your application to buy shares in Newstores plc has been accepted for the number of shares shown above. If this is less than you applied for, a cheque is attached for the difference.

2. General Information (in very small print).

3. Instructions for renunciation and registration, splitting and consolidation (in very small print).

Yours sincerely,
Chairman

Fig. 11. Letter of acceptance for new issue of ordinary shares.

- An off-market transfer of shares, for example between friends, requires a 'stock transfer form' to be completed and sent to the registrar. These forms can be obtained from legal stationers. One of the principal publishers of these forms, Oyez, is listed under Useful Addresses. An example form is shown on pages 91–92.

  Until the abolition of stamp duty, it will be necessary for Stock Transfer forms to be stamped, for which 0.5 per cent of the value of the shares is charged (at the rate of £5 for every £1,000 of shares, rounded up). This can be done by sending the form and a cheque to your local Stamp Office (not a post office!). The address of the local stamp office can be found in Appendix 20.

  However, certain exemptions from stamp duty are permitted and these are stated on the reverse of the stock transfer form. In particular, transfers at no cost between a husband and wife are free from stamp duty.

  Curiously, some, but not all, of the letters of acceptance of government privatisations could be traded through the Stock Exchange, but not privately, without incurring stamp duty for a few months after the letters had been sent out.

- Applying to become a private client of a stockbroking firm. This is much the most flexible option.

The London stockbrokers have very high overheads, so they are often interested only in clients with £200,000 or more to invest.

On the other hand, provincial stockbrokers, of which there are several chains, regard private clients as their bread and butter and in any case have a superior reputation for attention to private clients. Pick one out of your telephone directory and ask to be a client. Make sure that the broker is a member of the London (International) Stock Exchange, which has a partial protection scheme for clients in the unlikely event that the broker goes bankrupt in the course of a transaction. The broker will send an application form and will probably ask for a banker's reference.

It is almost a maxim that the average member of the public stands in awe of the stockbroker. Remember that he needs you much more than you need him. There are always plenty of alternatives if he does not like you – or vice-versa.

Typical broker's commissions are set at 1.65 per cent for each transaction, whether you buy or sell. The transactions are also known as bargains. There is typically a minimum charge to be paid of £30. In addition, a broker's levy for compliance with Stock

CON 40 (1963)

STOCK TRANSFER FORM

(Above this line for Registrars only)

Certificate lodged with the Registrar

Consideration Money £ .... *NIL* ....

(For completion by the Registrar/Stock Exchange)

Name of Undertaking.	*MEGASTORES plc*
Description of Security.	*ORDINARY 25p SHARES*

Number or amount of Shares, Stock or other security and, in figures column only, number and denomination of units, if any.	Words	Figures
	ONE THOUSAND	*(1000 units of 25p)*

Name(s) of registered holder(s) should be given in full; the address should be given where there is only one holder. If the transfer is not made by the registered holder(s) insert also the name(s) and capacity (e.g. Executor(s)) of the person(s) making the transfer.	In the name(s) of	*MR. A.N. INVESTOR OF NO FIXED ABODE LONDON AB1 9ZY*

I/We hereby transfer the above security out of the name(s) aforesaid to the person(s) named below.

Stamp of Selling Broker(s) or, for transactions which are not stock exchange transactions, of Agent(s), if any, acting for the Transferor(s)

Signature(s) of transferor(s)

1. *AN Investor*

2. ....

3. ....

4. ....

A body corporate should execute this transfer under its common seal or otherwise in accordance with applicable statutory requirements.

Date ....

Full name(s), full postal address(es) (including County or, if applicable, Postal District number) of the person(s) to whom the security is transferred. Please state title, if any, or whether Mr, Mrs, or Miss. Please complete in typewriting or in BLOCK CAPITALS.	*MRS. A.C. INVESTOR OF NO FIXED ABODE LONDON AB1 9ZY*

I/We request that such entries be made in the register as are necessary to give effect to this transfer.

Stamp of Buying Broker(s) (if any)	Stamp or name and address of person lodging this form (if other than the Buying Broker(s))
	AN INVESTOR OF NO FIXED, ABODE LONDON AB1 9ZY

Reference to the Registrar in this Form means the registrar or registration agent of the undertaking NOT the Registrar of Companies at Companies House.

Fig. 12. Stock transfer form (Oyez). The 'Crest' transfer form is similar.

FORM OF CERTIFICATE REQUIRED WHERE TRANSFER IS EXEMPT FROM STAMP DUTY

Instruments executed on or after 1st May 1987 effecting any transactions within the following categories are exempt from stamp duty:—

A. The vesting of property subject to a trust in the trustees of the trust on the appointment of a new trustee, or in the continuing trustees on the retirement of a trustee.

B. The conveyance or transfer of property the subject of a specific devise or legacy to the beneficiary named in the will (or his nominee). Transfers in satisfaction of a general legacy of money should not be included in this category (see category D below).

C. The conveyance or transfer of property which forms part of an intestate's estate to the person entitled on intestacy (or his nominee). Transfers in satisfaction of the transferees entitlement to cash in the estate of an intestate, where the total value of the residuary estate exceeds that sum, should not be included in this category (see category D below).

D. The appropriation of property within section 84(4) of the Finance Act 1985 (death: appropriation in satisfaction of a general legacy of money) or section 84(5) or (7) of that Act (death: appropriation in satisfaction of any interest of surviving spouse and in Scotland also of any interest of issue).

E. The conveyance or transfer of property which forms part of the residuary estate of a testator to a beneficiary (or his nominee) entitled solely by virtue of his entitlement under the will

F. The conveyance or transfer of property out of a settlement in or towards satisfaction of a beneficiary's interest, not being an interest acquired for money or money's worth, being a conveyance or transfer constituting a distribution of property in accordance with the provisions of the settlement.

G. The conveyance or transfer of property on and in consideration only of marriage to a party to the marriage (or his nominee) or to trustees to be held on the terms of a settlement made in consideration only of the marriage. A transfer to a spouse after the date of marriage is not within this category, unless made pursuant to an ante-nuptial contract.

H. The conveyance or transfer of property within section 83(1) of the Finance Act 1985 (transfers in connection with divorce etc.).

I. The conveyance or transfer by the liquidator of property which formed part of the assets of the company in liquidation to a shareholder of that company (or his nominee) in or towards satisfaction of the shareholder's rights on a winding-up.

(L.) The conveyance or transfer of property operating as a voluntary disposition *inter vivos* for no consideration in money or money's worth nor any consideration referred to in section 57 of the Stamp Act 1891 (conveyance in consideration of a debt etc.).

M. The conveyance or transfer of property by an instrument within section 84(1) of the Finance Act 1985 (death: varying disposition).

(1) Delete as appropriate.

(2) Insert "(A)", "(B)" or appropriate category.

(3) Delete second sentence if the certificate is given by the transferor or his solicitor.

(1) I/We hereby certify that the transaction in respect of which this transfer is made is one which falls within the category(2) ~~L~~ above. (1)I/We confirm that (1)I/We have been duly authorised by the transferor to sign this certificate and that the facts of the transaction are within (1)my/our knowledge (3) ~~,~~

Signature(s)

AN Investor

Description ("Transferor", "Solicitor", etc.)

TRANSFEROR

Date *1st JUNE 200X*

NOTES
(1) If the above certificate has been completed, this transfer does not need to be submitted to the Controller of Stamps but should be sent directly to the Company or its Registrars.
(2) If the above certificate is not completed, this transfer must be submitted to the Controller of Stamps and duly stamped. (See below.)

FORM OF CERTIFICATE REQUIRED WHERE TRANSFER IS NOT EXEMPT BUT IS NOT LIABLE TO AD VALOREM STAMP DUTY

Instruments of transfer, other than those in respect of which the above certificate has been completed, are liable to a fixed duty of £5.00 when the transaction falls within one of the following categories:—

(a) Transfer by way of security for a loan or re-transfer to the original transferor on repayment of a loan.

(b) Transfer, not on sale and not arising under any contract of sale and where no beneficial interest in the property passes: (i) to a person who is a mere nominee of, and is nominated only by, the transferor; (ii) from a mere nominee who has at all times held the property on behalf of the transferee; (iii) from one nominee to another nominee of the same beneficial owner where the first nominee has at all times held the property on behalf of that beneficial owner. (NOTE—This category does not include a transfer made in any of the following circumstances: (i) by a holder of stock, etc., following the grant of an option to purchase the stock, to the person entitled to the option or his nominee, (ii) to a nominee in contemplation of a contract for the sale of the stock, etc., then about to be entered into; (iii) from the nominee of a vendor, who has instructed the nominee orally or by some unstamped writing to hold stock, etc., in trust for a purchaser, to such purchaser.)

(1) Delete as appropriate.

(2) Insert "(a)", "(b)".

(3) Here set out concisely the facts explaining the transaction. Adjudication may be required.

(1) I/We hereby certify that the transaction in respect of which this transfer is made is one which falls within the category(2) .... above. (1)I/We confirm that (1)I/We have been duly authorised by the transferor to sign this certificate and that the facts of the transaction are within (1)my/our knowledge.

(3) ....

Signature(s)

Description ("Transferor", "Solicitor", etc.)

Date ....

Conveyancing 40

Fig. 12. Stock transfer form (Oyez) continued.

Exchange Regulations of about £5 may be charged and an Exchange levy of £1 for bargains in excess of £10,000, plus stamp duty. Stamp duty is 50p per £100 (rounded upwards) for shares purchased through Crest, but since 1 October 1999 has been increased to £5 per £1,000 (rounded up) for all other share transactions. This includes transactions between the owner of shares and a nominee account. Stamp duty applies only to purchases of shares, not to sales.

Some brokers require you to maintain nominee accounts (ISAs also require this). It means that the broker retains the share certificate, but it is written in their records as though it belonged to you. More commonly though, the broker sends the share certificate directly to you, although many months may have elapsed since you bought the stock. The purveyors of nominee accounts claim that it reduces paperwork and expense for them, and saves the client from receiving the paperwork. Nominee accounts are dealt with in more detail below. Your attention is drawn particularly to the section on the potential for fraud.

Finally, many brokers will require you to settle your first share purchase with cash by return of post, before entrusting you with the Crest system.

TAURUS/CREST

Taurus

Taurus was the name given to the Stock Exchange's proposed system for paperless share ownership. Instead of holding a share certificate, the investor would find that his share holding had become a computer entry in a nominee account.

Taurus was a project begun in the mid 1980s, but was put to one side during the government-promoted package of reforms introduced in 1986 and known as 'Big Bang'. However, work on Taurus subsequently was set in motion again and it was planned to introduce the system in 1991. Numerous teething problems finally caused its cancellation in mid-1993.

Crest

In its place, the Bank of England instituted a system of paperless trading known as **Crest**.

The effects of Crest are these:

- *Electronic settlement system*
  Crest is an electronic settlement system matching trades against payments and informing the company's registrars. Items already handled by the 'Talisman' Stock Exchange system are excluded. Crest does not handle takeovers and rights issues.

- *Changes in costs*
  The advantage of Crest is that removal of much of the paper-work makes share dealing cheaper for the stockbroker. However, the brokers have to pay for the huge costs of computerisation, and this represents a flat-rate burden on all share-dealing, regardless of size. Alternatively, the broker may levy a fixed yearly fee for maintaining a nominee account for the investor. Consequently, the net effect to private investors is likely to be that charges from brokers will rise.

- *Broker nominees*
  Private investors can elect to be nominees of their own stockbroker. This will enable them to benefit from the cheaper costs of trading with Crest, which may cancel out the increase in other broker charges. Nominee accounts should be kept separate from the broker's own affairs so that bankruptcy, or other disasters affecting the broker, ought not to affect the nominee accounts. There is, however, no certain way of ensuring that the broker has actually placed anything in the nominee account.

- *The potential for fraud*
  A number of frauds came to light in the early 1990s when it was revealed that shares supposedly held in nominee accounts did not exist at all. The investor was just being sent a yearly slip of paper purporting to show that he held stocks which had not been bought.
  The potential for fraud in this area is immense, and there appears to be little proposed by way of controls on the sponsors of nominee accounts. The reader is warned to select his broker *very* carefully. Some large brokers now provide huge insurance cover against most risks. Check the cover with your broker.

- *Voluntary use*
  No one is obliged to use the Crest system, unlike the compulsory use of its Taurus predecessor. Those who insist on retaining paper certificates are permitted to do so, although they are likely to find that they have to pay higher dealing costs. Private transactions, without the intermediacy of the Stock Exchange, are still possible using a standard stock transfer form.

- *Effect of Crest on settlement*
  A 'rolling system' of settlement was introduced to the London stockmarket in 1994, in anticipation of Crest becoming operational. Previously, purchases and sales of shares were settled about twice a month; now all settlements were to be made within ten working days. In 1995, this was reduced to five working days, and in 2000 to three working days with most companies signed up for Crest registration.

  It is evident that it will be difficult for a private investor to send a share certificate or cleared cash payment to his broker within three days. At present, many stockbrokers are allowing clients and broker to settle within ten days, with no penalty to either side. It is likely that charges for such slow settlement must rise eventually.

  A side effect of the need for accelerated settlement was that the registration of shares had to be steeply accelerated from its previous lethargic state. There was a major consolidation of the registrars in 1995–96, as many felt that they could not justify the cost of improved registration procedures. Another side effect has been that there is less cash chasing shares when transactions have to be settled quickly.

- *Sponsored membership*
  Investors who deal frequently may benefit from becoming a sponsored member of Crest (sponsored by their broker or a bank), and thereby becoming able to deal directly through Crest without having to use a nominee account. CrestCo charges the broker £10 per annum per investor for this service; brokers may pass on any charge they like to the investor. The London Stock Exchange can now be the sponsor for private individuals with Crest at 'competitive rates'.

  It is at present impossible to say how popular this service will become. Most investors who seldom trade will probably be better advised to retain share certificates – at any rate until the dust settles.

- *Bonds too*
  It is now possible to trade most types of bond through Crest.

- *Alternative electronic systems*
  It has been pointed out that the best electronic solution to paperless trading would be to register all share certificates on one giant computer. However, this proposal has met with fierce

opposition from all those who make a living as company registrars (principally the clearing banks).

- *Other countries*
  Numerous other countries now use fully electronic registration of share holdings. A good local example is France.

- *Experience with Crest*
  Take up of Crest membership by individuals has been very poor since it was first introduced in 1997. Most private investors prefer the security of personally holding share certificates, rather than having to pay expensive nominee charges to a broker who can't even be bothered to send the company reports. Thus all-electronic share dealing has failed to take off in the UK. There are currently (2003) proposals by the Stock Exchange that those who hold share certificates might consider transferring to an electronic share account just like that used by the successful overseas electronic accounts rejected previously in the UK as impractical. If this occurs, all broker-sponsored nominee accounts are likely to be abandoned by most investors immediately.

Dealing services
Many brokers offer three types of dealing service:

- The **dealing-only service** will accept and execute your orders only, without proffering advice. Charles Schwab is such a service. The dealing-only service is normally the cheapest.

- The **advisory service** is more expensive and the broker will, on request, offer advice on a proposed transaction. A special, more expensive, variant of the advisory service is available from some brokers, who will volunteer advice on investments without being asked. The investor usually needs a great deal of money to qualify for this treatment.

- The **discretionary service** also requires a substantial minimum outlay by the investor and permits the broker to switch investments on his behalf without consultation. This service has laid itself open to the charge of 'churning', where a broker keeps trading his clients' shares unnecessarily in order to boost his own commission. Some of the more reputable brokers avoid this suspicion by charging a flat rate (at a high price) for their discretionary portfolios, regardless of the number of deals.

Others enroll new clients in the broker's own unit trust. The latter entails quite high charges (like a normal unit trust), but means that the portfolio can be traded around without the individual investors incurring Capital Gains Tax on their transactions. This is clearly beneficial to most investors.

A SUMMARY OF CHARGES

A summary of typical charges by different types of agent for share investment is given below. It used to be the case that VAT had to be paid on stockbroking commissions, but this was ended in 1990. The abolition of VAT caused a small increase in commissions, since the brokers were no longer able to obtain interest on VAT payments received by them but not yet passed on.

Through broker
Commission normally 1.65 per cent, minimum £30 plus stamp duty (0.5 per cent on purchases only) plus broker's compliance levy up to £5 and PTM levy of £1 on bargains in excess of £10,000. Also market maker's 'spread' (1–10 per cent, depending on marketability).

Through unit trust manager
Manager's spread of bid-offer normally 5–6 per cent plus annual fees (1–2 per cent of trust value).

Through investment trust savings scheme
Buying: commission 0.2–0.5 per cent plus other fees as for broker's commission. Selling: normally as for broker's commission.

Charles Schwab (Tel: 0870 601 8888)
Commission 1.5 per cent to £3,000 (0.75 per cent to £5,000, 0.1 per cent above) maximum £75, minimum £20 plus other fees as for broker's commission. (Schwab no longer deals in certificates.)

Bank or building society
Current charges for share-dealing are typically: (NatWest Stockbrokers Ltd, Tel: (0345) 224488) – Commission 1.50–1.75 per cent, minimum £25 plus other fees as for broker's commission. Special, cheaper charges for government privatisation issues.

COUNTRYWIDE STOCKBROKING LIMITED

(Incorporating Country, Town and Co.)

1-4 Broker Street, Thames Valley, TV1 9SB Telephone: 0123-987654

Branches in: Birmingham, Dundee, Edinburgh, Littlemarch-under-Water, London, Manchester, Swansea

Registered Office: Countrywide House, Hampstead, London NW1 9XX

Registered in England No. 1234567 VAT Registration No. 123 4567 89

Regulated by the Financial Services Authority.
Member of the London Stock Exchange

CONTRACT NOTE AND TAX INVOICE

MR. ANTHONY INVESTOR
OF NO FIXED
ABODE
LONDON
AB1 9ZY

Bargain Date and Tax Point	Security	Client	Contract Ref.	Settlement Date
06FEB0X	+0123456	W12345D	A98765	10FEB0X

WE THANK YOU FOR YOUR INSTRUCTIONS AND HAVE BOUGHT ON YOUR BEHALF AS AGENTS
MEGASTORES ORD 25P

Time	Quantity	Price	Consideration
13:55	1000	1.97	£1970.00
			£1970.00

TRANSFER STAMP (N)	10.00
COMMISSION	32.51
V.A.T. EXEMPT	NIL
COMPLIANCE CHARGE	5.00
TOTAL	
	£2017.51

Subject to the Rules and Regulations of the Stock Exchange including any temporary regulations made by or under the authority of the Council of the Stock Exchange.

E. & O.E. V.A.T. Invoice for services rendered (N) = Not subject to V.A.T. Please retain this document for Capital Gains Tax and V.A.T. purposes.

Fig. 13. Contract note for the purchase of shares.

Several building societies offer special dealing rates for handling the sale of government privatisation issues. The general dealing services once offered by a number of societies have mostly been discontinued.

Discount broker
Brokers who provide an 'execution-only' service, and normally hold all their clients' shares as nominee accounts.

Example: Halifax Share-Dealing. Tel: 08457 225525. Commission minimum £15, maximum £40 for deals up to £60,000 plus other fees as for broker's commission.

Company plan
Some companies employ agents to provide very cheap dealing services in the company shares.

Example: Rio Tinto dealing through Hoare Govett Corporate Finance Ltd. Commission 1 per cent per £100, no minimum plus other fees as for broker's commission.

THE MECHANICS OF SHARE DEALING

Appoint an agent
For most share dealing, you will need a broker. The Stock Exchange (see Useful Addresses) will provide, in addition to several useful booklets about investment generally, a list of brokers prepared to deal for small private clients. Provincial brokers will usually be cheaper and have a reputation for being more approachable. See page 90 for more details.

Ensure that the broker is regulated by the Financial Services Authority (FSA), which has a compensation fund. This will reimburse most, or all, of the loss suffered by private clients in the unlikely event of a broker going out of business before a transaction is completed. Some brokers are also well insured against losses.

For investment in the savings schemes of an investment trust, write directly to the trust's managers asking for an application form for the scheme. A list of trust managers and their addresses can be obtained from the AITC, address in 'Useful Addresses'.

Buying shares
Suppose you want to buy shares in a company XYZ whose middle price in today's paper is 105 pence.

- Phone the broker (ask for him by name), then give your name and probably your account number.

- Ask 'What price is XYZ?'

  The broker will reply something on the lines of 'Buying price 110p, selling price 100p', or even just '100–110p'.

- If you don't like the current buying price (110p), just say 'too much' or 'not interested' and there is no further obligation.

- Otherwise, give your order such as 'buy one thousand XYZ at maximum 110p'. It is **strongly advisable** to state a maximum price (buying) or a minimum price (selling). *Never say 'at best'! However, you might be willing to say 'at maximum 113p'.*

Get the broker to repeat this order to you, especially if you are placing several orders at once, otherwise embarrassment could be caused.

Virtually all brokers now tape-record their telephone calls.

- That ends the transaction.
- Say 'goodbye' and ring off.
- Once you have rung off, you **cannot change your mind**.

You should receive the Contract Note the next day. It will state exactly what has been done for you by the broker, giving the full price including details of the commission, stamp duty (where appropriate) and the Stock Exchange levy. Check that the details agree with what you wanted, complain if they do not.

Later, you will receive a statement, listing all your transactions and requiring settlement by the stated day. You write out a cheque, make it payable to the broking firm (not to the individual broker) and post it off with your client number or other form of identification so as to arrive before the stated day. It is necessary to take action to ensure that you have cleared funds in the bank in time to meet the cheque. If you normally keep the money in a building society, it will have to be transferred to your bank account in good time.

Owing to a number of frauds perpetrated on cheques 'lost' in the post, the Cheques Act (1992) provided that cheques crossed 'A/C Payee only' could only be paid to the bank account of the named individual or company.

Important – purchases of gilts and traded options must be settled on the next working day after purchase. Unless you live next door to the broker, this requires that you leave a sufficient sum on deposit with the broker before making the purchase. Some brokers will allow late settlement of gilts – ie on Account Day – for a slightly higher purchase price.

In order to purchase shares in an investment trust through its savings scheme, it is necessary only to fill in the form and send a cheque. Make sure this will arrive in good time before the day, usually at the end of the month, that the trust buys the shares on the open market.

Retain all the contract notes for possible inspection by the Inland Revenue. Keep old notes for seven years. After weeks or months, your broker or the investment trust will send to you the Share Certificate. You were, however, the owner of the shares as soon as you bought them and have a full entitlement to any dividends which they paid after that date (but see page 65 for shares sold 'cum' and 'ex' dividend).

Nationality declaration

A number of companies have charters which limit the extent to which non-British citizens can buy their shares. Typical are several of the de-nationalised industries, such as Rolls-Royce and British Aerospace. The government deemed that these strategic industries should not be subject to foreign control.

Investors seeking to buy shares in these companies will be required to state that they have British nationality before the change in ownership is registered. Investors unable to make the declaration may or may not be able to complete the transaction, depending on the proportion of foreign-held shares already registered.

Companies exacting this requirement from their investors tend to have lower share prices than their less discriminatory peers, since there is a smaller pool of potential buyers.

The share certificate

The share certificate is issued by the registrar (frequently a major bank) of the company in which you have bought shares. (Note that share certificates will not be issued to investors using the Crest or nominee system of share registration, see pages 93 and 103.) It takes weeks or months to arrive, and several months should be allowed for the arrival of a share certificate from overseas. The certificate is made out with the number of shares held by the stated owner, and there is always a unique identifying code on the certificate (the certificate number, the allocation number, the transfer number or

CERTIFICATE NUMBER TRANSFER NUMBER DATE OF REGISTRATION NUMBER OF SHARES

AB001001 0001234 20MAYOX - - - 1000 - - - -

ORDINARY SHARES OF 25 p EACH

MEGASTORES plc

(Incorporated under the Companies Act 1948)

THIS IS TO CERTIFY THAT

MR ANTHONY INVESTOR
OF NO FIXED
ABODE
LONDON AB1 9ZY

is/are the registered holders of **ONE THOUSAND**
ordinary shares of twenty-five pence each fully paid in Megastores plc, subject to the memorandum and
articles of association of he company.

Issued under the common seal of the company

S-E-A-L

NOTE: No transfer of any of the shares comprised in this certificate will be registered until the certificate has been
surrendered to the registrar's office: Megabank plc, Registrar's Dept, PO Box 111, Threadneedle Street, London
EC1 2CE.

Fig. 14. A typical share certificate.

sometimes all of them). **Check that the details are correct**.

The share certificate is valuable and should be kept in a safe place, such as a bank. For the same reason, you should make note of, and keep safe, the unique code on the certificate. Store a copy of this code separately from the certificate itself. If you lose the certificate (in the post, through theft or through fire), then it is possible to obtain a replacement by writing to the registrar of the company (so be sure to keep that copy of the registration code). You will be obliged to agree to indemnify the company if the original share certificate is fraudulently used (although a thief would find it very difficult to dispose of without your signature). The registrars may charge a substantial fee (£10–£50) for this service.

Important exceptions are **bearer** share certificates, rare in the UK but quite common in Continental Europe. Unlike most UK share certificates, bearer certificates can be sold by anyone who has them in his possession. In this respect, they are as valuable as the equivalent sum in bank notes, and they must be as well protected. An ordinary UK share certificate signed away by the investor can also be regarded as a bearer certificate.

Share certificates are normally sent through the post 'at the investor's risk'. Usually first class post suffices, and this is used by most issuing companies and brokers. However, the nervous private investor might prefer to send these documents by registered post instead.

Nominee accounts

Some brokers or fund managers hold your shares in nominee accounts. This means that they hold the original share certificate, but you should still receive a statement confirming that you are the beneficial owner of these shares, ie the one to whom all dividends will be paid. PEPs and ISAs are, without exception, nominee accounts. Shares registered with Crest are held predominantly in nominee accounts.

Nominee accounts reduce the amount of paperwork necessary for the agent, which may help to reduce the costs to the investor. There are proposals that all share dealing will in future be carried out through electronic nominee accounts, to save the use of share certificates altogether. These proposals are not universally popular.

Unit trusts

Unit trusts can be purchased by clipping the form from a newspaper and sending it to the fund managers. Alternatively, any broker can

COUNTRYWIDE STOCKBROKING LIMITED

(Incorporating Country, Town and Co.)

1-4 Broker Street, Thames Valley, TV1 9SB Telephone: 0123-987654

*Branches in: Birmingham, Dundee, Edinburgh, Littlemarch-under-Water,
London, Manchester, Swansea*

Registered Office: Countrywide House, Hampstead, London NW1 9XX

Registered in England No. 1234567 VAT Registration No. 123 4567 89

**Regulated by the Financial Services Authority.
Member of the London Stock Exchange**

CONTRACT NOTE AND TAX INVOICE

MR. ANTHONY INVESTOR
OF NO FIXED
ABODE
LONDON
AB1 9ZY

Bargain Date and Tax Point	Security	Client	Contract Ref.	Settlement Date
06FEBOX	+0123456	W12345D	A98766	10FEBOX

WE THANK YOU FOR YOUR INSTRUCTIONS AND HAVE SOLD ON YOUR BEHALF AS AGENTS
NEWSTORES ORD 25P

Time	Quantity	Price	Consideration
13:55	1000	1.64	£1640.00
			£1640.00
COMMISSION			30.00
V.A.T. EXEMPT			NIL
COMPLIANCE CHARGE			5.00
			TOTAL
			£1605.00

Subject to the Rules and Regulations of the Stock Exchange including any temporary regulations made by or under the authority of the Council of the Stock Exchange.

E. & O.E. V.A.T. Invoice for services rendered (N) = Not subject to V.A.T. Please retain this document for Capital Gains Tax and V.A.T. purposes.

Fig. 15. Contract note for the sale of shares.

buy units for the normal commission. Unit trusts also represent a form of nominee account. Each 'unit' assigned to the investor comprises a stake in a wide range of companies held by the fund manager.

They may be sold through their fund managers. The prices of each trust are usually quoted at least in the *Financial Times* and often in other newspapers. Unit trusts may also be sold through your broker.

When you buy units in a trust, you pay for more of the forthcoming dividend than you will receive. The managers will make a one-off payment in compensation. This is known as **equalisation**.

Selling shares

Selling shares through a broker involves virtually the same procedure as buying. You must normally have possession of the shares, perhaps in a nominee account, that you are selling. However, if you are still waiting for the share certificate from your broker, he should permit you to sell the shares without the certificate (but not if another broker is involved). Very few brokers will now permit their private clients to 'sell short', ie, sell shares which they do not own.

When the contract note arrives, it will be accompanied by a 'transfer note'. This releases your ownership of the shares. Check the details of both contract and transfer notes are correct, then sign the transfer (not the share certificate), and return the transfer and the share certificate to your broker.

The broker will send you payment within a few days. He will not send payment until he has received the share transfer and share certificate.

If the investor dies while holding a portfolio of shares, then the original broker will normally sell the investments for the executor of the estate once probate has been granted.

Selling investment trust shares can be more complex. Any broker will sell the shares in exchange for the share certificate and the full commission. Some trusts will sell the shares for you at a reduced price, others will give you the name of a broker (not your own broker) who will sell the shares at a reduced commission rate. Yet other trusts will have your share holding, if purchased through a savings scheme, in a nominee account and the shares will have to be released from this before you, or the trust, can sell them.

Renunciation/splitting/consolidation

Temporary share certificates are provided in the first instance for new share issues (eg government privatisations) and rights issues.

Forms X, Y and Z are available for use until 3.00 p.m. on 4th December 199X provided that payment on acceptance has been made by 3.00 p.m. on 13th November 199X.

	CONSOLIDATION LISTING FORM	
	Serial number	Number of new ordinary shares

FORM X FORM OF RENUNCIATION

To the Directors of MEGABANK plc

I/We hereby renounce my/our right to the new ordinary shares specified in this Letter in favour of the person(s) named in the registration application form relating to such shares.

All allottees must sign

In the case of a corporation the form must be executed by affixing its common seal or otherwise in accordance with the Companies Act 1985

Signature(s) of allottee(s)   *AN/nvestors*

Dated...............*1st NOVEMBER*...199X

Forms of renunciation on Split Letters will be marked "Original duly renounced".

FORM Y REGISTRATION APPLICATION FORM

Not for use by original allottee(s)

In the event of renunciation, this Form and Form Z below should be completed IN BLOCK CAPITALS by or on behalf of the person(s) in whose name(s) the shares are to be registered.

1. Forename(s) (in full).............................Surname ....
   (State Mr., Mrs., Miss or Title)
   Address ....
   ....Post Code.................

2. Forename(s) (in full).............................Surname ....
   (State Mr., Mrs., Miss or Title)
   Address ....
   ....Post Code.................

3. Forename(s) (in full).............................Surname ....
   (State Mr., Mrs., Miss or Title)
   Address ....
   ....Post Code.................

4. Forename(s) (in full).............................Surname ....
   (State Mr., Mrs., Miss or Title)
   Address ....
   ....Post Code.................

Total number of allotment letters	Total number of new ordinary shares
Serial number of principal letter	

To the Directors of MEGABANK plc

Registration is requested in the above name(s) of the new ordinary shares specified in this Letter and in the provisional allotment letters (if any) detailed in the Consolidation Listing Form, totalling [   ] new ordinary shares, subject to the memorandum and articles of association of the company.

    Stamp or name and address of
    person lodging this Form for registration

*Insert the number of new ordinary shares to be registered, which must equal the number of new ordinary shares stated in Box 4 overleaf or, if the Consolidation Listing Form is used, the total entered in that Form.

FORM Z MEGABANK plc

In the event of renunciation, this Form and Form Y above must be completed by the person lodging this Letter for registration.

LODGED for registration by ....
of...
....
allotment letter(s) for [   ] new ordinary shares to be registered in the
name(s) of...
....
....

Registration of renunciation will not be recognised unless the stamp of the Bank appears in this box.

Fig. 16. The 'X, Y, Z Form' (which may appear in various versions).

106

These are complicated documents filled with legalistic jargon in very small print. Summaries are given on an adjacent page showing the important features.

These temporary certificates are valuable documents and must not be lost. They are used to support changes in ownership before the permanent share certificate is issued, and then have no further value. Details of how to handle the temporary forms vary slightly from case to case, so it is essential to read the document thoroughly. The following provides a typical example.

If you sell your temporary certificate, then you are said to have 'renounced' it. Fill in 'Form X' (Form of Renunciation) on the back of the certificate and send the certificate to the stockbroker or other agent. This new purchaser will fill in 'Form Y' (Registration Application Form) to register his new ownership. Several purchased temporary certificates can be registered together (consolidation). The broker, or agent, will fill in 'Form Z'; in the case of a private transaction, without going through a broker, fill in the buyer's name in Form Z. Forms 'X, Y and Z ' are traditionally printed on the back of temporary certificates.

If the investor wishes to sell only part of his share holding on the temporary certificate, then he is said to split the certificate. The same forms 'X, Y and Z' are filled in and sent with a covering letter to the company registrar stating how many shares should be sent on to a new purchaser and how many sent back on a temporary certificate to the original investor.

A complication is caused by rights issues. The temporary certificate has a small value of its own even while the purchase price of the shares on it has not been paid and the shares are known as 'nil-paid'. After the payment has been made for the new shares, the temporary certificate will be stamped by the registrar and returned temporarily to the original investor, pending arrival of the definitive certificate. These shares are known as 'fully paid' (or as 'part paid' if payment is to be made in several instalments).

'Splitting' the temporary certificate for rights issues can normally be done on or before two separate dates:

- an early date for 'nil paid' shares
- a later date for 'fully paid' shares.

If the investor declines either to take up his rights issue (ie, purchase the shares he has been allocated) or to sell them nil paid, then many companies issuing the rights shares will attempt to sell the rights nil paid in the open market and will then send the investor any proceeds so obtained, less expenses (normally subject to a minimum).

'Bed-and-breakfast'

'Bed-and-breakfasting' used to mean selling shares and buying them back again on the following working day. This was invariably done for tax reasons, usually to settle the capital gains liability on the day the shares were sold. This tax avoidance scheme was banned in 1998.

Share registers are public documents

The share registers of public companies are, in effect, public documents. Anyone can demand that the company makes its share register available, and the law requires that the register must be provided.

Several marketing agencies have trawled the registers of some of the government's privatisation issues (notoriously those of British Telecom and British Gas), so that anyone who subscribed for shares in these companies is likely to find themselves on numerous junk mail lists. Those investors who are found on several share registers are likely to receive special attention from charities and the sellers of holiday homes, gold-plated pens, luxury yachts and other up-market paraphernalia.

WHEN TO BUY AND WHEN TO SELL

Don't stay in too long

It is not always necessary or desirable to remain fully invested in the stockmarket. The ability to match the average performance of the market is of small comfort when the average is falling. If you can predict a market crash, then it will pay you to anticipate it by 'going liquid' – selling out for cash.

Recent experience suggests that index-linked gilts may provide the best home for funds pulled out before a bear market, assuming, of course, that the bear market occurred. This is because in recent years inflation has been a serious worry and the cause of share price underperformance.

However, index-linked gilts would be a poor investment if a depression occurred. Under these circumstances there is no money anywhere and inflation may even be negative.

Index-linked gilts show an increase in capital value (at the repayment date) which is based on the government's official inflation rate, the Retail Prices Index (RPI). Any alteration in the basis of calculation of the RPI permits investors to demand instant repayment. The government has indicated that index-linked gilts would not drop in value if inflation were negative.

Ordinary gilts have proved in recent decades to be a poor investment since their fixed income repayments are reduced in real terms by inflation. They ought to be a good investment in a depression and have indeed performed well in the early 2000s.

The start of a bull market

Bull markets start only a few times during an investor's active career, so it is essential not to miss them. Various warning signs of the start of a bull market are known, for example:

- Short-term interest rates fall.

- The 'yield gap' narrows (page 34).

- There is a sudden fall in the market as everyone agrees that it is not worth hanging on any longer and sells out.

- The Coppock Indicator starts to rise from a negative index.

THE COPPOCK INDICATOR

Historically, one of the most reliable predictors of the start of a bull market has been the Coppock Indicator. This indicator has also been used, less reliably, to predict the start of a bear market.

The Coppock Indicator is loosely based on 'Wave Theory', which says in substance that stock market performance ebbs and flows in cycles (the economic cycle). It follows that the Indicator is only of value for predicting long term changes in investment sentiment, and is useless for predicting sudden surges of enthusiasm or moments of panic like the October 1987 crash. The Indicator may be regarded as a general measure of underlying investor confidence.

The Coppock Indicator is calculated in a complex manner:

1. Take this month's average share price index and subtract the average index for the same month twelve months ago. Multiply the result by ten.

2. Repeat this arithmetic for last month and multiply the result by nine (instead of by ten). Repeat this sequence for a total of ten months, multiplying each successive result by eight, seven, six and

so on down to one.

3. Add up all the figures calculated in steps (1) and (2). The result may be positive or negative. Divide the result by ten. The figure so obtained is the Coppock Indicator for this month.

These laborious calculations are done for you and published monthly by the *Investors' Chronicle*.

An average indicator value of zero is taken as the base line. If the Coppock value is above zero, a bull market exists, while a figure below zero indicates the existence of a bear market.

The start of a bull market is predicted when the points plotted below zero first start to become less bad. Thus, if the figures for January, February, March and April were –100, –110, –112, and –110, then April would give the first sign of a new bull market.

The Coppock Indicator has worked well in the past (and is self-fulfilling if everyone believes it), but has been criticised for being too slow to respond. Therefore, a certain measure of anticipation is needed by the investor. Start to buy shares when the Indicator looks as though it is about to turn and hope that there is no sudden reversal.

The Indicator is particularly slow to respond after a market crash. The Coppock Indicator recommended selling stock in December 1987, just as the market bottomed! It can be a useful tool then, but must be used with caution. In particular, it is only of value if there have been no violent changes in the stockmarket indices in the preceding twelve months.

The Coppock Indicator last turned up again from a negative value in May 2003.

6

Stockmarket Strategies

SOME STOCKMARKET INVESTMENT STRATEGIES

This section deals with some known stockmarket strategies which have performed, for short periods, above average expectations. It is important to remember that no stockmarket strategy can be consistently successful, or everyone would adopt it causing share prices to fluctuate in a way which would undermine the original strategy.

By far the commonest strategies involve the identification of individual 'under-valued' or 'growth' shares. These strategies are examined in Appendix 10. Several *general* strategies are listed below.

High yielding stocks

Mention was made earlier of the strategy of buying shares only in those companies which had the highest yields and whose share price is higher than it was 12 months previously. Lists of stocks meeting these criteria are published six-monthly by the *Investors' Chronicle* and the strategy is claimed to be quite successful in giving above average returns in the medium term.

Recovery stocks

Investment in a wide range of recovery stocks often gives good performance in the long term, where the spread of risk enables several winners to offset losses from a few losers. M&G's 'Recovery Fund' has been one of the world's most successful unit trusts.

Average down

This is the name given to the process of buying more shares in a company as it falls in value, in order to maintain its overall position in the investor's portfolio.

For example, you buy 1,000 shares at 100 pence (total outlay £1000, neglecting dealing charges). Two months later you buy 1,000 more shares at 50 pence each (an extra £500). Two months on from

111

that you buy 2,000 shares at 25 pence each. The total value of your shares is now 4,000 × 25p = £1,000, so that the value of the company in the portfolio remains the same.

If the company recovers to a value of 100 pence per share, then you have made a useful profit. In this example, the profit is 4,000 × 100p minus 1,000 × 100p minus 1,000 × 50p minus 2,000 × 25p which equals £2,000.

However, if the company goes bankrupt, which is clearly on the cards judging by the way its share price is collapsing, you have spectacularly sent good money after bad.

Never, ever, average down, unless you are sure that your view of the company is right and everybody else's is wrong. Remember that the professionals rarely average down.

Success breeds success?

One old and well-tested strategy is called the 'Simple Reversal System'. It says, substantially, that in any four week period a share should be bought when its price has risen above its high prices of the previous four weeks, and sold when it starts to fall below its low prices of the previous four weeks. This is one of the very few strategies which has been objectively tested and found to deliver a good performance relative to the relevant stock market indices. Also it represents an unusual case where the effect of everyone joining in is to reinforce the correctness of the strategy. However, it has always seemed to me to be a very risky game to buy a share when it rises above its previous high value, since this invites a sudden fall in its price. This system is well known to have a potential for creating occasional large losses, which can be checked by the use of a 'stop-loss' system (see below).

Pound-cost averaging

Owing to the difficulty of getting timing decisions right when buying into the stockmarket, some authorities advocate pound-cost averaging. This strategy means buying a fixed sum of stock at regular, short intervals, regardless of how well the market is doing. This procedure inevitably means that some shares will be bought too expensively, others very cheaply. However, more shares will be bought when they are cheap.

A possibly superior strategy is to buy a different line of stock at regular intervals, but to try to pick a stock which appears to be undervalued at the time of selection.

Invest at once
Research has shown that it is *usually* better to invest a lump sum all at once, rather than piecemeal over several years. This is because markets tend to rise over time. I would invest a large lump sum over two years.

Avoid losers
The strategy of diversification of shares is intended to enable many winners to offset a few duds. An alternative strategy is to avoid picking losers in the first place. If you have a portfolio of shares in ten companies, then one bankruptcy has to be offset by gains of 11 per cent in value of *all* the other stocks. So avoiding one loser has at least the merit of being more efficient than trying to pick nine winners.

A strategy of 'buy the index, less losers' can be expected to be more successful than copying the index over long periods. It means buy a diversified range of shares (more-or-less to mimic the FT30 index) while avoiding the purchase of those companies that appear to be consistent losers.

Do not recover original price
Many private investors adopt the strategy that they will not sell shares for less than the price they originally paid. This is most unwise, since you can be locked into a dud investment for years, or even see it decline into bankruptcy. Always be prepared to sell at a loss, if you think the money could be invested more profitably elsewhere. Institutional investors never seek to recover the original price.

Stop-loss policy
Some authorities suggest that if the value of a share falls after you have bought it, you should automatically sell. Thus you cut your loss as soon as the price falls below the level you determined before buying (typically after a fall of 15 per cent).

This practice is known as a stop-loss policy and guarantees that you will never lose more than 15 per cent of your original investment. As the saying goes, 'the first loss is always the easiest to bear'. Of course, you feel pretty silly if the share price then rises again! A stop-loss policy is probably best implemented relative to the market as a whole. That way you do not have to take action against your newly-acquired shares just because the whole market has given a sudden lurch downwards.

However, if the relative loss is stopped even despite a general fall, the money must be re-invested in the market to minimise the original loss.

There are various theoretical disputes about the value of stop-loss, mostly based on the fact that the investor guarantees himself a loss by selling instead of hanging on until the price recovers. As has been mentioned previously, inflation creates a strong upward drag on all shares traded in Britain. I hold no very strong view on the subject with respect to investment vehicles with a long life, such as shares. However, short-lived investment vehicles, such as Traded Options (Chapter 7), should, in my view, be subject to stop-loss constraints.

All investors get bitten once
It is a fact of life that nearly all new investors start buying shares after stock markets have been rising too long and the newspapers are full of stories about how much money has been made by those already invested.

Nearly all investors, therefore, suffer an ensuing bear market while still 'green'. The most important thing is to sit tight and wait for the market to recover, rather than to sell out in a panic at the bottom of the bear market.

Sell underperformers?
Some authorities recommend that stocks which are underperforming relative to the market average should be sold, and the money reinvested in stocks which are performing well.

However, it has been shown that this year's underperformers often outperform the average in the following year, while star stocks tend to do worse. The reason is fairly obvious. Companies which are underperforming will take radical steps to do better, or will become the target of bids, while the growth of the hot stocks tends to fall away.

Disagree
An oft-stated stockmarket adage says that when everyone agrees on a course of action, do the opposite (the 'contrarian view'). Unfortunately, it is rare that market analysts ever agree about anything.

Guaranteed strategies
A new, innovative strategy was made possible by one-time high interest rates. The investor is guaranteed to receive most, or all, of his money back after a year or two. In addition, he may receive a considerable bonus.

The secret is that some 90 per cent of the investor's cash is placed in bonds or other high interest vehicles. The remainder, some 10 per cent, is used to buy warrants (see page 59). This is known as a 'Cash and Calls strategy'.

If the market goes up, the warrants increase rapidly in value, giving a geared appreciation in capital value and a good return to the investor.

Should the market fall, the warrants become worthless but the high interest paid on the 90 per cent of cash ensures that the investor at least gets his money back.

A modern alternative is for the guarantor to use the dividend income from the shares to purchase a 'put option' (Chapter 7) as insurance against a market collapse. This is known as a 'Stock and Put strategy'. The value of the guarantee then depends critically on whether the writer of the put option (the final guarantor) can meet its obligation in the event of a market collapse.

These strategies have been extremely popular. However, they can only be expected to succeed as long as interest rates remain high. As with all lower risk strategies, the long term financial return will usually be less than that from a direct investment in shares.

Program trading

Program trading (American spelling) is principally seen in the USA. When the relevant index falls to a preset limit, computers immediately sell the stocks owned by those institutions using the computers to preserve previous gains. When the index rises, the computers buy stock automatically, or sell off shares, as pre-programmed.

The central feature of this activity is that it is all automatic, without human intervention. The catastrophic 'knock-on' effects of this can easily be imagined, since each programmed sell-off causes a fall in share values, triggering other computers to start dumping stock.

This auto-disaster is widely believed to lie behind the great market crash of October 1987, which began in the USA. The American public raised a great outcry against program trading. Numerous US brokers no longer deal in such trades, nor permit their clients to do so, and at one time it seemed likely that it would be banned altogether.

In the meantime, the US authorities have introduced circuit breakers to try to break the chain of automated selling. Whenever the Dow-Jones index falls by a certain large amount, all trading in the US markets is suspended for one hour (there are other embellishments, irrelevant to the UK investor). The idea is to permit time for human intervention at the computers.

It is unlikely that program trading will become a problem in the UK. Firstly, no one wants to start the system when the likely consequence will be an immediate government veto. Secondly, it is not possible to trade bundles of stocks simultaneously in the UK, unlike the USA. Thirdly, the cost of stamp duty, when applicable, makes automated selling and rebuying an expensive business.

Whether this is a good or bad thing for the British private investor is unclear. Certainly, no one likes periodic market crashes. But the idea of institutions pointlessly dumping stock cheaply at the behest of a computer program should surely make the private investor lick his lips.

Sell shares/buy calls

A consequence of program trading, but also an independent strategy, is that of selling shares when the market falls (to lock in profits already made). Then buy the much cheaper 'call' options (ie the right to buy shares, see Traded Options, Chapter 7) in the same shares.

If the market then rises, the calls will rapidly appreciate in value. If the market continues to fall, the calls will become worthless but little money will have been lost on them.

Private investors may have to pay tax on capital gains made when they sell their shares.

MODERN PORTFOLIO THEORY/RISK MANAGEMENT

Modern Portfolio Theory (MPT) is the name given to an investment strategy which manages risk. The name is a misnomer since the theory is no longer modern.

MPT acknowledges that specific risk is reduced by spreading it over many investments. It also recognises that the performance of a wide spread of investments is nearly certain to follow the relevant index closely. Conversely, having a small spread of investments gives the possibility of outperformance relative to the index with an associated greater risk of underperformance.

Therefore MPT suggests that the investor should have a moderate spread of safe investments (ie, those with a low beta risk, see page 74) together with a carefully selected handful of high risk (high beta risk) companies which will with luck add spice to the overall portfolio performance.

This is where the risk management comes in. Cautious investors will want all low risk investments, others will be prepared to accept an increasingly high risk in the hope of gaining a better performance.

The capital asset price model (CAPM)

If a common rate of interest is available to all investors, then Tobin showed in 1958 that all investors could share the same, 'efficient' stock portfolio, adjusting their risk by holding back some cash (low risk) or by borrowing to buy more stock in the efficient portfolio (high risk).

Modern Portfolio Theory need not be applied only to investments in shares. It can also be used to balance the investor's risk/benefit aspirations from a mixed portfolio of gilts (very safe), building society (quite safe), property (less safe) and shares (least safe). The investor can pick and choose to give his own mix of safety and potential high performance.

THE LOGICAL INVESTMENT STRATEGY

After reading this far, the reader should we hope have been convinced of four principles:

- No fixed strategy and no fund management can guarantee to outperform the market (inside traders excepted).

- The investor needs a spread of shares to reduce specific risk.

- The total return (share price rises and dividends) to the investor will be enhanced if other people (fund managers, brokers) do not keep taking cuts.

- Dividends are needed to underpin the performance of the portfolio.

These four central beliefs form the foundation of the Logical Strategy for investing in shares on the stockmarket.

Most of the reasons for this strategy have been described previously. The most fruitful line of strategy can be seen to be one of accepting an average performance while minimising charges. This simple expedient will put the investor's performance ahead of 50 per cent of the highly paid professionals (see the zero-sum game, page 85).

Stock selection is based very much on buying shares of companies in which you have long-term confidence, while avoiding obvious disaster companies. This is not a new idea, but it has consistently proved over the long term to be a profitable one although, once again, past performance is not necessarily a guide to future performance. Two of the world's most successful pooled fund groups have adopted this approach. M&G, the unit trust manager, is famous for its steady long-term strategy, while the Templeton International Fund of Bermuda has proved to be one of the world's most single-minded investors. Over the short term it has occasionally done disastrously badly when the shares it held were out of fashion, but over the long term it has held one of the most consistently high ratings among pooled funds. Its strategies are summarised (by Templeton Unit Trust Managers, Templeton House, 20 Castle Terrace, Edinburgh EH1 2EH Tel: (0131) 469 4000) as these:

- Buy near the bottom of a bear market.
- Sell near the top of a bull market.
- Common sense and patience by investors and fund managers.
- Global diversification to spread risk.
- Flexibility in investment.
- Buy the 'relatively few under-valued opportunities'.

Another example of the value of patience and spread of risk can be seen in the private pooled fund of one of the Cambridge colleges. In the 1950s, its financial staff became seriously worried about the absurdly high rate of inflation (5 per cent!). The college involved decided to sell out of gilts and other bonds and reinvest in the stockmarket for long term growth of assets and dividends.

However, the staff knew nothing about equity investment. They had a 'round table' meeting of the heads of the college and in half an hour picked a selection of widely spread stocks out of the *Financial Times*. These shares were purchased.

Thereafter, there was a meeting once a year to discuss progress, although the college bursar had daily authority to take up rights issues and other matters needing immediate attention. Changes in holdings were only made at the yearly meeting, by mutual agreement of those present, and based largely on common sense. The college sold a lot of shares before the 1987 crash, reasoning that share yields were too low (see The Yield Gap, page 34).

This simple strategy by self-confessed market illiterates has since its start in the 1950s produced a performance well ahead of the stockmarket indices, aided by selling out of stock at the right times, and with a minimum of expensive share trading.

The beneficial effects on investment performance of reducing management charges have been well documented by the life assurance industry. It has been observed that mutual assurance companies which have no shareholders to pay out and which, in the case of a few mutuals, pay no commissions to middlemen either, consistently give better long term returns to their policy holders than the ordinary life assurance companies which lack these advantages. Again, management skill appears to have only a secondary effect on investment performance.

SUMMARY OF THE LOGICAL INVESTMENT STRATEGY

The Logical Investment Strategy may be summarised thus:

- Decide whether you want capital growth, income growth or a combination of both (income growth has in the past proved to deliver superior capital growth too).

- Do not buy shares if you believe a sharp fall is imminent. Pay attention to the yield gap and do not buy when the gap exceeds 6 per cent for a long period.

- Watch out for the beginning of a bull market, when you should try to be invested in shares. Lead indicators include a fall in short term interest rates, a rise in gilt prices and an upturn in a previously negative Coppock Indicator.

- Compile a wishlist (see 'Wishlist' on page 121) of shares which you want to buy and monitor their progress at least weekly.

- When you judge the time to be right – ie, when you expect shares in general to rise, or believe that one stock is undervalued – buy that stock. Do not buy that stock if your chart of the share price shows that it has recently risen steeply. You will, of course, occasionally miss a stock which explodes upwards in this case. Do not buy a stock that has just been 'tipped' until at least two weeks have passed. If you are unable to judge the timing of a purchase, then adopt the 'pound-cost' averaging method, buying stock at regular intervals.

- Ensure you buy a wide spread of stock from the outset. At the beginning, when you own few shares and are therefore exposed to high specific risk, buy only blue chip shares. When you select your spread of shares, be sure to have at least one company from each of the principal market subdivisions (see Chapter 2).

Alternatively, if you cannot afford to buy many stocks at once to give a good spread, buy investment trusts to spread the risk. You can always sell these later, in order to fund the purchase of several individual stocks.

- When you have assembled your core holding of ten diverse stocks, you can consider buying shares on the basis of hunches or with an emphasis on smaller companies, which have greater potential for growth. Investment trusts are ideal vehicles for spreading risk for investment in smaller companies or in shares bought for their recovery potential. If you already have a holding in as many shares as you think are sufficient, it is a good idea to use additional funds to top up your holding of those shares which you think show promise. This may reduce broker's charges when you come to sell all the stock. Moreover, many authorities agree that the average private investor cannot properly follow the fortunes of more than about 20 shares.

- Do not chase stockmarket fashions. Fashions come and go, and good profits can be made if you get in at the beginning. It is, however, unwise to keep chasing fashionable stocks once they have started to move. You do better to sell such fashionable stocks before the collapse.

- Investment trusts are the best vehicle for global diversification, investing in overseas markets. Japan, Europe and the USA are the principal overseas market domains. Unless you have strong views on the strength of the overseas market, it is wise to invest in a trust which makes its own decisions about when to be invested and when to be in cash. Currency movements can considerably alter gains or losses made in overseas markets.

- Prefer stocks which pay good dividends. Do not place too much reliance on the ability of growth stocks to fulfill their promise.

- Do not be afraid to take a profit. Pull out of a stock when you think it has peaked. Sell out of most stocks if you think the market as a whole has peaked, or if the yield gap exceeds 6 per cent for a protracted period. Leave a bit for the next man. Do not try to wait for the price to top out before selling. You will never guess right and markets tend to fall faster than they rise. But do not be too keen to sell out of a company just because it has recently underperformed, unless you have reason to suppose that the fall will get worse.

- Never let yourself be a forced seller of shares, always have enough spare cash for your likely needs. Sell shares only when you choose to. Never borrow money to buy shares. Leave that to the professionals.

- Do not keep changing shares. Unless you are very lucky, you will not benefit and you will keep incurring broker's charges. Remember that underperformers tend to come good in later years, while strong performers slow down.

CONSTRUCTION OF A WISHLIST

It should by now be apparent that, in the first instance, a wishlist of companies to buy should be constructed from about 20 major companies with a wide spread of sectors.

Go through a financial newspaper, such as the *Financial Times*, and pick out 20 stocks from at least 12 sectors. Choose companies that you have heard of and, most importantly, in whose long term future you have confidence. If you do not recognise any of the companies within a sector, pick a stock with a good dividend cover, low P/E ratio (by the standard of the sector) and high yield. The high yield will provide some protection if the market falls since no one likes to sell shares which earn fat dividends.

Company reports

It is at this point that most standard texts about investment in shares advise the reader to study the company's published accounts carefully. While I would not deter the reader from doing this, one should not put too much emphasis on the results.

There has been a striking rise recently in the number of companies which went bankrupt shortly after publishing accounts purporting to show that they were making big profits. This is in part due to the dubious practice known as 'creative accounting' and in part due to the well known propensity of a company's management to make over-optimistic noises about its future. Of course, simple fraud may have played its part in a number of cases.

Read company accounts then, but do not believe everything you read. It takes a professional eye to disentangle some of the hidden problems, if the company bothers to report them at all. Moreover a recent court ruling declared that the obligation of the company's auditors was to the company (its employer) and not the company's shareholders. Perhaps the most important single item is the 'Cash Flow' statement. Is the company making cash?

Most of all, remember that even the professionals have repeatedly been caught out by the sudden collapse of a company which had just stated record profits. The amateur investor would do well to rely rather on knowledge and analysis of the company published by magazines and other independent judges.

Company reports now come in two forms, the full accounts and a shortened summary. Most companies will send shareholders only the summary, unless specifically requested to do otherwise.

All public companies in the UK have a legal obligation to send a copy of their most recent report to any shareholder and will often provide reports on request to enquirers. This can provide a useful starting point for a wishlist. At the very least you can discover what the company actually does for its living. The *Financial Times* offers a service by which an investor can receive many different company reports at no charge.

Follow your selection

The 20 or so shares should be monitored at least weekly (daily, if you can manage it) plotting charts of share price versus date so that you can see the trend of movement. Incidentally, it is customary to plot the logarithm of share price versus date. This is because a stock which doubles in value every year will rapidly explode out of the top of a normal price-date chart, but will rise steadily on a logarithmic share price versus date graph. You can buy semi-logarithmic graph paper from many stationers.

Try to identify good buying moments, then buy the stocks singly or together (or use pound-cost averaging), always adding new stocks to the wishlist to replace those bought, usually from the same sector. These will serve as reserves, or replacements, for the original companies.

You might also like to follow a few general investment trusts and the relevant indices to see how well your selection performs over a period of time.

As time passes, you may wish to replace the original members of your wishlist with more speculative stocks or overseas investment trusts. Remember, however, to continue to monitor the performance of the previously purchased stocks, so that you can identify the best time to discard them if necessary. This latter practice is only recommended when a share is clearly overvalued.

Once the core share holdings of your portfolio have been assembled, there is plenty of scope to follow personal ideas for investment. If you believe that a company has a bright long term future, then it is worth adding to the wishlist to be followed until its performance can be established. Conversely, if you hear a tip about a retail store chain but know from observation that your local branch is a shambles, then you would be well advised not to buy its shares.

One of the primary features of keeping a wishlist is that you start to observe published information about the companies on the list, which would previously have passed unnoticed. Thus your memory (or a notepad) can compile a dossier of information about your target companies before you buy them.

It has been in the course of following this practice that I have on many occasions noticed how completely inaccurate the predictions of the chartists (technical analysts) have been about 'my' companies. I have often wished that I could nerve myself to do always the opposite to what the chartists recommend.

CONSTRUCTION OF A HITLIST

The opposite of the wishlist is the hitlist, containing those companies of whose shares the investor wishes to dispose.

The hitlist should not normally contain companies which are temporarily underperforming, but rather those which the investor feels either have no long-term prospects of good growth, or are shares which are temporarily absurdly overvalued (perhaps after becoming 'fashionable').

Companies on the hitlist should be disposed of when a good price can be obtained and not merely at the first opportunity. It is important never to be a forced seller of shares.

VALUATION OF SHARES

It is desirable occasionally to value a stockmarket portfolio, even if only to see how well it is doing. It can be particularly important to have the portfolio valued at the end of the tax year, for tax purposes. Many brokers provide a valuation service, but it is possible to do this for yourself.

Obtain a copy of the *Financial Times* for the next working day after the date in question (gives closing prices for the day required). Then write down a table with four columns, thus:

Name of company   No. of shares   Market price   Value

- In the first column put the name of the shares.
- In the second write the number of shares for this company.
- In the third column write the mid-market price for the company taken from the *Financial Times*.
- In the fourth column place the figure obtained by multiplying columns two and three.
- The nominal value of your portfolio is equal to the sum obtained by adding all the figures in the fourth column (this is particularly easy to do with a spreadsheet program, such as Microsoft's EXCEL^{TM}).

For certain purposes, such as valuation of the estate of a deceased investor, the Inland Revenue requires the 'quarter-up' valuation to be used. This requires the valuer to know the bid and offer prices (the spread) of each stock or share being valued.

First, obtain a copy of the *Daily Official List* of Stock Exchange dealings for the date in question. You may be able to obtain this from your broker, or to consult the guide at his office. If the last day of the tax year is at a weekend, get the guide for the preceding Friday.

The guide provides the 'quotation prices' for each listed stock in the form, 'pp99–119'. This means that the stock in question could be bought for 119p or sold at 99p. The spread therefore was 119–99p or 20p. The Inland Revenue states the value of a stock is equal to the sell price plus one quarter of the spread. For this example, the value of the stock is 99p plus one quarter of 20p, which equals 104p.

PERFORMANCE ASSESSMENT

Most investors calculate their wealth as their total holdings of cash and assets expressed as cash. In other words, if they started ten years ago with just one thousand pounds, but today have shares worth nine thousand five hundred pounds and cash worth five hundred pounds, all derived from investment exclusively in shares, then the investor's total worth is ten thousand pounds, a ten-fold rise from the original value. However, the value of ten thousand pounds includes all dividends received (and perhaps reinvested) in this period.

By contrast, the relevant Stock Exchange indices all consider only changes in the value of the underlying shares without taking dividends into account. In practical terms, this means that the indices always understate the true accumulation of wealth for the investor.

If you wish to compare the performance of your wishlist with a Stock Exchange index such as FTSE, it is necessary to construct your own index from your wishlist. This is most simply achieved by taking the average of all the percentage gains (or losses) of each stock in the wishlist over the period of time considered. Dividends must be ignored if the comparison is to be fair. Even so, this elementary procedure takes no account of the weighting of stocks used by indices like the FTSE (see page 41).

For this reason, I recommend comparison with the older, unweighted FT30 (also known as the FT-ORD) index. The FT30 index also has the advantage to the private investor that its constituent companies are chosen to reflect the stockmarket as a whole, whereas the FTSE-100 constitutes those companies that currently have the largest market capitalisation – often banks and utilities. The FT30 index has been criticised for not being updated frequently enough. Unlike the FTSE 100, where changes are made quarterly to keep the highest-valued 100 companies in the index, companies are normally only ejected from the FT30 when they are taken over or go bankrupt. The current list of companies can be found at *www.ftse.com/ft30.txt*.

Why beat the Index?
It is very easy to get carried away with the urge to beat a financial index with one's investments, but it is worth bearing in mind that the index is only an artificial mathematical concept.

The indices take no account of the *risk* of their underlying components. There is little merit in outperforming a falling index, if your own investments have fallen too.

The Prudential Portfolio Managers publish a thought-provoking advertisement. 'All fund managers talk about *growth*. But you can't achieve *growth* without *risk*. So we'd like to talk about *risk*'.

Before chasing any index, the private investor should ask himself why he is trying to do so.

Closet indexing
Most widely diversified holdings of shares (especially those of the institutional pension funds) may be described as 'closet indexers'. This means that the portfolio will, in the long term, behave as the underlying index would without replicating it exactly. Thus it is possible to mimic the approximate performance of a stockmarket index over long periods while owning only a proportion of the shares that make up the index.

7

Investing in Traded Options & Futures

INTRODUCTION TO OPTIONS

Options form a separate branch of normal Stock Exchange activity and are at present controlled by LIFFE (London International Financial Futures Exchange). The purchase of an option grants the buyer the right either to buy or sell (depending on the option type) shares at a fixed price agreed with the option writer (the initial seller of the option). The agreed price is also known as the 'exercise price', the price at which the buyer can force the writer to buy or sell shares.

Options are marketed as being an essential part of a large, balanced portfolio, since they help to manage risk. However, options are themselves very high risk vehicles for investment. Use of options requires a proper understanding of their mechanism and uses, and only a brief outline is given here. A full information pack about Traded Options, the most important class of options, can be obtained from LIFFE (see Useful Addresses).

Traditional options

Traditional options, also known as European Options, are held for periods of up to three months, and cannot easily be exchanged. They provide the holder of the option with the right to buy shares at roughly the price prevailing when the option was purchased (the exact price will be stated). Traditional options can be bought for almost any company and are usually underwritten by large institutions. They may be exercised on any day, and typically cost 10–20 per cent of the underlying share price. Other details are similar to those of traded options, below.

Traded options

Although a much more recent innovation than traditional options, traded options are far more widely employed. Their principal advantage is that the options can be traded through a central market (the Traded Options Market) at any time before they expire. Traded options for any particular company are sold in 'series' that last for up to three, six or nine months.

It is important to note that the buyer of an option pays a fixed sum (the premium) to the writer for the privilege. The writer keeps this sum. If the option is not exercised by its time of expiry, then the buyer loses all his premium.

Calls and puts

Purchase of a 'call' option in a company enables the buyer to purchase shares in that company from the writer at the agreed price, regardless of the current share price.

Purchase of a 'put' option in a company enables the buyer to sell shares in the same company to the writer at the agreed price, regardless of the current share price.

Investors may be buyers or writers of options, but in practice writing options is largely confined to the institutions.

The writer of an option may be required to buy shares if a put option is exercised, or to sell shares if a call option is exercised. In the first case, he must have the money. In the second, he must have the shares. If the writer does not already own the shares when he is called, he must buy them in the market to enable him to pass them on to the caller.

Potential for loss – the margin

Here there is the possibility for unlimited loss to the writer of traded options. He may have to pay all the agreed money to buy a share which has become worthless (put option exercised) or he may have to pay inflated prices to buy in from the market the called shares after a steep market rise. There is therefore a requirement by the Stock Exchange that the option writer put up 'margin' – currently some 20 per cent of the value of the option if it is exercised – as a security against payment (the money is refundable when the option expires).

Generally, today brokers only permit very creditworthy investors, such as institutions, to put up the margin on a written option. Most private clients must put up **all** the purchase price for a put option, or deliver the actual number of shares before writing a call option. If the investor already owns the shares, there is no danger that he will have to buy them in the open market at an excessive price.

On the other hand, the buyer of a traded option has limited risk (the maximum loss is that of his premium). There is no limit to the buyer's potential gains.

Purchase of options

Options are currently available on many of the most traded shares of the FTSE index and the number is steadily increasing each year. Options pay no dividends. The spread (touch) is very high on traded options (typically 15 per cent), while the broker retains his normal commission and minimum charges. This makes trading on a small scale very expensive.

Options are usually traded in bundles representing 1,000 shares (one contract = 1,000 shares), but a very few expensive shares may be traded in bundles of 100. A 'class' of options comprises all options of the same type (call or put) pertaining to one company. Any traded option has a choice of three expiry periods spaced at three monthly intervals. The closest expiry date may be much less than three months away, though. A 'series' of options refers to options of the same class which have either the same exercise price or the same expiry date (an example is given on page 133).

All option purchases must be settled, like purchases of gilts, within one working day. This means that the investor must lodge money with the broker in cleared funds before making a transaction in traded options. Some brokers offer money market interest accounts, ie, accounts which pay interest at typical three-monthly market rates. The interest may be paid monthly or quarterly, and these provide a suitable home for funds earmarked for options.

MEGABANK plc

PO Box 111, Threadneedle Street, London EC1 2CE
Tel: 020 7123 4567 Ext. 9876
Regulated by the Financial Services Authority.

MEGABANK DEMAND ACCOUNT

Client	Account No.	Statement No.	Currency
A. N. Investor	123456.789	001/0X	Pound Sterling

Date	Detail	Ref	Payments	Receipts	Balance
01Jan0X	Opening Balance				0.00
01Jan0X	Remittance	XYZ10		1,000.00	1,000.00
06Apr0X	Interest Net	Int1		25.00	1,025.00
07Apr0X	Closing Balance				1,025.00

Please quote dates and reference numbers in regard to any queries.

INCOME TAX AT 20% HAS BEEN DEDUCTED FROM
ALL CREDIT INTEREST ARISING ON THIS ACCOUNT.

Fig. 17. Typical statement of a money market account.

Agreements

No broker will deal in traded options for a client without having previously received two written agreements from the client, saying that he has read LIFFE's Trading Options booklet and is aware of the risks involved in trading options. The written agreements are LIFFE's 'Letter of Authority' and the Financial Services Authority's 'Risk Disclosure Statement'.

Volatility

The gearing element of options relative to the shares they represent (see example given in 'Why buy options?' page 130) ensures that they are much more volatile than the underlying shares. Options are high risk investments, and must be monitored daily. A stop-loss policy (see page 113) is usually recommended.

Price movement of options

The movement of option prices is controlled by the market forces of supply and demand. The value of traded options generally moves in line with the underlying shares. A share going ex-dividend can cause a big drop in the option price as the share value falls, since ownership of the share will no longer earn a short-term dividend.

It is possible to work out the theoretical value of an option, taking into account its time value and the underlying value of the shares, according to the Black-Scholes theoretical model (briefly outlined in Appendix 2). It is also possible to calculate a delta value (hedge ratio) for the option, representing the amount by which the option premium should move for every one point move in the share price. Thus, if the delta ratio for a share is 0.5 and the share moves by 10 points, then the option premium should move by 5 points.

If the actual value of an option is much below its theoretical value, then the option is underpriced. A strategy of buying underpriced options presumably ought to pay in the long term, although there appears to be no evidence for this.

Closing the account

Neither buyer nor seller is compelled to hold traded options until the end of the expiry period. The buyer may sell the option to close his account. The writer may buy the option back from the current owner of the option, again closing the account. In both cases, the price paid will be the current one prevailing as the market value of the option, not the initial premium.

In addition, most options, traded or traditional, may be exercised at any time. A randomising computer called London Options Clearing House (LOCH) decides which of many option writers is the one who has to settle up with the buyer of the option. Buyers or writers of options will exercise their sell/buy back alternatives if they feel that their initial judgement of the movement of the underlying share was incorrect.

Why buy options?

There are many alternative reasons or strategies for buying options, several of which are quoted by the booklets of LIFFE's Traded Options Group. A few of the most important strategies are given here.

An investor buys options primarily for their gearing effect (see under warrants, in Chapter 3) relative to movements of the underlying shares. If the investor thinks that the shares of a company, currently valued at 100p, are going to rise, then he could buy the shares. If they rise to 120p, the investor has made a profit of 20 per cent (less dealing charges). If, however, the investor buys 90p call options at their market price of 20p (ie, he buys the right for 20p per share to buy the shares at 90p each regardless of their current market value), then, all other things being equal, the options will rise in value to 40p – a 100 per cent profit.

If the shares were to drop in value, the investor would lose some or all of his premium, although he might recover some of his loss by selling the 90p call options at, say, 10p.

Put options can be purchased as insurance. Suppose the investor owns 1,000 shares worth 120p after talk of a takeover. The investor does not want to sell his shares in case the takeover bid emerges, and the shares rise higher. On the other hand, if the bid fails to materialise his shares may fall to 80p each. The investor can protect his position by buying 120p put options for, let us assume, 20p each. If the shares rise, he loses his insurance money, the put premium, but gains from the value of the shares. If the shares fall to 80p as feared, the put options will be worth about 60p each – quite a consolation!

Put options can similarly be purchased by anyone who expects the value of a share to fall, perhaps in anticipation of a bear market. Some authorities recommend that only about a quarter of the threatened share holding should be covered by put 'insurance'.

Why write options?

Writing options guarantees the writer an extra income. If an institution holds shares worth 100p each, paying 4p dividend, writing 100p call options on the stock may give an extra income of 7p per share. Eleven per cent makes a good return, particularly if the institution has already decided that it would like to dump the stock on the grounds of underperformance.

If the market rises and the writer has to provide the stock at the agreed price of 100p to the buyer, then the writer has effectively sold the stock at 107p (agreed price plus premium). This is more than the writer would have got if he had sold the shares in the first place. If, however, the market value of the shares remains steady, or falls, the writer of the option simply keeps the premium.

Put options may be written by an investor or institution who wants to buy a stock, but does not like the current price. If the investor wants to buy stock at 100p, but it is currently worth 120p, he writes put options for 100p and collects a premium of, for example, 15p. If the price falls to below 100p, the investor effectively gets his stock at a price of 85p(100 − 15). If the price stands still or rises, the investor has missed his chance to own the stock, but has 15p per share to help swallow his disappointment.

FTSE options/FTSE-Eurotrack

It is also possible to buy or write options on the FTSE index itself. No shares change hands. Instead rises or falls in the index are paid off in cash by the writer at the rate of £10 for every one point rise or fall in the index. This represents simple gambling, although purchase of a FTSE put option does provide insurance against a general market fall. Conversely purchase of a call option gives the buyer a stake in a sudden general market rise.

As well as the normal series of short lived options, it is also possible to buy 'long dated' FTSE options with a life span of up to twelve months. FTSE-Eurotrack options, which speculate on the FTSE-Eurotrack index comprising a basket of typical European (non-British) companies, are additionally available.

It is also possible to gamble directly on various UK share indices through a number of London-based betting organisations such as I.G. Index Ltd, Ladbrokes or City Index. The reader is warned that use of these gambling services can subject the investor to the possibility of unlimited loss. These institutions advertise themselves in the financial newspapers.

A trainee accountant earning £7000 per year acquired notoriety after the October 1987 market crash when he went bankrupt owing £1m to his broker, one of the clearing banks. How could this happen?

It seems that he was receiving income by writing many FTSE put options, without having the cash to cover his position in the event of a crash. In addition, it would appear that he was not being required (as he should have been) to put up the necessary 20 per cent margin. Had he been required to do so, it would have cost more than the value of the income and would soon have exposed his lack of capital.

It is disturbing to note that the trainee had nothing, ended up with nothing (the bank sustained all the loss ultimately), but could have pocketed some £30,000 in option premiums if the market had not collapsed. Effectively he took no risk and received no punishment.

In and out of the money
With fluctuations in share prices, some options could be exercised immediately with profit to their owners. These options are said to be 'in the money', whilst the remainder are 'out of the money'. For example, if a share is worth 100p, an 80p call option is 'in the money' since the buyer can demand delivery of shares at 80p, while the 120p call option is 'out of the money'. Naturally, options 'in the money' are worth much more than those 'out of the money'.

Time value
With each successive day that passes, an option 'out of the money' has less of a chance of being exercised before its expiry date. It is therefore progressively worth less and the time element of the option's value is declining. On the day before expiry, the time element effectively becomes zero and the option is only worth its exercise value (if it has one).

Public limit order
This is a limiting system operated by LIFFE. The investor can ask to buy or sell a traded option at a maximum or minimum price which will be 'GD' or 'GTC'. LIFFE will only execute the order if the price is within the investor's limit during the stated time.

'GD' means Good for the Day and the limit only applies for the current trading day. If the transaction is not made within the investor's limit by then, it will be cancelled.

'GTC' means Good Till Cancelled, ie cancelled by the investor. Limits set GTC will be considered daily by LIFFE until the transaction is completed within the investor's limit or the investor cancels the proposed transaction. It would be most imprudent to leave a GTC instruction open for any long period of time.

Many stockbrokers dealing in traded options for private clients will, in addition, operate their own limit systems. An investor could ask to buy a call option at a maximum of 100 pence today, or 110 pence tomorrow or 120 pence the day after, then cancel. The stockbroker's computer will translate this somewhat eccentric series of instructions into a succession of appropriate GD orders.

Capital Gains Tax

Losses incurred through the use of traded options for shares (not gilts), for example if they expire with no value, can be set against capital gains made elsewhere for tax purposes. This is provided that the options were traded through recognised intermediaries (such as a stockbroker) on a recognised stock exchange, and gains are not so regular as to be counted as 'income'.

Miscellaneous

No stamp duty is paid on the purchase of traded options. However, a special traded option charge may be levied as well as the £5 charge made by many stockbrokers for compliance with Stock Exchange regulations.

Interpretation of the traded option data in the *Financial Times*

The *Financial Times* devotes a large part of one page to the last closing prices of traded options. Here is a typical example for Glaxo-SmithKline on one day in January 2003:

		Calls			Puts		
		Jan	Apr	Jul	Jan	Apr	Jul
Glaxo	1200	37	107	135	28	99	127
(*1208)	1250	15	81	109	55	124	150

The price marked (*1208) represents the current price of a Glaxo share, in pence. There are two classes of traded options, calls and puts.

There are two price-series of options, 1200 and 1250, the first 'in the money' (calls) and 'out of the money' (puts). The second is 'out of the money' (calls) and 'in the money' (puts). Alternatively, there are three date-series, ie, January, April and July. The options expire at the end of these months. Note that there are far more price series than those shown. The *Financial Times* has only space for a few.

Thus, an optimistic investor in December, expecting Glaxo's share price to rise, would buy a 1250 call option (Class = Glaxo Call) for April (Series = 1250, Apr), at a middle price of 81 pence per

COUNTRYWIDE STOCKBROKING LIMITED

(Incorporating Country, Town and Co.)

1-4 Broker Street, Thames Valley, TV1 9SB Telephone: 0123-987654

*Branches in: Birmingham, Dundee, Edinburgh, Littlemarch-under-Water,
London, Manchester, Swansea*

Registered Office: Countrywide House, Hampstead, London NW1 9XX

Registered in England No. 1234567 VAT Registration No. 123 4567 89

Regulated by the Financial Services Authority.
Member of the London Stock Exchange

CONTRACT NOTE AND TAX INVOICE

MR. ANTHONY INVESTOR
OF NO FIXED
ABODE
LONDON
AB1 9ZY

Bargain Date and Tax Point	Security	Client	Contract Ref.	Settlement Date
06FEB0X	+0654321	W12345D	A56789	07FEB0X

WE THANK YOU FOR YOUR INSTRUCTIONS AND HAVE BOUGHT ON YOUR BEHALF AS AGENTS:
MEGASTORES
CALL OPTIONS/JUNE 0X/1050
DEC. DATE 25 JUNE0X STRIKING PRICE 10.5000

Time	Quantity	Price	Consideration
09:55	1	0.850	£850.00
			£850.00
TRAD OPTION CHG			.60
COMMISSION			30.00
V.A.T. EXEMPT			NIL
COMPLIANCE CHARGE			5.00
		TOTAL	
			£885.60

Subject to the Rules and Regulations of the Stock Exchange including any temporary regulations made by or under the authority of the Council of the Stock Exchange.

E. & O.E. V.A.T. Invoice for services rendered (N) = Not subject to V.A.T. Please retain this document for Capital Gains Tax and V.A.T. purposes.

Fig. 18. Contract note for the purchase of traded options.

share (the real price, allowing for the trading spread, would have been about 85 pence).

A pessimistic investor would buy a 1200 put option for April for 99 pence plus spread.

Remember that options are normally traded in contracts of 1,000 each. The minimum purchase cost of just one call option by the optimist, as illustrated above, would be 85 pence × 1,000 = £850, before dealing costs are added.

How to deal in traded options

As previously stated, it is necessary to sign two agreements with your stockbroker before he will let you deal in traded options. Many brokers will not deal at all for private clients. Charles Schwab (see Useful Addresses) started dealing in traded options in March 1992. It is now the largest dealer. **Warning**: It is absolutely essential that the investor knows what he is doing before trading in these high risk derivatives. A serious error could result in unlimited loss and bankruptcy!

When you speak to your broker, you need to provide the following information:

- Your name and client number (if applicable).

- The number of contracts to buy or sell (remembering that one contract is normally for 1000 options).

- The class of option (name of company and whether a call or put is required).

- The series: the expiry date and exercise price of the option.

- Whether you are opening or closing a position (see page 129).

- (Optional) your public limit order (see page 132) and whether it is GD (Good for the Day) or GTC (Good Till Cancelled).

- How you intend to pay within 24 hours, including any margin or deposition of share certificates that may be required.

The professionals always win

Anecdotal evidence suggests that the market professionals always beat amateur investors at traded options. Expert traders can judge the odds on the value of a traded option better than an amateur, although there are published technical details about the calculation of the 'theoretical value' of a traded option, using the Black-Scholes model (see Appendix 2). Only five per cent of traded options are ever exercised.

Other types of traded option

Traded options can be bought for selected gilts, in blocks of 50,000 gilts per contract. Special traded options are made available by LIFFE for use in bids or takeovers, applying only to the target company for the duration of the bid.

Warrants

Warrants (see Chapter 2) can be regarded as long-lived call options, since they can be exercised at regular intervals to provide the underlying shares. Their cost is higher than those of the related traded options, reflecting their long 'time value'. The purchase of warrants also requires the investor to sign a formal risk warning.

A typical example is provided by Hanson plc. In December 1993, the following prices were quoted:

Hanson ordinary shares	266p
260p call options August 1994	21p
Warrants (300p to be paid before September 1997)	28p

Penny shares

Penny shares (see page 51) represent, in effect, a type of undated, traded option. The cost of these shares is so low that investment requires little more than option money. The shares can be traded and the time element is set by bankruptcy (loss of the option) or a turn-around in the fortunes of the company when the shares can be sold.

INTERPRETATION OF CHARTS

Examination of share price charts (plotted logarithmically) against time provides a number of features of interest even to those who are not dedicated 'chartists'.

The most important single feature is the 'trend'. A series of higher peaks and higher bottoms indicates a rising trend in share price. Conversely a series of lower peaks and lower bottoms indicates a falling trend. Trend lines may also be sketched by drawing two lines joining the highest peaks and the lowest bottoms. If both lines move in the same direction, then that direction is the trend (see Figure 19).

Many chartists also plot 'n-day moving averages', comprising the average share movement of the last 'n' days to the point at which the average is plotted. Graphs commonly show the 20 day and 50 day moving averages. When the share price is above the most recent 20 or 50 day moving average, it is deemed to be:

- overvalued, or

- starting a new trend in the direction it has moved.

This difference is important, but it is very difficult to distinguish the two alternatives except with the benefit of hindsight.

Chartists rely heavily on previous patterns to tell them which way a share price is moving, but the patterns may not always apply. From private observations, I believe that some patterns apply in bull markets, but do not apply in bear markets. For this reason, they will not be described here. If a share price exceeds its 50 day moving average in a bull market, it may well be set to explode upwards. On the other hand, in a bear market, panic at the high price is likely to set in, causing the share price to revert to the long term average. Certainly, there appears to be plenty of scope for the private investor to invent his own rules for following chart patterns, so long as he realises that past performance is not a certain guide to the future.

Another instructive feature of charts is the concept of the 'resistance level'. A share may keep rising until it seems to hit an invisible wall at a certain price. The share drops in value, then rises until it hits the wall again. Again it falls and again it rises to the wall. The value of the wall is known as the (upper) resistance level of the share.

After the wall has been hit several times, one of two things normally happens:

- Investors give up, and the share price falls sharply downwards.

- The wall collapses, and the share price rockets upwards.

An example of an upper resistance level can be seen in the 1993–98 chart of the FTSE index (Figure 19), where it seemed to be impossible to break the wall at 6,000 in an upwards direction over several months.

A lower resistance level can also be encountered, where buyers flock in whenever a share falls in value to a certain level. A good example can also be seen in Figure 19, where the FTSE index had a clear lower resistance level at 3,000.

It can be seen then, that charts can provide a great deal of information to private investors, if used with common sense.

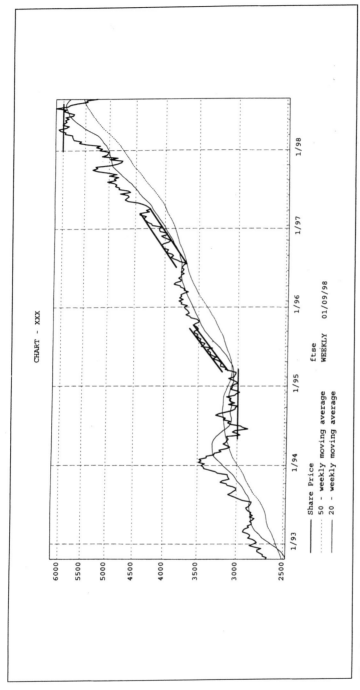

Fig. 19. The chart of the FTSE index shows the range of weekly price movements with the 20- and 50- week moving averages. On the left is a 'lower resistance level' at 3,000, sustained for over 20 weeks. I recall that the big institutions bought heavily whenever the index fell below 3,000. Subsequently there was a steep rise. On the right is an 'upper resistance level': over many weeks the index failed to push decisively through the 6,000 level and subsequently fell back steeply. Two trend lines are shown centrally.

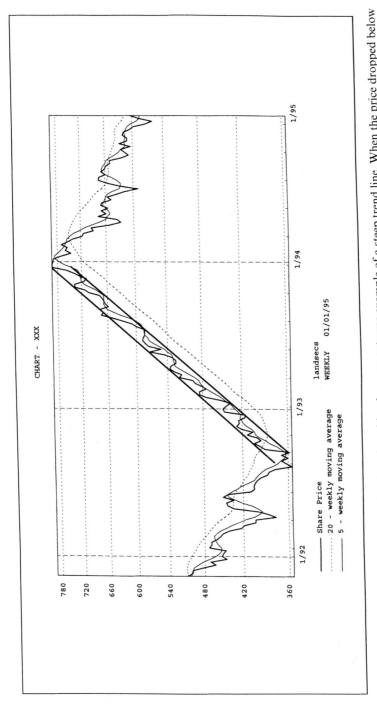

Fig. 20. The chart of Land Securities plc, plotted weekly, shows an extreme example of a steep trend line. When the price dropped below the trend in January 1994, the shares fell steadily in value.

139

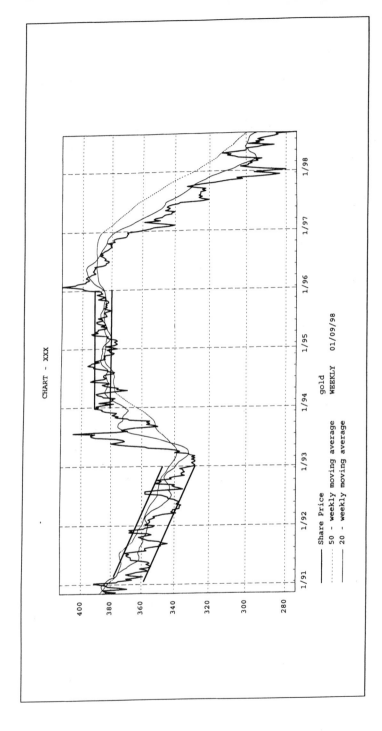

Fig. 21. Gold shows a declining trend to 1993, when a consortium of speculators bought heavily. Then a steady trading range (centre) was established. Finally the price of gold resumed its decline.

However, the finer points of the chartist's art – it is certainly not a science – require a great deal of faith and are distinguished by the number of exceptions to the rules.

A good account of technical analysis (study of charts) is given in one of the references in the Further Reading section of this book. Ready-made charts can be purchased from many sources. Those published in this chapter were provided by my program 'Chart-XXX'.

FUTURES

Options give the purchaser the *right* to buy or sell shares.

Futures give the *obligation* to buy or sell shares, bonds or commodities.

Futures therefore expose the investor to **unlimited** risk. AVOID!! – strictly for professionals only.

OTHER DERIVATIVES

The recent slow downturn in stockmarkets has increased the demand for investment products that will make money even when share prices decline. Derivatives of shares, such as traded options, fit this role. All are linked to an underlying company share (or to an index of shares), but have the characteristic that they can be bought and sold separately.

Since derivatives generally are not classified as shares, most are not subject to stamp duty when purchased in the UK. In addition, most allow the purchaser to 'go short' (that is, to profit when the stockmarket falls), most are 'geared' (ie a small movement in the price of the underlying share has a large effect on the value of the derivative), most are subject to wide spreads or commissions, and gains on most are subject to Capital Gains Tax. Nearly all have time limitations imposed upon them, which means that it would be very dangerous for the investor to leave the derivatives unattended – indeed, most require hourly or daily monitoring. In nearly all cases, investors will be required either to sign an agreement with the broker stating that they are aware of the risks involved, or even to present evidence that they are experienced investors with good knowledge of derivatives.

See Appendix 18 for a list of alternative derivative types.

8

Bonds/Gilts/Interest-Bearing Deposits

INTRODUCTION TO BONDS AND GILTS

A bond is an instrument by which the seller receives money from the buyer in exchange for giving:

- an amount of interest
- (usually) repayment of the money on a stated expiry date, or between two stated repayment dates.

It is important to note that the buyer pays the current market price for the bond, while repayment is normally made at the face value of the bond. The face value of the bond, referred to as the 'par value', is usually £100 per bond.

Types of bond

Gilts are interest-bearing bonds issued by the UK government as a means of borrowing money to finance its various activities not covered by income from taxation.

Foreign countries' governments also issue bonds. These are usually denominated in the country's own currency.

Companies issue bonds, or 'debentures', to raise money. Some of the oldest bonds were issued by newly formed railways.

Debentures are bonds secured on company assets and have first claim on those assets in the event that the company goes bankrupt. Debentures may be 'fixed', secured on specific assets, or 'floating', secured on the company as a whole.

Loan Stocks are unsecured bonds, ie bonds with no claim on a company's assets if the company goes bankrupt. However, loan stocks are usually paid back ahead of the ordinary shareholders after bankruptcy.

Loan Notes are loan stocks which are repaid only when the company's life is for some reason ended ('wound up'). They are usually issued by investment trusts with a specific date for winding-up. See also page 72.

142

Certificate Number	Transfer Number	Date of Registration	Number of Units
CON01001	C001234	22MAY0X	—1000—

Units of 5.75 percent Convertible Unsecured
Loan Stock 2010 ('Stock') of 500p each

MEGASTORES plc

(Incorporated under the Companies Act 1948)

THIS IS TO CERTIFY that

MR ANTHONY INVESTOR
OF NO FIXED
ABODE
LONDON AB1 9ZY

is/are the registered holders of   **ONE THOUSAND**
units of Stock of 500 pence each fully paid in Megastores plc,
subject to the memorandum and articles of association of the
company, the Instrument dated 1st January 200X constituting
the Convertibles and the Particulars endorsed hereon.

Issued under the common seal of the company

NOTE: No transfer of any of the units comprised in this certificate will be
registered until the certificate has been surrendered to the registrar's office:
MegaBank plc, Registrar's Dept, PO Box 111, Threadneedle Street, London
EC1 2CE.

Fig. 22. Example of a convertible certificate. Note: the date and conditions
of conversion of the stock into shares, and the dates on which interest
payments will be made on the stock, will be given on the reverse of the
certificate in very small print.

Cumulative Bonds are entitled to collect arrears of interest, from a company which has previously had to miss some payments of interest due to financial hardship, before any other interest or dividends are paid.

Non-cumulative bonds are not entitled to collect arrears of interest. Redeemable bonds can be bought back by the issuer before the expiry date.

Convertibles (see Chapter 2) represent another type of bond issued by companies. They pay a fixed interest rate until their expiry date, when they are paid back in full. The special feature of convertibles is that they can, at certain times, be converted into the ordinary shares of the issuing company.

Step-up and Call Bonds can be redeemed at a distant date. If the bond is not redeemed, the interest paid will be increased from that date.

Reverse Convertible Bonds (RCBs) are mostly issued by banks and combine a share price-link to a blue chip company or an index, coupled with a put option (Chapter 7): the issuer can dump a predetermined number of shares in the company onto the bond-holder (the investor) instead of repaying the loan. In exchange, the bond-holder receives an abnormally high interest payment on the bond. At maturity, the bond-holder receives the lesser of:

a) the bond's par value
b) the value of the company shares (or of the index).

The value of the shares is fixed at launch, typically at the share price on that day. RCBs are traded fairly readily on the Stockmarket.

Example:

UBS 12% 19/12/03 (Legal & General, 157p)

UBS is the (Swiss) issuing bank. Legal & General is the company whose shares may be dumped on the bond-holder on 19th December 2003 if L&G's share price is less than 157p then. The bond-holder will receive a yield of 12% until December 2003.

It is perfectly feasible for a bond to be issued by a company bearing a combination of the above designations. For example, a '3% Cumulative Convertible Preference Stock 2010'. This bond will pay 3 per cent gross or net interest per annum (depending on whether it ranks as a loan stock or as a preference share), and any arrears will be made good in preference to other loanstock- and share-holders. The bond will be repaid preferentially in the event of the company going bankrupt, and it will be possible to convert the bond into the company's shares at certain dates before the year 2010. Since many of the terms described above are in practice used rather loosely by the companies issuing bonds, it is very important to read the exact terms of the bond before investing in it.

The Eurobond Market is a rapidly increasing market for international governments, institutions and companies. Interest payments are normally paid at 12 month intervals (six months is common for the British bond market).

Local authorities (such as city councils) and utilities (such as water companies) issue bonds similar to gilts.

Some building societies issue bonds, either on the Stock Exchange or directly to their investors. The first type of bond is freely negotiable on the Market. The second, held by private investors, can only be sold back to the building society, usually with a financial penalty. PIBS are described in Appendix 8.

Safety of bonds

Gilts are the safest forms of UK investment, since the government is less likely to default than any other UK agency, such as banks, building societies and the like. However, it is possible for private intermediaries or agents to reduce this security by their incompetence or dishonesty. Although gilts are safe, their market value will fluctuate in a way similar to, but normally much less than, shares. All gilt prices move together. Therefore diversification of gilts (a portfolio) serves no purpose – the risk remains the same. This is not true of other bonds.

The bonds issued by foreign governments are of variable safety, depending on the ability of the government to pay the interest and repay the debt at the stated time. Similarly, bonds issued by local authorities and utilities are regarded as less safe than UK gilts. The yields of the less safe bonds are normally slightly higher than those of the corresponding gilts to compensate for the increased risk.

It is, regrettably, not unknown for institutions or even for governments to default on their obligations either to pay interest or to pay back the outstanding capital sum. If this happens, the investor has lost some or all of his investment. Sometimes partial settlements of the outstanding sum may be agreed. On other occasions all that remains is the intrinsic value of the piece of bond paper. Some very old bonds were particularly attractive in appearance, and have acquired value as collectors' pieces. Very occasionally, a defaulting government may agree to redeem its bonds years after they apparently became worthless. Recent examples include payments made by the Communist Russian and Chinese governments to settle the debts of their imperial predecessors. Not, let it be acknowledged, out of any sense of honour but because it makes the issue of new bonds so much easier if the old have been repaid.

Mezzanine finance
Companies can fund expansion, or a management buyout, by two main routes:

- borrowing money
- issuing shares.

Money is borrowed with a view to the return to the lender of his original capital, with interest. Shares give the shareholder a continuing stake in the business and, therefore, borrowed money is normally repaid to the lender in preference to dividends to the shareholders. In the event of bankruptcy, the money lenders will get their money back from remaining company assets before the shareholders, in accordance with the maxim that greater return equals greater risk.

The borrowed money which will be paid back preferentially is known as 'senior debt' (eg debentures). However, it is worth noting that the last pound of senior debt is scarcely less risky than the first pound of equity. If a bankrupt company owes its lenders one million pounds and its shareholders one million pounds then, unless its assets are worth exactly one million pounds, some of its money lenders and all of its shareholders are bound to be treated similarly (not necessarily alike).

This created the demand for 'mezzanine' or 'junior' (loan stock) debt. Mezzanine finance rates below senior debt for repayment in the event of bankruptcy, but ahead of the shareholders. To compensate for the increased risk, mezzanine loan stock pays a few percentage points of interest more than the senior debt.

The big difference between mezzanine finance and 'junk' bonds (see below) is that the latter are securities issued by the company which can be traded on open markets. Mezzanine finance is not openly traded, but is usually retained by the issuing lender (normally a bank). A technical advantage to the bank is that the mezzanine debt can be retained on its books at face value, instead of having to be adjusted to market value.

Junk bonds
Junk bonds, seen mostly in the USA in the 1980s, were frequently

issued by managers to finance their purchase of the companies for which they worked from the original shareholders. Other junk bonds were issued as an innovative means to finance the huge sums needed when one company took over another. Interest charges consumed a very high proportion of the company's profits, so that the bonds were of very high risk. In turn, this meant that higher interest had to be paid to persuade investors to hold the bonds, reducing the company's profit margins further.

Many of the US companies concerned finally defaulted on at least some of their repayments on these bonds as the recession of the late 1980s took hold and their profits could not cope with the interest payments. Consequently, the prices of these junk bonds fell rapidly, although there was for a time a vogue for 'bundles' of junk bonds in the belief that the bundle offered a very high average yield and not all of the companies could go bankrupt (could they?). Alas, many of them did.

It is possible to invest in the shares of a handful of investment trusts which trade in junk bonds and mezzanine debt. An old example was 'Mithras Investment Trust', managed by L & G Ventures but now directed towards a different objective.

Bond ratings

Most bonds are now rated for credit-worthiness by either or both of two US organisations – Standard&Poors and Moody. The most credit-worthy bonds are rated A-something; the more As the better, Aa1 or AA+ count higher than Aa3 or AA−. Company bonds, which are more speculative, are generally rated B-something. High-risk, or 'junk', bonds, are rated C-something. Bonds in default are rated D.

The more risky that a bond is, the higher the yield that investors demand in compensation. This has led to the recent issue (especially by telecoms companies) of some bonds whose interest payment during any repayment period depends upon their credit rating.

Long-dated company bonds are riskier than the short-dated. Will the company still be around in 20 years' time? However, in the event of a takeover, the bonds will normally be converted in some way (eg repaid at a premium, or renamed and continued).

The price of bonds

Market forces

The price of gilts and other bonds is fixed by supply and demand in the usual way. Their value goes up and down according to changes in general interest rates. When interest rates are high, the nominal return on fixed-interest bonds becomes less attractive and the price of the bond falls. Conversely, when interest rates fall, the price of bonds tends to rise. These changes are often caused by changes in inflation.

A new release of existing government gilts is known as a 'tap', and the initial release price is fixed at whatever the government thinks the market will bear. New types of gilt are released by tender in partly-paid form through 'gilt auctions'. Private investors may apply. Details can be obtained from the Debt Management Office at the Bank of England (address at the back of this book).

At the time of writing, the government will probably need to issue many more gilts to fund its public spending plans.

Accrued interest
It is essential to realise that, in the case of government gilts and most other bonds, the price which is quoted in the newspapers is the 'clean' price of the gilt, free of interest. However, the price which you pay for the gilt is the clean price plus the accrued gross interest to the purchase date.

Gilt Price = Quoted Price + Accrued Gross Interest

Example: Treasury 8% 2015 could be bought on 7th December 2003 for £131. It pays £8 per annum in interest, *ie* £4 every 7th December and 7th June. If you purchased the stock ex-dividend on 7th December, you would pay, near enough, £131 per gilt. If you bought the gilt cum-dividend on 7th December you would pay about £135 per gilt (quoted price plus interest). If you bought on 7th March and the quoted price was still £131, you would pay roughly £131 plus £2.00 which equals £133.00.

Gilt strips
In order to facilitate the sale of new gilts, in 1995 the government permitted the separation of their capital value and their coupons. This is known as 'gilt stripping', a practice long known for bonds in the USA. The prospect of gilt stripping created changes in the taxation of gilts, discussed below. Gilts that *can* be stripped will often trade in their conventional form. Stripped gilts will not be offered through the Post Office/National Savings Stock Register (see below).

Types of gilts
There are three principal types of gilt:

* fixed interest, dated
* fixed interest, undated
* index-linked.

Fixed interest, dated gilts
Ordinary gilts are dated, ie have fixed expiry periods. Some of the dates of expiry are fixed to a certain year, others cover several years and can be repaid at any time during the fixed time range.

Dated gilts are divided into three classes:

* shorts – to be repaid within five years of the present date
* mediums – to be repaid within five to 15 years of the present date
* longs – to be repaid more than 15 years after the present date.

1. **Interest rates**

    Gilts are bought for their ability to pay interest. As their price goes up, the yield paid goes down. Prices tend to rise in times of low interest rates and to fall when interest rates are high. The nominal interest rate of a gilt, ie the interest paid per £100 of stock, is known as the 'coupon' of the gilt. The coupon is normally paid twice yearly and is subject to income tax. The name 'coupon' derives from times past when a coupon had to be clipped off the bond certificate and sent for payment.

2. **Indices**

    Indices of the performance of dated gilts are available, usually measuring either the average capital value or the average interest rate of the 'longs'. One such index is the FT-Gilts Index, printed in the *Financial Times*.

3. **Redemption**

    When the life of a dated gilt expires, the government repays the gilt 'at par', usually £100 per gilt. As the life of the gilt nears its end, its price becomes closer and closer to that of its par value. It never quite reaches the par value, partly due to the fact that money in hand is worth more than money owed by the government, no matter how briefly, and partly owing to the cost of any transaction just before repayment. In the case of gilts with a variable life, such as Treasury 8% 2002–2006, the government can decide the repayment date. Alternatively, the government may elect to redeem some of the gilts at any time between the stated dates. The sum repaid by the government on gilts is generally tax-free. This is not always the case when other bonds are repaid.

4. Interpretation of Gilts Measurements

The values of gilts are published daily by the *Financial Times*. Gilts may pay nominal coupon rates of between two and 15 per cent. Their price fluctuates so that the actual price gives a real yield close to what the market wants, allowing for current interest rates. In April 1989 and then in May 1991, the *Financial Times* quoted the following prices for two 'short' gilts:

(Issue)	(Coupon)	(Date)	(Price)	(Int.)	(Red.)
*Treasury	10%	1992	97 3/16	10.29	11.18
*Treasury	3%	1992	83 5/8	3.59	9.02
†Treasury	10%	1992	99 5/8	10.04	10.45
†Treasury	3%	1992	95 1/16	3.16	8.00

* = April 1989 prices   † = May 1991 prices

The column 'Int.' shows the actual interest paid to anyone who buys the gilts at the current price. The column 'Red.' shows the overall yield that will be gained by a buyer who holds the gilts to redemption, assuming all coupons received are reinvested in the same gilt at today's price. In practice, the price of the gilt will vary as perceptions of interest rates change, so that it may not be best to buy the gilt currently showing the greatest yield.

Note that the price of the gilts comes closer to par (£100) as the redemption date approaches.

Low coupon gilts used to be very popular with higher rate tax payers since gilts can be bought below their par value, the coupon paid is too low to attract much income tax, and the redemption payment is tax free. This has become of less value in recent years as income tax rates have been reduced.

5. Difference between shorts, mediums and longs

Shorts are closest to their expiry date, and so a primary feature of their price will be the expected, tax-free redemption. As the redemption date approaches, their price will trade closer and closer to the redemption value. The principal interest of shorts to a private investor is as a means of making a tax-free capital gain.

Longs are more volatile in price, since their value depends on expected inflation over a long period (more than 15 years). They perform better when the rate of inflation is expected to decline and offer greater scope for making capital gains by active trading. High coupon longs also provide a long term, stable source of income, although this may be at the long term expense of capital.

Mediums provide a half-way house between the two extremes of the shorts and longs.

Fixed interest, undated gilts

Undated gilts are those which pay interest, but have no set redemption date. Most of them are very old, with low coupon rates from the days when inflation was low.

Examples are Consols 2.5% and 4% from the nineteenth century and 3.5% War Loan from the World Wars. Successive governments never repaid the War Loan at par and they won't find it so easy to borrow in another war.

As with dated gilts, the price of the undated stocks is adjusted to bring the actual interest rate into line with current rates. Thus the 3.5% War Loan was priced in January 2003 at £75.40, yielding 4.6 per cent gross interest at this price (£3.50 being paid per bond).

As long as inflation is high, successive governments have no incentive to repay these low coupon, undated gilts.

Index-linked gilts

These are of comparatively recent origin, arising from the inflationary 1970s. The first was issued in 1981. Index-linked gilts are, without exception at present, dated and pay a low coupon yield of a 'fixed' 2 to $4^5/_8$ per cent. However, their redemption payment will not be £100, but rather £100 adjusted to allow for inflation, as measured by the Retail Price Index, since the day the gilt was issued. Moreover, the 'fixed' coupon rate will also be adjusted to allow for inflation. However, it should be noted that the inflation adjustments always lag about eight months behind the actual current rate of inflation.

The *Financial Times* calculates what the *real* rate of interest will be to a buyer who holds an index-linked gilt to redemption assuming (a) 5 per cent and (b) 3 per cent inflation in the intervening period. In January 2003, the real yields were around 2.0–2.2 per cent for all the long-dated index-linked gilts, higher real yields being seen with the lower projected inflation rate of three per cent. Unfortunately, index-linked gilt yields are at present very low owing to high demand (high prices = low yields). The government forced many pension funds to buy these gilts to match their liabilities with their assets, but there were not enough index-linked gilts to go around.

Conversion gilts
Conversion gives the investor the right to switch to another gilt instead of accepting repayment at maturity.

Rump gilts
Gilts that have mostly been converted to other types. The handful that have not been converted may be very hard to trade.

Partly-paid gilts
The government frequently sells gilts in partly-paid form (as it often does when privatising the shares of nationalised companies). The partly-paid gilts normally trade at a higher price than would be expected from their partly-paid value. The reason is due, at least in part, to the interest which can be earned on money which would otherwise have been used to pay the whole price of the gilt.

TAX IMPLICATIONS OF PURCHASES OF BONDS AND GILTS

Taxation of the interest from bonds in general is usually quite straightforward. You are liable to income tax at your normal rate and the interest must be declared on your income tax form. In many cases, 20 per cent tax will have been deducted from the interest paid to the investor, which may discharge the liability completely. Higher rate tax payers will have to pay further income tax at the end of the tax year, while non-tax payers can reclaim the interest paid.

The situation is much more complicated for government gilts. The interest is usually paid twice yearly and may be paid to the direct investor, by request since 1998, gross or net of 20% tax. However, if your gilts are held in a nominee account, the account operator will probably make its own choice, gross or net. The investor is subject to income tax on the coupons paid (if the Treasury deduction of 20 per cent tax was insufficient, or the coupon was received gross) and they must be declared on the yearly tax form. It may be possible to reclaim tax if you are not subject to income tax. In addition, it may be possible to reclaim from the Inland Revenue the excess payment which you made when you paid for the accrued gross interest on buying the gilt, but received only a net coupon payment from the Treasury (see page 148). Eligibility for repayment depends on a complex formula from the Inland Revenue.

Income from the coupons of stripped gilts is paid gross, and therefore must be declared on your tax form.

Security Code
0–123–456

95

9 PER CENT TREASURY STOCK, 200Z

Principal and interest charged on the National Loans Fund, with recourse to the Consolidated Fund of the United Kingdom. Repayable at par on 20th November 200Z. Interest payable half-yearly on 20th May and 20th November.

ACCOUNT NUMBER		CERTIFICATE NUMBER
98-76-54321	£ 3,000.00***	135-246802

MR ANTHONY INVESTOR
OF NO FIXED
ABODE
LONDON AB1 9ZY

THIS IS TO CERTIFY THAT THE ABOVE-NAMED IS/ARE THE REGISTERED HOLDER(S) OF

THREE THOUSAND POUNDS 9 PER CENT. TREASURY STOCK, 200Z. 15TH APRIL 200X

Exd. ______________________ BANK OF ENGLAND
CHIEF REGISTRAR

No transfer of the whole or any part of the holding represented by this certificate wil be registered until the Certificate has been delivered at the Bank of England.

The Stock is transferable in multiples of 1p.

Fig. 23. A typical gilt certificate.

Capital gains made from trading in most types of bond are subject to new, complicated rules.

Liable to *income tax* are capital gains on holdings that exceed £200,000 from most gilts, PIBs (see Appendix 8) and all corporate debt (debentures and loan stocks, including those that are index-linked). Also all capital gains on gilt strips (any value holding).

Liable to *CGT* are capital gains made on preference shares (including zero dividend) and most convertibles.

Exempt from tax are capital gains made on gilts and qualifying corporate debt whose aggregate value is less than £200,000 as well as any gains on government (but not corporate) index-linked stocks that are due to their inflation protection. Also exempt are some classes of National Savings issued by the Post Office.

Both income received, and capital gains made from the purchase and sale of unit trusts or other funds dealing in gilts, are subject respectively to income tax and Capital Gains Tax.

See Appendix 16 for a general overview of Capital Gains Tax.

STRATEGIES FOR BUYING GILTS

For income

The principal reason for a private investor to hold gilts is that of income with safety. Purchases of gilts are particularly suited to pensioners who are more interested in augmenting their pension than in capital growth.

A typical pension plan strategy, for those still earning a living, would be to hold a private pension plan in shares until five to ten years before retirement then, choosing a time when shares appeared to be overvalued, to transfer the accrued sum into a gilts fund.

Another important feature of fixed interest gilts is that the income from them never varies unlike, say, building society interest rates. Consequently, long term planning is extremely easy for the purpose of, for example, arranging school fees. However, the nicely calculated income may prove to be insufficient after inflation!

High interest gilt funds

Some pooled funds dealing only in gilts provide very high income at the expense of capital. For example, they buy a ten per cent coupon gilt (with a par value of £100) for, let us say, £130. This gives a steady yield of £10 per gilt (an interest rate of 7.69 per cent), but at redemption only £100 of the original capital invested will be repaid for each gilt.

Some shrewd fund managers might be able to dispose of the gilt at an opportune time towards the end of its life for more than £100, but one should not count on this.

Purchase of high-coupon gilts is completely unsuited to those seeking appreciation of their capital.

Bond washing
This is mentioned mainly for historical reasons. Gilt interest is paid gross and is liable to tax. Capital gains on gilts are not taxable. In the days before the price of a gilt and its accrued interest were separated, the price of gilts tended to rise just before the coupon was paid.

It used to be feasible, and legal, to buy a gilt at a low price ex-dividend, hold it for six months then sell at a higher price just before the dividend was paid. The gain was tax-free.

Changes in taxation have ended this dodge and the accrued interest on gilts is now taxed as income. The price of gilts is now quoted in papers such as the *Financial Times* 'clean' of all accrued interest. An extra sum has to be paid when the gilt is purchased in respect of the gross interest accrued to the purchase date.

The merit of gilts
Recently, gilts have been of benefit only to the government and not to the investor. Returns have in general lagged well behind other forms of investment (see Figures 1 and 3). Holding fixed-interest gilts is in general a poor policy in inflationary times. The recent decline in inflation has caused interest rates generally to fall steeply, resulting in gilts and other bonds enjoying their best run in decades (high gilt price = low gilt yield). Certainly gilts have outperformed equities in the past three years. Yet, unless inflation falls still further, it is hard to see how gilts can continue to outperform shares, at any rate in the near future.

Index-linked gilts have fared better, but most of the benefit will only be seen at redemption. At the time of writing, the Post Office's own 38th Index-Linked issue, with a coupon of 1.00 per cent, does not offer a better opportunity to private investors, the maximum which one person can hold is limited to £15,000 and the bonds have to be held for five years to gain the maximum benefit.

There is no limit to the number of gilts which can be bought and held by any one investor.

HOW TO BUY AND SELL GILTS

Through a gilt fund manager

The principles are just the same as for buying unit trusts. It is important to realise that, although gilts are safe, the fund manager may not be. Never put all your funds with one manager.

Remember that all income from a unit gilt fund will be paid net of standard rate tax, and the implications of Capital Gains Tax must be considered whenever units are sold.

Through a stockbroker

Again, this is similar to dealing in shares with three exceptions:

- The commission rate is lower.
- Cash settlement is required within one working day. In practice, some brokers allow later settlement, but you then pay a slightly higher price for the gilts.
- Stamp duty is not payable.

Gilts bought through a broker are owned by the investor personally.

Through the Post Office

This is the cheapest and best route, and is now applicable to all gilts (ask the Post Office for the current list). Gilts can be purchased through any main post office, although you have no control over the timing of the purchase (the gilts will be purchased within a week or so). At present, it costs 0.7% for the first £5,000 and 0.375% above £5,000, minimum £12.50.

The Post Office holds all the gilts it purchases in a giant nominee account (see 'The Broker', Chapter 5) now administered by the Bank of England. Interest on the gilts is paid to the investor gross. It is liable to income tax for tax payers, but is particularly well-suited to those who do not pay income tax.

Through the Bank of England

The cheapest way of all to buy gilts is to apply directly to the Bank of England when it advertises a new issue in the newspapers. You may be able to buy the gilts at a fixed price (preferred) or submit a bid (better avoided).

Through Computershare

A new, popular route to buy gilts is through the independent registrars Computershare. Current costs for buying and selling are 0.7% to £5,000, or £35 plus 0.35% above £5,000.

HOW TO BUY AND SELL BONDS

Bonds issued by British companies are best bought through your friendly stockbroker. It can often be very difficult to obtain precise information about yields, conversion terms, security and status of these rarely-traded instruments, and this is where professional advice can be very helpful indeed. Trading charges are much the same as those for buying shares.

Foreign bonds should be regarded as inaccessible, unless you are very wealthy. They are very expensive to trade owing to minimum dealing charges (typically £50 or more), so that it is not worth buying foreign bonds in bundles worth less than £20,000 each. Moreover, the cost of converting interest received in foreign currencies into sterling can also take a disproportionate sum away from its value.

Bonds may be placed in ISAs. Unit trusts of company bonds can be purchased. Investment trusts are not, however, available owing to the unfavourable tax treatment of bonds in the hands of companies (such as investment trusts).

Distribution bonds are special bonds invested roughly 60:40 in equities:bonds which pay out income net of income tax (the tax cannot be reclaimed). The Inland Revenue currently permits tax to be deferred on the return of 5% of capital and income per annum for 20 years, which may be beneficial to higher-rate taxpayers.

9

Six Typical Case Studies

A number of typical examples are given below. All the cases given are fictional, as are the companies involved.

Warning: The examples given are intended to illustrate how a typical investor might think when confronted with various situations. Actual investment strategies depend critically on an investor's circumstances and inclinations about risk versus profits. **Under no circumstances** should the examples be construed as 'best advice'.

In the examples which follow, it is assumed that all the investors concerned (except, perhaps, 'Desperate Dan') have previously secured their financial positions, so that they have taken out sufficient insurance, 'rainy-day' money, basic pension arrangements and so on, and are not about to undertake an expensive venture, such as moving house or setting up in business.

EXAMPLE A: MR SMITH CHOOSES SAFETY FIRST

Mr and Mrs Smith are both aged 40 and have two children of school age. Mr Smith is the sole salary earner and he would like to protect his standard of living for when he retires. However, he does not wish to take the chance of tying up all his pension contributions indefinitely. He has many years to look forward to before retirement, is already a member of a company pension plan, but with little in the way of savings cannot be certain that he will not need to dip into them occasionally.

He therefore considers the possibility of opening an Individual Savings Account, which will give him tax-free savings to retirement and good long term capital growth from an investment in shares. Also it will be relatively easy to close the fund if it becomes necessary to do so.

All ISAs are managed funds, so Mr Smith reckons that whatever he does, he will be stung by management charges. He would prefer the fund to be managed for him (often cheaper than self-selected funds).

This, plus a good investment trust or unit trust, will provide almost as much spread of risk as a proper pensions fund. Mr Smith knows that there is little to choose between the costs of an expensively managed unit trust with no extra ISA charges, and a cheaply run investment trust with heavy additional ISA charges, so it does not matter much for which class of fund he aims. However, unit trusts, being real trusts, are possibly less risky than investment trusts. Mr Smith is primarily concerned that his money should be safe.

Finally Mr Smith picks the 'SuperGrowth Investment Trust' whose management has a good reputation and a satisfactory track record across a range of funds. Its charges are at the low end of the investment trust spectrum and there are comparatively cheap additional ISA charges. SuperGrowth will normally reinvest into its ISA the dividends it pays out, but undertakes to provide tax free income from the ISA on request. This is ideal for pension income. Its charges for premature closing of the ISA appear to be reasonable relative to competing funds.

SuperGrowth is a general fund investing in shares, of which more than 50 per cent are in companies in the UK for income growth. The remainder comprises shares in America, Europe and Japan. This provides a useful spread of risk.

Mr Smith could acquire greater security, if he wished it at the expense of some drop in performance, by investing in 'SuperFund Unit Trust', having the same spread of investments as SuperGrowth but being regulated by a board of trustees. SuperFund cannot (yet) jeopardise its viability by making excessive borrowings, unlike the investment trust.

Currently, Mr Smith is allowed to invest a maximum of £7,000 per year in SuperGrowth. He takes advantage of their savings scheme to pay £200 per month (£2,400 per year) into the fund, thereby obtaining a pound-averaging effect which will ensure that he will buy more shares when their price is cheap.

Note that Mr Smith could instead have opted for an Additional Voluntary Contributions scheme (AVC), a Stakeholder Pension or a Self-Invested Pension Plan (SIPP) to improve his pension. The payments for any of these would have been made from his gross income (ie, before deduction of income tax), but the retirement income would be taxed and new plans cannot be cashed in at any time, nor can they be commuted into cash at retirement. By contrast, Mr Smith's ISA plan will be paid for out of taxed (net) income, will deliver tax-free income at retirement (or earlier) and can be cashed in at any time without tax penalty.

EXAMPLE B: THE JONESES TAKE AN ACTIVE INTEREST

Mr and Mrs Jones are also 40 years old, but are 'dinkies' (Dual Income – No Kids). Consequently they have a much higher disposable income than the Smiths, while investment errors can more readily be tolerated. In other words, the Joneses are prepared to take higher risks for higher returns reasoning that dud investments will be amply compensated by winners over the next 30 to 40 years. They are seeking long-term capital growth.

As before, the Joneses check carefully that they have fully covered all likely contingencies before investing money into the stockmarket. They reckon that they can invest £2,000 every three months in shares. Mr Jones notes that in order to avoid minimum dealing costs, he needs to make minimum transactions of £2,000 each time. He has already registered with a local stockbroker, having taken the trouble to check the broker's reputation and local history. Mr Jones could use a dealing-only service like Charles Schwab, but feels happier checking his decisions with the local broker. There is the comforting knowledge that his friendly broker will warn him if his planned investment is in any way 'dodgy'. He would not get this reassurance from Schwab. Besides (thinks Mr Jones), he might want to dabble in gold, for which Schwab and similar operations currently provide no service.

His next step is to compile a wishlist. Since he is starting from scratch, there could be a grave danger that he will face high 'specific risk', ie the risk that the company whose shares he buys will go bankrupt before he can benefit from the compensatory gains of other shares. This risk could be avoided by buying shares in investment trusts to get a foothold in the market, then selling them at a later date to fund the purchases of the shares of individual companies. However, he prefers to concentrate on blue chip companies, adding smaller companies for spice at a later stage. (I started my investment career with the purchase of five investment trusts, subsequently adding individual companies.)

Mr Jones now picks up his *Financial Times*, turns to the back pages and starts to select stocks. He wants, ultimately, to pick 20 shares for a good spread of risk, of which the first ten should be blue chips. The *Financial Times* classifies the various shares on which it quotes prices into several categories. Mr Jones elects to pick shares out of Banks, Beverages, Construction, Information Technology, Electricals, Engineering, Insurance, Leisure & Hotels, Oils, Real Estate, Retailers (Food, General) and Transport (13 sectors). There are others, according to taste.

First he looks at Banks. His bank account is with Megabank plc, so naturally he looks at them first. This is what he sees:

Stock	Price	+ or −	200X High Low	Div Net	C'vr	Volume 000s	Y'ld	P/E
Megabank	578	-5	630 480	30.5	1.4	953	5.0	14.3

(This table is a composite construction of data gleaned from the *Financial Times*, Saturday and Monday issues.)

Megabank is an alpha stock (easily traded) and is trading comfortably within its high and low prices for the year. The yield is a tasty 5 per cent (net). However, the C'vr (cover) is only 1.4; the payment of the dividend is covered only 1.4 times by the bank's profits. The price-earnings (P/E) ratio (14.3) tells the number of times the current share price exceeds the bank's profits (earnings) per share which can be distributed as dividend, and appears to be typical for the banking sector.

Hmmm! That low cover is a little worrying (ideally it should be 3 times or more). No wonder the yield (5.0 per cent) is so high. The professionals must be expecting a cut in the dividend.

Mr Jones looks at the other banks. All the bigger names seem to be on high yields and have low cover. There is, of course and as usual, a banking crisis reported in all the newspapers. Mr Jones makes up his mind. Even after a dividend cut, the yield is still likely to be better than the market average. Megabank looks no worse on paper than other banks of its sector, and he is a satisfied customer. Megabank goes onto the list.

Moving down to brewers, Mr Jones adopts the same principle to select Real Ales plc, suppliers of one of the country's most celebrated beers. He has seen it in every pub he visits and is not averse to a pint himself.

After picking a respected local builder, Mr Jones's eye alights on Chemicals. ICI is the big name there, but their price has been inflated by rumours of a bid. It is probably too late to get involved with ICI, and Mr Jones does not recognise the names of any of the other companies listed in the sector. He moves on to the next sector.

In the Retailers sector, Mrs Jones is enthusiastic about Newstores, the newly launched fashion chain. The local branch is packed with shoppers every Saturday ('but do they buy?' wonders Mr Jones). Newstores has a high P/E ratio by the standard of the sector – it is a growth stock. Mr Jones pencils it tentatively onto his wishlist as a second choice stock.

In this way, Mr Jones goes through all the sectors in the *Financial Times*. He likes the oil and food companies ('unexciting, but safe enough', he thinks). By the finish he has selected 13 blue chip stocks and Newstores makes a good speculative addition. Mr Jones pads his wishlist out to 20 stocks with a few companies with good reputations and even adds a hunch or two. He knows that smaller companies generally perform better than larger, in the long term, and he does not want to stick solely to the blue chips. The smaller companies form the reserve of second line stocks.

Mr and Mrs Jones now track the performance of the shares on their wishlist at least weekly (preferably daily), writing down the prices taken from *Ceefax, Teletext* or daily newspapers and (if possible) plotting them onto semi-logarithmic graph paper (prices on the logarithmic, vertical scale, dates horizontally). Alternatively, the Joneses could enter the share price data into a computer program which does all the plotting for them. (If they own an Atari ST computer and printer, they would be able to use my CHART.XXX program for this purpose.) While doing this, the Joneses collect and collate all the information which they learn about the companies underlying the shares on their wishlist, for example) in a card index.

After three months, the Joneses have their expected £2,000 in cash and review the list. SuperOil plc is a blue chip, appears to be trading towards the bottom of its recent price range and there are no adverse comments about it in their card index. If they have fallen for the seductive charms of technical analysis (Chapter 7), they will also wish to examine their charts to see whether a fall in the share price looks imminent. Assuming that this is also satisfactory in their eyes (I am sceptical about the whole principle), Mr Jones will, holding his breath, buy £2,000 of SuperOil's shares (and, if he is like me, will spend the next fortnight anxiously scanning the price).

Mr and Mrs Jones have previously agreed a 15 per cent stop-loss limit for two weeks against the market. If the price of SuperOil falls more than 15 per cent relative to the market as a whole (which may be going up or down of its own accord) within the next two weeks, they will acknowledge their error and sell the stock at a loss, thereby ending the immediate danger of taking losses heavier than 15 per cent.

Three months later, the Joneses purchase another blue chip, Megabank. They continue to buy shares at three-monthly intervals. Firstly the blue chips and then the second line stocks. This represents an example of pound-averaging, and will ensure that the ups and downs in share prices will, on aggregate, be evened out.

The Joneses also maintain a hitlist. It transpires after a year that Megabank's debt problems were much worse than had originally been foreseen by the market professionals. Its share price has been in slow decline over the period concerned. Megabank's name is transferred to the Joneses' hitlist, and a reserve company is now monitored as its replacement on the wishlist. Megabank will be sold on the first upturn in its price caused by a hint of good news.

They also wish to spread their risk internationally. As funds permit, and probably before they have acquired all the shares on their wishlist, they will buy investment trusts investing in all the main foreign markets (America, Europe and Japan). If ever they become sufficiently knowledgeable, they will 'form a view' and buy investment trusts specialising separately in America, or in Europe or in Japan. Additionally investment trusts provide a good way to spread risk over many smaller companies.

Because the Joneses are long-term investors, it will probably reward them to place some of their investments into self-selection or corporate ISA schemes. The latter can be very cheap in terms of management charges, and between them the Joneses can have a total of two ISA schemes per year. Altogether, the Joneses can place up to £14,000 per annum into ISA schemes. Mr Jones might well also consider buying an ISA based on an international investment trust with a 'top-up' facility in shares of his own choosing up to the general ISA scheme limit of £7,000.

When the Joneses acquire more disposable income to invest in shares, as might occur after a salary increase, they intend to increase the rate at which they buy shares from quarterly to bimonthly or even monthly. Once they have accumulated the 20 stocks on their wishlist, Mr Jones will reinvest further money in existing shareholdings. At the same time, he will continue to monitor the performance of all the companies on the wishlist, replacing them as necessary with reserve companies.

EXAMPLE C: CAUTIOUS INVESTMENT OF AN INHERITANCE

Mr and Mrs Black are 50 years old, have two grown up children, are moderately well off and have just inherited £100,000 from the sale of a deceased relative's house. They wish to invest this money for capital and income growth to be accessible on demand but otherwise to provide an increasing income stream for retirement – which will not occur for another ten years. The Blacks are cautious investors and do not expect to be able to make up disastrous losses once incurred.

Substantially they decide to follow the same strategy as the Jones couple, but drip-feeding their capital into the purchase of shares at the rate of £5,000 per month.

Their selection of shares is based on blue chips for safety and ease of marketability, while exposure to overseas markets and to smaller companies will be obtained through investment trusts. Cash awaiting investment will be held on deposit in a building society (making use of ISAs for each of them as far as the limits allow).

If the Blacks are very nervous about inflation or the current state of world stockmarkets, they will move some of their money into index-linked gilts ('and don't forget Post Office index-linked granny bonds', adds Mrs Black, pointing out that the latter often pay a higher rate of interest than index-linked gilts although there is a limit [currently £15,000] on the amount which can be held by any one individual, and the bonds have to be held for five years to derive the maximum benefit).

EXAMPLE D: THE WIDOW SEEKING EXTRA INCOME

Mrs Brown is a 70-year-old widow living alone on a state pension and the residual pension of her late husband. She has a capital sum of £20,000, but no other income. Her principal concern is to augment her income, but she has to decide which of three options to take:

- to preserve her capital in real terms
- to preserve her capital in paper terms (ie, neglecting the ravages of inflation)
- to convert her capital into income.

The last option will provide the greatest addition to Mrs Brown's income, but she might want to leave some, or all, of her savings to her children.

If Mrs Brown chooses the first option, her only real investment opportunities are either:

- to buy index-linked gilts and/or granny bonds (the latter usually providing the better yield). Both from her Post Office so that the interest is received free from income tax (but remembering that income tax is ultimately payable on interest from gilts).

or:

- to buy shares, preferably in the form of a high-yielding investment trust through the medium of an ISA, when the income will be paid to her free of tax (gross).

The yield from the investment trust will normally be greater than that from index-linked gilts in the long term. However, the gilts are safer. High-yielding unit trusts in an ISA would provide an alternative option to investment trusts.

The second option would allow her to put her money into an ISA, up to the maximum limit, with a building society. She would then withdraw only net income over the life of the plan while depositing the remainder of her money into a building society (if she expects interest rates to rise) or into gilts (if she expects rates to fall).

Mrs Brown needs to consider her tax position. With a pension on top of the state pension, it is likely that she will be a standard rate tax payer. If she pays no tax, she can sign a declaration to that effect and collect interest payments from banks and building societies without paying tax on them. Tax withheld on most investments in shares can no longer be reclaimed from the Inland Revenue. If Mrs Brown does not have to pay income tax, then an ISA's only attraction will depend on the rate of interest which it pays on savings relative to other cash deposits.

By choosing the third option, she may feel that her best bet is to buy an annuity from a pensions company. All types of annuity are possible (fixed rate, limited rates of increase, index-linked) and she should shop around for the best offer. However, Mrs Brown should note that all the money used to purchase the annuity will be lost to her after purchase – she cannot get any of it back if she wants to buy a new car. Also residual money in the annuity will revert to the pensions company after her death. Mrs Brown should certainly keep some 'rainy day' money in reserve before buying the annuity.

Other sensible alternatives which provide income at the expense of capital, but without tying up or losing the capital for good, include investment in high coupon (ie high-interest) gilts and in the income shares of split-capital investment trusts.

The following is an example of high-coupon gilts. In January 2003, Treasury 8% gilts expiring in 2015 cost £133 each, providing a fixed yield to expiry of 6.02 per cent (gross; this does not include reinvestment of the interest paid). In 2015 the gilts will be repaid at par, ie £100 for each gilt.

The income shares of split-capital investment trusts (see Appendix 6 for more details) receive all the income payment from the underlying trust (the capital shares receive, usually, all of the capital growth in the value of the shares). Therefore, the income shares ought to provide a large, increasing income. At the expiry date, Mrs Brown's shares will be repaid at par although the precise terms vary with the investment trust. There are also other types of income-bearing investment trust shares. Mrs Brown should certainly seek professional advice before taking this course of action.

A random example of the income shares of a split-capital investment trust follows. Throgmorton Dual Trust Income shares in December 1993 could be bought for 78 pence each, providing a gross yield of 11.6 per cent. In August 1996, the same shares cost 38p each, with a gross yield of 23.4 per cent. In late 1996 the income shares were repaid at the rate of 35 pence each.

If Mrs Brown had more money available, say a lump sum of £50,000 or more, then further options would be open to her. She could construct a composite portfolio to mix-and-match different investment vehicles to give the exact blend of income, risk and capital appreciation that she wanted.

For example, Mrs Brown could put a third of her money into each of gilts (safe and high yield), convertibles (less safe, medium yield but with the scope for conversion into a share which may have risen steeply in value) and blue chip shares, providing reasonable prospects of growth, moderate security and an above average (by share standards) yield. This kind of combination product will provide a yield intermediate between gilts and shares, and with intermediate growth prospects to reduce (although not avoid) the effects of inflation too.

EXAMPLE E: SID AFTER PRIVATISATION

Sensible Sid has been purchasing small packets of government privatisation shares for the last few years, beginning with the great British Telecom issue in 1984. However, since the success of the British Telecom flotation he has been unable to buy the size of share stake that he would like.

Sid's appetite has been whetted for a further venture into shares since he has made good paper profits on his privatisation stocks, which he still retains. He would like to invest £1,000 per year in shares.

He will therefore buy the shares of an investment trust through its savings scheme. Also he could make use of an ISA, but the charges of the plan may well outweigh the tax advantages (the saving to a 20 per cent tax payer on a 6 per cent gross dividend from an initial investment of one thousand pounds is only £6; dividends taxed at 10 per cent).

If Sid is lucky, he may well be able to find an investment trust manager who will provide him with a good exchange deal between his privatisation stocks and shares of the investment trust at a very favourable price. The Association of Investment Trust Companies (AITC; see Useful Addresses) will supply a list of trusts which provide this service.

He will be careful to select a trust with a wide range of shares, preferably a general trust with at least 50 per cent of its stocks held overseas. Specialist trusts investing in a narrow area of the market, either in terms of market sectors or in terms of national markets, should be avoided.

Sid will employ the trust's cheap scheme (a commission of 0.2 per cent or less) for reinvestment of the dividends from his shares within the same investment trust. In years to come, he expects to find that he has built up a very useful nest egg.

EXAMPLE F: DESPERATE DAN

Finally we turn to 'Desperate Dan', the Gambling Man. Dan Gambler has heard about the high returns that can sometimes be made on the stockmarket. He wants a piece of the action for himself.

Dan spends a fortune on tip sheets, but loses money on the tips. He buys traded options, having heard that you can turn £1,000 into £10,000 overnight, but his choices always seem to decline in value. Writing options would bring gains too small for his greed – luckily for Dan, since he would never think to cover his position after a market change and would be wiped out (infinite loss).

He writes to the financial magazines asking how best to turn £1,000 into £2,000 in the shortest possible time. If he reads this book at all, he will certainly think that he knows better.

Dan has 'nous'. He would never buy shares from an expensive and reputable broker when he can buy them from a cut price spiv working in the local bucketshop. He buys shares recommended by the spiv, or by strange telephone callers with American accents phoning from the Antilles.

Buying unit trusts when the market has peaked ('fantastic gains; market up 50 per cent in the last six months'), he is then forced to sell after the temporary fall in market prices to pay for his holiday.

Today, Dan is probably a 'day trader' on the Internet, buying and selling 'spiv.com' stocks.

One day Dan will retire hurt from share investment. And the stockmarket will be just a little better, and more stable, in consequence.

CONCLUSION

The ideas presented in this book represent the most logical way to invest in the UK Stockmarket, given current market and economic conditions. The strategy has performed well in recent years – better than the FTSE index, in fact – but past performance is no guide to the future.

The reader is wished the best of luck!

Appendix 1
Government Privatisations 1977–1998

COMPANY	YEAR	PRICE [p]
British Petroleum (I)	1977 (June)	70.4
British Petroleum (II)	1979 (October)	121.0
British Aerospace (I)	1981 (February)	150.0
Cable & Wireless (I)	1981 (November)	56.0
Amersham International	1982 (February)	142.0
BritOil (I)	1982 (November)	215.0
Associated British Ports (I)	1983 (February)	56.0
British Petroleum (III)	1983 (September)	145.0
Cable & Wireless (II)	1983 (November)	137.5
Associated British Ports (II)	1984 (April)	135.0
Enterprise Oil	1984 (June)	185.0
Jaguar	1984 (August)	165.0
British Telecom (I)	1984 (November)	130.0
British Aerospace (II)	1985 (May)	375.0
BritOil (II)	1985 (August)	185.0
Cable & Wireless (III)	1986 (March)	293.5
British Gas	1986 (December)	135.0
British Airways	1987 (February)	125.0
Rolls-Royce	1987 (May)	170.0
British Airports Authority	1987 (July)	245.0
British Petroleum (IV)	1987 (October)	330.0
British Steel	1988 (December)	125.0
Water Companies	1989 (November)	240.0
Electricity Distributors	1990 (December)	250.0
Electricity Generators	1991 (March)	175.0
Scottish Generators	1991 (June)	240.0
British Telecom (II)	1991 (December)	320.0
Forth Ports Authority	1992 (March)	110.0
North Ireland Electricity	1993 (June)	220.0
British Telecom (III)	1993 (July)	420.0

Rail Track	1996 (May)	380.0
British Energy	1996 (July)	203.0
AEA Technology	1996 (September)	280.0

Notes:
1. Several privatisations were conducted in more than one tranche.
2. BritOil was taken over by British Petroleum in 1988; Jaguar by Ford in 1989.
3. B.A.A.'s share price excludes a simultaneous, separate sale by tender struck at 282-283 p.
4. British Steel is now known as Corus.
5. Rail Track has been returned to public ownership.

GOVERNMENT 'GOLDEN SHARES'

(Protect newly privatised companies from takeover)

Indefinite	**Redeemed**
British Airports Authority	BritOil 2/88
British Aerospace	Amersham Int. 7/88
British Gas	Enterprise 12/88
British Telecom	Jaguar 10/89
Cable & Wireless	British Steel 12/93
Rolls-Royce	Water Cos 12/94
	Electrical Distributors 12/94
	AEA Technology 9/99
	National Power 8/00

The European Union deemed the government's 'golden shares' to be illegal in 2003. They were abolished during 2004.

Appendix 2
The Black-Scholes Model
for Traded Options

In the early 1970s, Black and Scholes developed a method for estimating the 'fair' value of options and futures relative to their underlying securities.

The model uses complex arithmetic calculations, which are best handled by computer. The 'fair' price of the option is calculated by consideration of the current market price of the underlying stock, the exercise price of the option, the computed market volatility and the amount of interest which could be earned before the option expiry date if the option payment were placed on deposit instead.

Implicit in the model are the following assumptions:

1. The price of the underlying stock or security rises exponentially throughout the option life. The rise need not be uniform but there should be an underlying normal distribution of the log of the market price of the stock at the expiry date of the option. In other words, the price of the underlying stock should not move significantly away from its expected gentle rise and there should be no violent price changes.

2. The volatility of the underlying stock should remain constant (as implied in 1), and can be calculated as the standard deviation of the recent past reported prices.

3. There is a constant rate of interest available as an alternative for cash invested in an option.

4. No early exercise of the option is possible before the expiry date.

These are highly dubious assumptions, particularly 1. Moreover, traded options can be exercised early, negating assumption 4, so that the Black-Scholes model frequently understates the 'real' value of a traded option. This is because the ability to exercise an option early can sometimes be of advantage to the investor.

The Black-Scholes model is very popular with institutional investors despite its assumptions and inaccuracies. In fact, the difference between the 'fair' price of an option and its real price is sometimes taken as a measure of the market's 'implied volatility'.

The main attraction of the Black-Scholes model is to enable large institutions to balance their books in a range of traded options. There is no definite evidence that a policy of investing in 'undervalued' options, according to the model, provides long term gains.

It is highly improbable that the private investor needs to consider these abstruse calculations.

Appendix 3
Personal Equity Plans (PEPS) and Tax-Exempt Special Savings Accounts (TESSAs)

PEPS were announced by the Conservative Chancellor Nigel Lawson in 1986 as a tax-free shelter for shares. Cash sums could be placed in a PEP each year for investment in shares (and later bonds). They became very popular after an initial slow uptake, but were ended in 1998 by the new Labour government. However, existing PEPS are allowed to continue indefinitely, but they cannot be added to.

TESSAs had been introduced by the Conservative Chancellor John Major in 1991. They permitted a total sum of up to £9,000 to be saved in a bank or building society account over a period of five years, with interest received completely free of tax. These have also been ended by the Labour government, but existing TESSAs will be allowed to run their five-year course, with further instalments of added cash being allowed.

PEPs and TESSAs were closed allegedly on the grounds of high tax losses to the Inland Revenue. In their place was substituted a much cheaper (to the government) scheme called Individual Savings Accounts (ISAs, see Appendix 4). We assume that any readers currently holding PEPs and/or TESSAs already know the rules; therefore they will not be repeated here.

Government regulations changed recently so that PEPS can now hold the same assets (including gilts) as ISAs, see Appendix 4. Single-company PEPS can now be treated as general PEPS. Part-transfers of PEPS (as well as complete transfers) to a new manager are now allowed.

Appendix 4
Individual Savings Accounts (ISAs)

ISAs replaced PEPs and TESSAs (see Appendix 3) from April 1999. They have a lower annual investment limit (£7,000) than their forebears and are much more complicated for fund managers to administer.

The function of an ISA is to serve as a vehicle in which shares in quoted companies, bonds and, optionally, cash and life assurance may be held free of all tax charges.

The benefits of an ISA are therefore:

- No tax on dividends/interest received. (Up to year 2004 the plan manager may also reclaim a ten per cent tax credit on dividends paid by shares.)

- No Capital Gains Tax is payable when shares in the ISA are finally sold.

- The investor is not required to hold an ISA for a minimum number of years (no 'lock-in').

- Tax benefits guaranteed for at least ten years from 1999.

- The ISA does not even have to be declared to the Inland Revenue.

The investment must be made through one or more authorised plan managers. A different plan manager may be used by the investor each year. The dividend or interest will normally be reinvested by the plan manager. The manager will make a charge for these services. Many managers now make only the normal unit trust charges for investment in ISAs through their unit trusts.

The following outlines the current (2006) rules:

Three ISA components and their investment limits

The maximum, overall investment in an ISA is £7,000 per annum, in one or more of three components:

- shares and bonds (max. £7,000 per annum)
- cash (max. £3,000 per annum)
- life assurance (max. £1,000 per annum)

If the maximum sum is invested in shares and bonds, no contribution can be made to the cash or life assurance elements. Once cash has been subscribed to any component part, it may not later be switched (eg money in the cash component may not be used to buy shares).

Properties of the ISA components

Share/Bonds component
A tax credit of ten per cent could be reclaimed by the fund manager for the first five years of ISAs (but no longer). Interest earned on uninvested cash in the shares component will be taxed at 20 per cent. Most ISA managers permit the investor the choice of a discretionary ISA (where the investor chooses his own shares, normally from a restricted list) and a managed fund in which the fund manager makes all the decisions (typically a unit trust). Discretionary charges, once higher, are now often lower than those for a managed fund.

The performance of many managed funds is now being monitored yearly by financial magazines.

The cash component
Most cash component schemes offer variable interest rates, which may move up and down over the investment period (in common with most other deposits).

A handful of schemes guarantee a fixed interest rate over the life of the scheme. These usually offer a lower initial rate than the floating rate schemes. The investor must decide for himself which type of interest rate to take.

Example benefit from a cash component:

If an investor were to deposit the maximum sum possible (£3,000) in each year over ten years then, assuming a constant interest rate of 5 per cent gross, the total tax savings would be as follows:

20% tax payer: Saving = £2,161
40% tax payer: Saving = £4,197

Eligibility for ISA components
The rules for eligible assets to place in the component parts of an ISA are more generous than those for PEPs and TESSAs:

Stocks and shares component
- Any company ordinary share listed on a recognised stock exchange world-wide (this excludes unquoted, AIM and OFEX shares).
- UK-based unit trusts, investment trusts and OEICs.
- Overseas funds that would qualify as UCITS (EU-approved pan-European unit trusts) and hold less than 50 per cent of their assets in bonds that are less than five years from expiry.
- Any qualifying bond or gilt with an expiry date more than five years from the date of purchase.
- Employee share schemes.
- Newly-issued shares (including shares from building societies that have newly demutualised) may *not* be entered in the scheme.
- Shares in property funds may *not* be entered in the scheme.

Cash component
- Cash held in banks or building societies.
- Cash unit trusts.
- Credit unions.
- National Saving products developed specially for ISAs.

Life assurance component
- The life assured must be that of the ISA investor, and must be paid as a single premium.
- With-profits funds are now permitted.

CAT (charges, access, terms) hallmark
The CAT hallmark will be designated for those investments that comply with tight criteria for low charges, easy access and reasonable terms. For example, index-linked unit trusts are likely to be the only share-based collective fund that will receive a CAT mark. The reader should clearly understand that:

- items which bear the CAT mark may not be suitable for him as an investment
- items which lack the CAT mark (eg virtually all investment trusts) may provide superior performance.

MAXI-MINI

Although individuals can open only one ISA per annum, they may choose to have:

> *either* a MAXI ISA, where one manager provides the shares and cash components of the ISA up to the £7,000 limit

> *or* one or two MINI ISAs, where different managers provide *either* shares (max £4,000) with the optional life insurance component included *or* cash (max £3,000).

It is now apparent that supermarkets intend to provide mini-CASH ISAs, fund managers will provide MAXI-ISAs (but without the life assurance component), mini-SHARES/BONDS and mini-CASH ISAs, the banks provide MAXI ISAs but, curiously, the life assurance offices have little enthusiasm for operating mini-LIFE ASSURANCE components (there are technical reasons for this to do with the way the offices' expenses are handled, and £1,000 per annum is probably too little to compensate). Instead several insurance companies are now offering investment in their with-profits funds, which average investment performance from shares, bonds and property over several years. You must hold these funds for many years to reduce the effect of high initial charges.

The fund managers' ISAs operate indistinguishably from the older PEPs, excepting the lower subscription level and the wider range of investments.

TESSA-ISAS

These can be used to hold the capital sum only (not the accrued interest) from a matured TESSA. They can be opened jointly with either MAXI or MINI ISAs, without affecting their qualifying limits, in any one year.

STRATEGIES FOR INVESTORS IN SHARES

ISA share/bond component

At the time of writing, a long-running ISA appears to be capable of providing tax-free income and capital gains, which can be realised at any time. The ability of the fund manager to reclaim a 10% tax credit on dividends paid on shares held within an ISA is set to end in 2004. If the government does not reinstate the tax credit, it is unlikely that standard-rate tax-payers will derive any benefit from holding their shares within an ISA, since manager's charges will exceed probable tax savings.

Accordingly, they can be used to pay off mortgages or education costs, to provide income and a lump sum at retirement and, after the death of the investor, can be realised by the beneficiaries of the will. Of course, all this supposes constant growth in the value of the ISA shares.

ISAs comprising bonds shelter high income from income tax, and may be of value to those who do not require capital growth.

However, ISAs may not be used as security against any kind of debt. Capital losses in ISAs may not be offset against Capital Gains Tax.

Cash component

Cash components can be used to provide tax-free interest on cash deposits which are unlikely to be required quickly (once money is removed from the fund, it cannot be replaced at a later date). Thus they can provide a convenient contingency fund, see page 14.

In some favourable circumstances, cash components from some deposit takers will provide a better net rate of return, if the scheme is prematurely ended, than ordinary, tax-liable funds from the same source.

Charges

The reader's attention is drawn expressly to the high management charges for some ISAs (see page 38), which may completely negate the tax benefit of the scheme.

Inheritance tax

ISAs provide no shelter from inheritance tax.

Appendix 5
The Price of Gold

Gold is a curious investment medium. It is dug out of the ground in order to be stored underground. It is yellow, very heavy and does not rust or tarnish. The price of gold used to be regulated by governments, but now rises or falls on a free trading market. Bullion (bars of gold) is rarely owned by small investors, but gold coins are commonly held. Purchase of South African 'Krugerrands' is now again permitted in the UK, alternatives being Australian, Canadian and American coins, and also the British-minted 'Britannia' coin.

Purchase of gold coins in the UK used to attract the punitive VAT rate of 17.5 per cent, but this was abolished in 2000. Gold is stored most safely in a bank. A small annual fee is charged by the bank concerned for storage and insurance.

It is much easier to buy gold coins than to sell them. Spink & Sons Ltd (Tel: (020) 7930 7888) is the best known dealer. The buying/selling spread is typically 7–10%. The supply of gold does not match the needs of economies, therefore the link to the gold standard was broken in the 1930s. The Bank of England has joined other central banks in recent years in reducing its reserves.

Gold pays no dividend – you actually have to pay to keep it – so the owner can only hope that the price of gold will rise. The price tends to reflect inflationary expectations: gold is cheap when inflation is low and bonds pay good yields, but high when inflation is high. Gold also tends to be sought after in times of uncertainty, such as international crises. The value of gold will always be recognised when paper money has become worthless.

At the time of writing, the purchase of gold is free from commission with the difference between buying and selling prices providing the dealer's profit. Capital gains are subject to CGT.

It is also possible to buy shares in gold-mining companies. Britain's Consolidated Gold Fields used to be one of the best known, but was taken over by Hanson plc and subsequently sold on. South Africa's Anglo-American company is now widely accepted in the UK as the best alternative, being traded on the UK stockmarket. The price of gold company shares tends to follow the price of gold.

In recent years the performance of gold has been poor relative to equities. As a non-payer of dividends, it is excluded from the Logical Investment Strategy described in this book. Nevertheless, the price of gold does remain an important indicator of expected trends in global inflation.

A web-site that provides an excellent overview of gold trading and history can be found at *www.taxfreegold.co.uk*. Trading in gold can also be carried out through derivatives, see Chapter 7 and Appendix 18.

There remains considerable uncertainty about which investments in gold attract capital gains tax when sold. In general, gold is subject to CGT. However certain British coins may be exempt and the Inland Revenue's own website is ambiguous. If in doubt, consult your local tax office for advice. Make sure you get a written answer.

Appendix 6
Split Capital Investment Trusts

A number of investment trusts are marketed as 'split capital'. This means that they issue different shares, each with a different stake in the trust.

The most common split involves the separation of capital and income shares. The income shares usually receive all the dividend income and are repaid at a fixed price after a stated number of years, on the so-called 'wind-up date'. The capital shares receive all the value of the assets remaining at the wind-up date after the income shares have been repaid.

It follows that the income shares pay out a very high yield to their owners, albeit at some loss of capital over the lifetime of the trust, while the capital shares should deliver a good rise in asset performance.

A good example is the Aberforth Split Investment Trust, which invests in smaller companies. The income shares receive all the income, but will be repaid at 10p each on the last day of June 2004. The capital shares will receive the remaining assets on the same date.

In January 2003, their prices were as follows:

Share type	Price(p)	Yield %	Asset value(p)
Aberforth Income	38	43.7	–
Aberforth Capital	424	0.0	474

Further complicated subdivisions are possible. Zero dividend preference shares receive no dividend, but get a stake in the capital performance. This is frequently expressed as an annual percentage increase which is compounded each year and can only be claimed when the trust is wound up. Stepped preference shares are an even more complicated hybrid, with a partially rising dividend payout. Other preferred shares may pay a fixed income, the same as bonds. Warrants may be added to the mixture.

Complicated split capital trusts have proved not to be successful and fell out of favour in the 1990s. The original purpose was to eliminate the discounts that have plagued investment trusts over the years, making them a prey to outside bidders (and thereby losing the fund managers their management fees), by providing something from the trust for every type of investor.

However, it has proved difficult to run the trusts to please all the stakeholders, and the killer blow came with the decline of interest rates. Many of the split funds had been set up when rates were higher, and therefore they had to provide a large yield on their zero dividend preference shares to attract investors. When inflation and interest rates declined, so did returns on share investments in absolute terms (although real returns actually increased), so that payouts to the holders of the zero dividend shares dominated performance, leaving less for the other classes of investor.

Consequently the mid-1990s saw the premature wind-up or take-over of many split capital trusts, including the example that illustrated this appendix in earlier editions. But when inflation had remained low for some time, the institutions were willing to accept the issue of new zero dividend preference shares with low annual percentage increases, causing a renaissance of the whole split-capital sector.

The reputations of all split-capital investment trusts have again been newly besmirched by a number of their managers. They firstly took on giant bank loans (thereby increasing their fees for funds under management), then bought shares in each other to prop up each other's share prices. When the stockmarket fell, the trusts concerned all collapsed like dominoes, triggering the sector's first ever failures of the supposedly safe zero dividend preference shares.

However, not all split-capital trusts were involved in this debacle, and there is always likely to be demand for the simple split trusts (capital shares and income shares; no borrowings).

It is highly desirable to seek professional advice before dealing in a split-capital investment trust. These combination products are mostly aimed to suit the specialist needs of the institutions, and have little place in a private investor's portfolio (and no place at all in the Logical Investment Strategy). Never buy a 'package', nor accept a package from the reconstruction of an existing investment trust, of a combination of shares of this type. Moreover, trading in some of these specialist vehicles can be difficult.

Appendix 7
Business & Enterprise Schemes

SUMMARY

Business Start-Up Scheme (BSS, 1981–3)
Business Expansion Scheme, (BES, 1983–93)
Enterprise Investment Scheme (EIS, 1993 –)
Enterprise Zone Trusts (EZT)
Venture Capital Trusts (VCT, 1995 –)

The schemes were originally intended to provide venture capital for new businesses or to expand existing small businesses.

Introduced in April 1981 as the **Business Start-Up Scheme**, successive Chancellors made repeated alterations to the scheme to find a formula attractive to investors.

The principle underlying each scheme is that substantial sums can be invested in a new small company for a minimum of five years while attracting income tax relief on the investment. The companies are expected to join the main stockmarket after a number of years, which provides the opportunity for the original investor to sell up; otherwise, marketability of the shares would be very restricted.

Unfortunately, the success rate of the early small businesses was very poor (bankruptcies in the late 1980s averaged 25 per cent, while many other companies struggled), so that tax relief even at levels of 60–75 per cent (available in the early 1980s) failed to provide sufficient compensation. Capital Gains losses on BSS and BES investments could not be set against CGT.

The history of the BSS and BES provides a salutary example of the struggle between the government's good intentions and what a cynical market will tolerate.

When it became clear that conventional small companies were proving to be too risky, pooled funds investing in several start-up ventures were initiated. Few held more than half a dozen companies and their track records were poor.

Consequently there was a vogue for asset-backed companies, such as farms. Restaurants with large wine cellars were, I recall, especially favoured! The rules were changed in 1986 to restrict investments in collectables (antiques, wine) and land. Investments in the BES dried up.

In 1988, the rules were changed again to favour investment in the government's new pet plan: the creation of homes for rent. New BES companies sprang up to buy housing.

By now the top rate of income tax was 40 per cent, so investors wanted more security. BES companies began to guarantee that investors would receive a fixed sum, typically 35–40 per cent higher than the original value, for selling their acquired housing at the end of five years. Property companies and other institutions provided the guarantee.

Finally, the last stage was reached: some banks would lend the investor cheap money against the guaranteed gains to be made when the housing was sold. This meant that the investor was each year handing over a sum of money topped up by income tax relief, and getting back larger sums on loan. The circle was closed after five years when the BES company repaid the loans from its guaranteed repurchase sum. The process has been described as 'arbitrage of the tax man'.

After unsuccessful adjustments of the rules, the BES was scrapped at the end of 1993. In its place was appointed the **Enterprise Investment Scheme**, an attempt to return to the basic idea of providing venture capital.

The most important change from the original BES was that investment losses could now be allowed against CGT. However, the same budget reduced this attraction by removing the ability to index capital losses for inflation. Moreover, the initial income tax relief was reduced to only 20 per cent for all investors.

The current (2005) rules for the EIS are these:

- Investments in qualifying companies of up to £150,000 per annum.

- Income tax relief restricted to 20 per cent.

- Capital gains free from tax.

- Capital losses qualify for (non-indexed) CGT relief.

- Dividends from EIS companies are liable to tax.

- Shares must be held for at least three years.

- The company can raise a maximum of £11 million through the EIS. Private housing, forestry, farming, nursing home companies do not qualify. Foreign companies that trade in the UK may be permitted.

- Investors can become paid directors (however, the rules for existing directors to become investors are complex).

- Venture capital trusts also qualify as EIS investments.

Venture Capital Trusts (VCTs) provide pooled funds for investment in a number of EIS companies. The rules are these:

- The VCT must invest not less than 70 per cent of its cash in qualifying companies within three years of the trust's launch.

- A maximum of £1 million may be invested in one company per year (and the company's assets must never exceed £10 million at the time of purchase). No single company may represent more than ten per cent of the trust's assets.

- Investors who purchase shares in the VCT *at launch* qualify for income tax relief at 20 per cent and can defer CGT on other investments sold within twelve months to pay for the purchase of the VCT, provided that the trusts are held for three years.

- Investments of up to £100,000 are free from all income tax on the dividends and from CGT. However, capital losses incurred on the trusts may not be set against CGT.

With VCTs, the original CGT bill is only deferred, and still has to be paid after the VCT is disposed of, whatever happens to the investment (even if it goes bust). With an EIS, the original CGT bill tracks the performance of the investment and may be zero (company goes bust) or huge (company has performed very well).

Those VCTs that have already been launched have been met with much less enthusiasm by investors than was expected. Management charges, at 2–3 per cent, are significantly higher than those for an ordinary investment trust, owing to the greater management time and skill needed in selecting investments. Investors will be required to sign that they are aware of the risks involved from investment in VCTs.

As more older VCTs pass their 'lock-in' period, after which the original investors can sell up while still retaining their tax advantages, there is an increasing market in 'second-hand' VCTs. These retain most of the tax advantages of the original investment, except the 20 per cent tax relief on the original investment and the ability to roll-over capital gains on purchase, and are actually safer investments than the original VCT since of the first investments the 'plums' will have been ripening while the 'lemons' will have been thrown out. However, even second-hand VCTs are of much higher risk than a conventional unit or investment trust.

ENTERPRISE ZONE TRUSTS

Enterprise Zone Trusts remain as BES-like plans for investing in commercial property. Tax relief is currently still available at the investor's highest income tax rate. However, the risk of investing huge sums of money in property – that may at any time lose its value or its tenants – for lengthy periods (years) makes EZTs unsuitable for most small investors.

Update for 2004–5

The maximum annual investment for VCT companies is now £200,000. For years 2004–5 and 2005–6 ONLY, income tax relief for VCT companies is 40% (was 20%). New VCTS can no longer be used to shelter existing capital gains.

Appendix 8
Permanent Income Bearing Shares
(PIBS)

Permanent Income Bearing Shares (PIBS) have been issued by various, mostly large, building societies since the first was issued by Leeds Permanent in June 1991.

PIBS are not shares in the sense of being equities. They are undated, non-cumulative loan stock bonds (see Chapter 8), paying a fixed rate interest (normally around 11.5 – 13 per cent). The actual interest varies with the market price paid, and is currently around 7 per cent (Bank base rate 4.0 per cent).

PIBS convert automatically to 'Perpetual Subordinated Bonds' after demutualisation of the building society.

As 'Qualifying Capital Bonds', CGT is not chargeable on most gains or losses made on the purchase and subsequent sale of PIBS. The income from PIBS is paid twice a year, and is paid *net* of standard rate income tax.

The PIBS may be traded through a stockbroker, like other bonds, which represents the only way for an investor to get his money back. However, the market in PIBs is becoming smaller with the conversion of many building societies to banks. The building society PIBs qualified for conversion bonuses; those of the new banks do not. The decline in the liquidity of the market means that there are now wide dealing spreads. Investors in PIBs should set limits on the price they are prepared to pay, and to wait some time before the order can be filled. Alternatively you could ask the broker which PIBs happen to be currently available.

Dealing charges are similar to those of other bonds. Owing to a legal technicality, stamp duty is payable on the purchase of those PIBS issued without the formal approval of the building society's members firstly being sought. At present, this applies only to the PIBS offered by the Coventry Building Society.

Prices of PIBS are now listed in the *Financial Times* (Saturday edition). The prices quoted are 'clean' of interest – as with gilts, the actual price paid will include the accrued gross interest up to the point of purchase. Minimum purchases of PIBS vary from £1,000 to £50,000 (face-value).

RISKS

The risks of investing in PIBS are not to be taken lightly, and are reflected in their high yields.

- PIBS must not be confused with building society fixed-interest investment bonds, issued by many societies to their members.

- PIBS rank for repayment behind *all* other creditors in the event of financial failure of the building society/bank.

- Interest payments to PIBS investors *must* be suspended if to pay them would threaten the society's capital asset backing, driving it below the legal minimum.

- Arrears of interest payments do not have to be made up by the defaulting society (the PIBS are non-cumulative).

- The price of the PIBS is acutely sensitive to general interest rates: when interest rates fall, the value of the PIBS will rise – and vice-versa.

- There is no compensation scheme for a failed PIBS, if the building society/bank cannot make its payments.

- Many private investors would be better served by the purchase of the 'Cumulative Irredeemable Preference Shares' of a bank or insurance company. An example is given below.

Example
The following provides a typical example of a PIBS available in January 2003. Included for comparison is the Cumulative Irredeemable Preference Share of a leading insurance company. Unlike the PIBS, the latter will pay arrears of interest and will receive more favourable treatment if the company goes bankrupt. It should be noted that CGT applies to Irredeemable Preference Shares, but not to PIBS.

Building Society (Nominal £1 PIBS)	Nominal Interest %	Price (£) on 4/1/03	Market Interest %
Bradford & Bingley	13	182.00	7.1
Aviva (*)	8 3/4	106.00	8.25

(*) - 8 3/4% Cumulative Irredeemable Preference Share £1.

DIVERSIFICATION OF RISK

As with most investments, much of the individual risk of owning PIBS can be reduced by buying a spread of them.

Portfolios can now be purchased in selections of PIBS offered by some unit trust providers (typically with five to ten building society/bank PIBS, sometimes with a few irredeemable preference shares of leading banks thrown in and occasionally even with some zero dividend preference shares added to the mixture).

These unit trusts are penalised by typical unit trust charges, are subject to CGT, but are compensated in the event of their failure by the Investors' Compensation Scheme.

PIBS STRATEGIES

PIBS are bought by private investors primarily for income (high yield), and can replace a temporary annuity.

Current financial advice is to use PIBS as part of an income-bearing bond portfolio, but *never* as the sole component! The rest of the bond component should be made up with gilts and other stocks (eg debentures) with first call on the assets of the issuing company in the event of bankruptcy.

Appendix 9
Bulletin Board – SEATS

Owing to the numerous complaints about the difficulty of dealing in the shares of small companies, the Stock Exchange created a new trading system.

The **Bulletin Board** was introduced in April 1992 to match bargains (see page 44) for some 120 UK-listed and USM companies as a central market for two-way trades, being more visible, more flexible and lower cost than conventional SEAQ trades. The Bulletin Board appears on the TOPIC Stock Exchange price-listing computer system.

In November 1992 the **Stock Exchange Alternative Trading System (SEATS)** modified the Bulletin Board. If there is just one market maker for a company listed on the Bulletin Board, it has to display a bid-offer quotation at all times. Brokers dealing through the Bulletin Board are obliged to give the market maker first refusal on any bid or offer they receive.

The last ten trades executed are always shown on the Bulletin Board, together with the brokers involved. All trades must be reported to the controller within three minutes.

SEATS and the Bulletin Board have greatly boosted total trade in smaller companies. In practice, the investor can phone his stockbroker and ask to have his buy/sell order in a little-traded company posted on the Bulletin Board at the investor's price for as long as the investor chooses.

The reader should note the similarity between SEATS and SETS (Appendix 14).

Appendix 10
Value/Tactical/Bottom-Up
Investment Strategy

One of the most popular, and common, means of deciding which shares to buy is based on the assumption that, by careful study of company reports, it is possible to identify and purchase shares in under-valued individual companies. A portfolio is constructed from several such stocks.

This principle is known as **value** or **tactical** or **bottom-up** investment. The principle runs contrary to the Efficient Market Hypothesis and, even if it is true for some professional fund managers in daily contact with the market, the idea that a private investor can pick up a bargain in one of the larger companies which has somehow been overlooked by the armies of full-time professional analysts seems to the author to be naïve.

Nevertheless, this system provides the stock-in-trade for most 'tip sheets', which tend to feature the smaller companies.

Even more optimistic is the idea that the private investor can find, *and continue to find*, hot 'growth' stocks before the professionals spot them. Such stocks can be expected to rise steeply in value as earnings explode. Polly Peck was always the most-cited example – until it went bust.

A variety of systems are commercially exploited, often in book form, which seek to select such growth stocks. All are extremely successful at picking *past* winners. The reputation of few persists after the following three years.

Many professional investors accept that it is not possible to beat the market consistently. Instead they use Modern Portfolio Theory to match risk and gains. The 'Logical Investment Strategy' set out in this book follows this path, relying for long-term success on the individual investor to select stocks with good long-term prospects since the market is notoriously short-sighted.

Strategic or **top-down** investment is the name given to the strategy of selecting different classes of assets (eg shares in the UK or overseas, property, cash, bonds) in which to invest and then to try to match the appropriate index within each class. The skill comes in selecting the proportions of each class in which to invest.

There is one little-recognised, but major, difficulty with 'value' investment. The portfolio of shares that you create is not properly diversified. Since it often happens that an entire stockmarket sector may be undervalued, it is quite easy to build up a portfolio of undervalued stocks that are all, say, property companies or all banks. This is fine if the whole sector recovers, but what if it does not? Then you have a portfolio of intertwined duds. Thus a policy of seeking undervalued shares can actually be a very high-risk strategy. It is much wiser to diversity your portfolio and let general stockmarket movements work their magic over all your investments.

Appendix 11
FRS-3: New Accounting Rules

The accounts of companies listed in the *Financial Times* have been restated to conform with the FRS-3 accountancy standard.

Introduced in October 1992, the aim is to encourage companies and investors to pay more attention to cash flow and asset value, and less to the (easily manipulated) 'earnings per share' (eps).

The old accounting standard distinguished 'extraordinary' items, mostly one-off items such as redundancy costs which were deemed not to affect the yearly 'true' profit, and 'exceptional' items, which occurred rarely but did affect the yearly profit. The scope for creative accounting under the old system is evident.

The new rules make 'extraordinary' items much, much less common. Accordingly, profits and the eps will become more volatile. In addition the 'accrual concept' ensures that the yearly cash-in-hand statement will take account of money still owed or due.

Further accounting improvements are also being recommended.

Appendix 12
AIM/OFEX

EU regulations required a relaxation of the rules governing admission to the main stockmarket, thereby reducing much of the appeal of the 'junior' market, the Unlisted Securities Market (USM). The latter was closed at the end of 1996.

However, there remained a demand from small companies for a cheaper route to market and the Stock Exchange introduced the Alternative Investment Market (AIM) in June 1995. Admission is after nomination by one of a list of sponsors approved by the Stock Exchange.

AIM has proved to be unexpectedly successful. It received a good lift when companies trading on the USM or under Rule 4.1 were required to find new markets, and now boasts its own index (FT-SE AIM, started at a value of 1,000) and numerous companies whose share prices are listed in their own section with the other share prices in the *Financial Times*.

However, marketability of many stocks is poor – frequently there is only one market maker – and these companies are much more risky than those traded on the main market, although AIM is regulated by the London Stock Exchange. At present, two investment trusts trade in AIM companies.

Far riskier still are companies listed on the OFEX market, which is run by the company PLUS Markets, a specialist in small companies. OFEX is since 2001 regulated by the London Stock Exchange, admission is decided by a nameless panel of 'wise men' and the only requirement of companies is that they must publish their accounts twice a year.

OFEX companies are not suited to amateur investors, owing to their high risk. After a number of scandals, the *Investors' Chronicle* magazine greatly reduced its coverage of OFEX in 1996 in order to avoid misleading readers as to the companies' status. Most company shares held in Aim and OFEX are now classified by the Inland Revenue as 'business assets', and capital gains made on such investments now qualify for accelerated taper relief. The shares are also exempt from Inheritance Tax after they have been held for two years. However, if the company concerned moves up to the Main Market, *all* reliefs are lost at once. See Appendix 16 for tax treatment of capital gains.

Appendix 13
Emerging markets

Emerging markets are those foreign stockmarkets enjoying growth in consumer spending, industrial prowess and sophistication in marketing the shares of local companies. Examples include the so-called 'Tiger' economies of the Far East (eg Singapore, Thailand, Malaysia, Korea; no two professionals can ever agree whether Hong Kong counts as 'emerging'); Latin American countries; Eastern Europe and South Africa. The USA was an emerging market in the nineteenth century.

Since their growth rate may be much higher than that of the established markets, the potential for making big profits is always present. However, the stockmarkets of individual countries tend to go up and down like yo-yos – today's winners are tomorrow's losers – so private investors should never invest heavily in a single emerging market. Individually, the markets are of high risk.

The best way of participating in this growth is through a pooled fund (unit or investment trust), where the manager can select from many countries. The best known such manager in the UK is Templeton Emerging Markets Investment Trust.

Even so, the reader should clearly understand that *all* the emerging markets can fall together if sentiment turns against them. Many emerging markets are linked to the US dollar, and share its successes and disappointments. Dividends are usually negligible. Standard financial advice is that *long-term* investors only should gamble five – 15 per cent of their capital in emerging markets.

Appendix 14
Order-Driven Markets/SETS

Until recently, the great bulk of share trading in the UK Stockmarket was done through 'market makers', institutions that buy and sell shares for their own account and charge a spread on the share price to compensate for the risk of accumulating dud stock that they cannot then off-load.

Some foreign stockmarkets, particularly in the USA, have an emphasis on an 'order-driven' market, where individual investors can place buy and sell orders on a central computer that brings together buyer and seller. The Bulletin Board (Appendix 9) is similar. Order driven markets tend to have much lower spreads than those operated through market makers, but trading can dry up if the market collapses (all sellers and no buyers).

There have been several proposals to introduce order-driven markets to the UK, some mediated by the Internet, and it seems increasingly likely that these will in time come to dominate the UK stockmarket. But at present market makers still make trades for the majority of companies traded there.

SETS (Stock Exchange Electronic Trading Service)

SETS is an order-driven market that was initiated by the London Stock Exchange in 1997 for all the FTSE 100 stocks and many others, with a view to reducing the spreads charged by market makers. Unfortunately, the big institutions showed less enthusiasm than expected, causing severe ebbs and flows in dealing spreads during trading. This has been particularly noticeable at the beginning and end of each day, when poor volumes (few institutional trades) have occurred.

The solution to this problem on other order-driven exchanges has been to encourage the private investor to fill the gap. The London Stock Exchange first discouraged such investors with a requirement for high order volumes on SETS, but these have since been abandoned. Even so, the potential for large dealing spreads, especially early in the morning, means that the reader should *never* deal 'at best'. *Always, always,* place a limit, such as 'buy shares at maximum 100 pence' or 'sell shares at minimum 90 pence'.

Appendix 15
The Internet

The Internet is essentially an electronic communications system joining all those connected with it, through a computer and a modem, by way of the telephone system locally and internationally. Calls through the service provider are usually charged at local rate. The Internet has many potential applications; here we are concerned only with those pertaining to share-dealing.

Some companies provide share price data on a fairly regular basis, by arrangement with the London Stock Exchange or even by tapping into American quotes of London stock prices. Foreign share prices are also accessible. The situation is constantly changing, and the interested reader will need to find his own best supplier. The provision of fast information is one of the Internet's strengths.

Charles Schwab and Barclays are among those stockbrokers now offering Internet trading in the UK. The security of such transactions is little understood, but the reader is reminded of the number of computer hackers who continually break into the computers of the world's defence agencies, and the rapid progress in decryption techniques for computer-generated codes. A further problem occurs if the system crashes while you are making a transaction. Have you bought the shares or not? The early uptake by enthusiastic investors of Internet dealing has now fallen to a trickle of new accounts.

Don't be tempted to deal in any financial instrument (stocks, shares, bonds, building society, bank account, gas bill) on the Internet (and don't give away your credit card number either). Do not believe that rubbish about how giving your credit card details over the Internet is no different from giving it to a waiter in a restaurant. If the waiter abuses the system the police have his address and his description. Does that apply to the Internet? Let it be the mugs who determine first just how secure such electronic dealing really is – and give them a few years in which to find out.

Don't believe everything that you read about companies on the Internet either. False rumours are deliberately propagated to manipulate share prices.

Don't become a 'day-trader' – one who daily gambles through the Internet on share movements. The majority of day-traders lose money in the long run, often large sums. Don't chase the value of Internet ('dot-com') stocks too far; many of the new issues are of dubious quality.

Don't succumb to the temptation to keep moving your deposit accounts to chase the highest rates found on your Internet screen. Sooner or later, there will be an electronic glitch resulting in the apparent disappearance of all your money (remember: the more you switch, the more likely the glitch), causing panic even if you manage to recover the money. Worse, sooner or later you will transfer your deposits to a rogue bank and then they will be lost for ever.

It is impossible to provide up-to-date information in a book like this when the environment is changing so quickly – check the latest situation with a current financial magazine. Despite my experience with computing, or perhaps because of it, I remain deeply suspicious of the Internet for financial transactions, and I do not recommend this procedure (yet). Don't blame me if your Internet transactions go wrong.

Five years have elapsed since an earlier edition of this book first made mention of the use of the Internet by trading investors. Yet still I cannot recommend this procedure for security reasons. Sadly, far too few companies dealing over the Internet have yet grasped the basic fact that no security chain can be stronger than its weakest link. There is absolutely no point in having state-of-the-art encryption of the line connecting investor and website if the company then deposits the de-crypted data all over its website for anyone to see. The number of reported instances of this serious security breach shows no sign of abatement, and has affected household names. The number of unreported instances is presumably much higher.

Somewhat ironically, perhaps, many former customers of the Internet brokers are giving up. Not for security reasons, but because the customers have lost too much money following their own ideas and now require the kind of advice that Internet brokers cannot give without returning to the old-fashioned telephone.

However, the Internet is an excellent source of information about companies. *www.LondonStockExchange.com* provides a good example.

Appendix 16
Capital Gains Tax (CGT)

Capital Gains Tax is a mess since recent government changes, and there is no point in trying to disguise this fact. The following provides only an overview, and the reader who deals in shares (or other assets) on a large scale, such as to exceed the yearly capital gains allowance, is strongly advised to seek professional advice.

CGT is a tax levied on all capital gains from most assets, including property, land, shares, most bonds and traded options. Gilts and certain other bonds are exempt, see Chapter 8 (bonds). Capital gains occur when an asset is sold for more than its purchase cost; capital losses when an asset is sold for less than its purchase cost. The purchase cost may have been indexed for inflation. The tax is charged at present at the investor's marginal tax rate – higher tax rate payers at 40 per cent, lower rate tax-payers at 20 or 22 per cent.

First, the good news. There is an annual capital gains exemption limit, currently (tax year 2006–7) of £8,800. The government has indicated that this allowance will be increased in line with inflation. Where total capital gains, from all assets sold during the current tax year, do not exceed the exemption, there is no liability to CGT.

Bed-and-breakfasting used to mean selling shares and buying them back again on the following working day. This was invariably done for tax reasons, usually to settle the capital gains liability on the day the shares were sold. For example, if you owned a stock which had risen by £5,000 in value and you expected it to rise another £5,000 in the following year then, bearing in mind the then-current capital gains limit of £6,500 before tax was payable, you might choose to bed-and-breakfast the shares in each year to avoid paying any capital gains tax (assuming, of course, that you had no other taxable capital gain). Another common reason to bed-and-breakfast shares was to establish a capital loss, to offset capital gains made on other shares.

Now, the bad news.

The new Chancellor abolished bed-and-breakfasting in 1998, by setting off any sale of shares (or other assets) against the repurchase of the same assets within 30 days after the sale. After 30 days the risk would be excessive that the share price might have changed steeply, between selling and re-buying.

Until April 1998 there was a (fairly) simple regime:

- Any shares or bonds held before 31 March 1982 should be considered to have been purchased at the higher of (i) their actual purchase price, or (ii) their market value on 31 March 1982.

- Tables produced by the Inland Revenue showed indexation for inflation between March 1982 and the date of sale of the shares. The adjusting indexation parameter can be found in publications such as *Taxation* and *Investors' Chronicle*.

- All shares or bonds of one type were held in a common 'pool', regardless of when they were bought. Thus, if you bought 1,000 shares in an investment trust on 1/4/1982, 1,000 shares on 1/4/1990 and 1,000 shares on 1/4/1997, you would be deemed to own 3,000 indistinguishable shares purchased for the sum of the 1982 cost (indexed from 1982 to today's date), plus the 1990 cost (indexed from 1990) plus the 1997 cost (again indexed). If today you sold 1,500 shares (half total holding), your capital gain would be sale price less half the total indexed cost. This principle is called **Apportionment**.

- Complications are caused by rights issues and share splits.

- The November 1993 Budget banned the use of indexation to create or increase a capital loss. Capital gains could still be reduced by indexation.

Example 1

One thousand shares in company 'XYZ' were bought on 20 December 1980 for a total cost of £1,025, including buying expenses. Their market value on 31 March 1982 is £2. Their price when sold in April 1998 is £5 per share, or £4,925 after expenses. The inflation multiplier is 2.047 from 31 March 1982 to April 1998. The capital gain (for tax purposes) is therefore:

$$4,925 - (2,000 \times 2.047) = £831.00$$

This will be taxed at your normal income tax rate (currently 22 per cent or 40 per cent), assuming that the tax-exempt limit (see above) has already been exceeded.

Example 2

One thousand shares in company 'XYZ' were bought on 20 December 1985 for £3 (total cost, including buying expenses, £3,025). Their price when sold in April 1998 is £5, less expenses gives £4,925. The inflation multiplier from 20 December 1985 to April 1998 is 1.693. The chargeable taxable gain is therefore:

$$4,925 - (3,025 \times 1.693) = £196.33$$

Remember that there is currently a tax-exempt limit on capital gains, so that neither of the above gains would of themselves be subject to tax. They would only be taxed if your total capital gains on other dealings had exceeded the exemption limit.

Remember too, that Capital Gains Tax is only payable when the shares are sold (not when they are merely held or 'valued').

The above rules still (2003) apply to companies, and also to shares and bonds held by private investors up to April 1998. But the 1998 Budget created a severe complication, under the title of 'simplification'. Capital gains for individuals and non-company groups are no longer to be indexed-and-pooled, but to be 'tapered'.

Tapering

A sliding scale is applied to reduce capital gains, according to the number of years that the asset has been held after March 1998. 'Business assets' attract a much faster taper relief than for ordinary shares. Originally aimed at entrepreneurs seeking to dispose of shares or assets in their own companies, business taper relief has been expanded. Since April 2000, employee shareholdings in their own business, or investment holdings greater than 5% of the issued shares, are both subject to the accelerated CGT taper for business assets, provided that the company is in a qualifying business. Qualifying shares traded on the AIM or OFEX markets similarly benefit from the accelerated taper. For ordinary company shares, the following table applies:

Tapering Scale

No. years asset owned after March 1998	Percentage of gain applied
0	100
1	100
2	100
3	95

4	90
5	85
6	80
7	75
8	70
9	65
10 +	60

An extra year of 'ownership' (for tapering purposes) is allowed for each asset that was held on 17 March 1998.

Example 3
Suppose you bought shares in 'Z plc' on 6 April 1999 for £3,000 and sold them on 7 April 2005 for £7,000. The capital gain is £7,000 - £3,000 = £4,000. Using the table above (shares held for six full years), the capital gain is reduced by tapering to £4,000 x 80/100 = £3,200.

Note that the above table gives no tax relief for shares held for fewer than three years, and that no compensation is now given for the effect of inflation in destroying the real value of the investment. Tapering will only be of benefit to investors (relative to the old 'index-and-pool' system) if inflation is low and capital gains are high. The Inland Revenue did its sample calculations on the incredible assumption that inflation will be only 2.5 per cent for the indefinite future.

The private investor should clearly understand that *indexation-and-pooling* applies to all shares held up to the end of March 1998, and *tapering* applies thereafter to the pool of shares held at that time.

Monthly savings
The Inland Revenue allows each monthly contribution to be counted: either as a monthly contribution (requiring 12 monthly calculations each year); or as one total payment made in the seventh month of the company's year (which may not be July).

CGT rollover relief
It is possible to 'roll-over' capital gains by investment of the entire realised gain (after sale) in certain qualifying companies. For example, if you buy shares in 'A plc' for £10,000 and sell them for £30,000 (for a capital gain of £20,000, assuming that no reliefs apply), you could defer paying CGT by using the gain (£20,000) to buy shares in a qualifying company.

The rules for qualifying companies are complex, but include these key criteria:

- The shares must be newly bought by subscription (*not* acquired by share dealing).
- The shares must be held for at least three years.
- The company must be in a qualifying trade, and remain qualifying during the three-year period.

Most EIS and VCT companies (Appendix 7) meet the above criteria, with the following additional conditions:

- Shares must be issued not more than twelve months before or 12/36 months (VCT/EIS) after the date of disposal of the original shares (or other capital assets).
- Maximum annual CGT rollover relief is equal to the EIS/VCT maximum annual qualifying sums (currently £150,000/£100,000). Some carry-back to earlier years may be permitted.

The reader should clearly recognise that this system for avoiding capital gains tax involves a three-year lock-in of the capital and is of very high risk (being invested predominantly in start-up companies). The rollover relief is really aimed at businessmen retiring after selling their own businesses, and is *wholly unsuitable for most private investors*. Always seek professional advice before taking this path.

Capital losses
It has always been possible to subtract capital losses from one asset against capital gains from another when computing the total capital gains bill. Thus, under the old 'index-and-pool' rules, if you had a gain from selling shares in 'A plc' of £5,000 and a loss after selling shares in 'B plc' of £2,000, your net capital gain would have been £3,000. Net capital losses in one year can be carried through to subsequent years (subject to some restrictions), to reduce the following year's capital gains. Remember that capital losses from *any* source (eg sale of farmer's land) must be set against capital gains.

The new tapering system requires this year's capital gains to be set off against this or previous years' capital losses *before* tapering each asset's gains. Each purchase of shares counts as a separate event, and the number of years taper that applies depends on how long each purchase has been held, on a last-in first-out basis. It is essential to keep records of every sale and purchase of shares and other assets.

Example 4

You bought 1,000 shares in an investment trust on 1/4/1998, 1,000 shares on 1/4/1999 and 1,000 shares on 1/4/2003, then sold 1,500 on 2/4/2007. You are deemed to have sold all your 1,000 shares bought in 2003 (four years' taper) and 500 of the 1,000 shares bought in 1999 (eight years' taper). Note that 'pooling' no longer applies.

However, where there are several losses and several gains, the rules permit the losses to be applied to the gains in the way that creates the smallest capital gain (after tapering) for the investor. Here there is room for big trouble. Since the investor is allowed to allocate his capital gains and losses in the way which gives the smallest capital gain, then in order to find the most tax-favourable combination he has to calculate the effect of setting every loss against every gain before tapering the result, and the number of combinations explodes exponentially. If an investor has five gains and five losses in the current tax year, there are 120 combinations to calculate. Ten gains and ten losses? Roughly 3.6 million combinations. Fifteen gains and fifteen losses? 1.3 million million combinations. Fancy working that out with a pencil and paper? The trick is to set any losses first against gains with no taper relief, then against gains qualifying for taper relief, starting first with those gains that have the lowest taper relief.

Capital Gains Tax is an unmitigated curse that raises very little income each year. The justification given for its continued existence is that, if the tax did not exist, avoidance schemes would spring into operation to turn income into capital gains, depriving the Inland Revenue of income taxes. Yet the continued existence of CGT results in the paralysis of rational investment decisions (and not only with shares). Shares may be retained to avoid large tax bills when they should certainly be sold on the grounds of underperformance.

For example, suppose an investor has held shares in a company for ten years. The company has been successful and the dividends paid have increased ten-fold, and are now £5,000 per annum. Unsurprisingly, the shares have also risen ten-fold in value from the purchase price of £10,000 to £100,000. However, the investor believes that the company now has reduced prospects of future growth, and wonders whether to sell his shares. The capital gain is nominally £90,000 (to illustrate the point, this calculation ignores the reliefs that may be available from Capital Gains Tax, such as exemption limits, indexation and tapering). If the investor now wishes to sell the shares, he will pay tax of £90,000 × 40% = £36,000, leaving £64,000. Where can he find a similar income (£5,000) from shares purchased for only £64,000? The investor will be reluctant to sell under these circumstances.

In view of the complications explained above, it may be good practice to send a list of all shares held with their purchase prices and dates of purchase to the Revenue with your tax return each year, in order to avoid any subsequent disputes about the size of your holdings and Capital Gains Tax.

Appendix 17
Reinvestment of Dividends

Many companies, but most especially investment trusts, unit trusts and OEICS, permit their shareholders to reinvest dividends in the same company. This provides a cheap means for the investor to increase his holding in the company, and also provides a form of 'pound-cost-averaging'; more shares will be bought when prices are low than when they are high. This type of reinvestment is known as a **roll-up fund**. It can be particularly effective in raising the value of a share-holding when the dividends are received without deduction of tax, as in a PEP or ISA.

There are two procedures by which a company can reinvest shareholders' dividends:

1. Purchase of its own shares on the open market.

2. Create and issue new shares while retaining the dividend cash (effectively a rights issue).

For technical reasons, virtually all collective investment funds (investment trusts etc.) adopt procedure (1) above. The investor receives the benefit of cheap share-dealing but has to pay stamp duty on the share purchase. Continual purchase of existing shares has the long-term benefit of providing a support for the company's share price.

Most ordinary companies – ie, excluding collective funds – have historically preferred procedure (2), when new shares are created and there is no stamp duty to pay. However, recent changes to tax law have favoured the purchase by companies of their own shares rather than the payment of dividends. Under these circumstances, there is little purpose in using such dividends as are paid to create new shares, so that procedure (1) is becoming more popular here too.

Whether the private share investor should bother with dividend reinvestment is hard to say:

Advantages
- Cheap acquisition of more shares.
- Pound-cost-averaging.

Disadvantages
- Complex record-keeping required for income and capital gains taxes.
- You may be adding to a failing investment.
- Often necessary to hold the new shares in a nominee account.

In my view, recent tax changes mean that the disadvantages outweigh the advantages, unless the company concerned is held tax-free in a PEP or ISA.

Appendix 18
Derivatives

The following gives a list of the most popular derivatives. They apply generally to shares, or to indices of shares, but often can be applied also to bonds or other assets. Traded options and warrants (Chapter 7) represent a classic type of derivative, and the reader should re-read that chapter to ensure familiarity with the terminology used below.

There is a large overlap between types of derivative, representing types of product available from different providers. It is quite instructive to read the promotional advertising for each type of derivative to learn the weaknesses of its competitors! Brokers love short-dated derivatives, since the investor is forced to keep replacing them – and pay the commissions. It is difficult not to imagine that soon another financial scandal will break over the indiscriminate and widespread marketing of these products. Claims that they aid risk management are false, since the dealing charges are too high relative to the size of portfolios that most private investors will have. It is, however, true that the institutions use futures a great deal to manage risk.

1. HIGH RISK OBLIGATION

The following derivative types confer the **obligation** (not the right) to buy or sell the underlying shares, although usually the investor will buy back the obligation at the prevailing market price before the expiry date of the derivative. All can be used to go short of a company (bet it goes down in value), as well as to go long. All require that a variable margin be deposited with the broker; all employ gearing so that gains and losses on the investor's original payment are greatly magnified. All are of *very high risk of infinite loss* to the investor, although some brokers may operate stop-losses to protect the investor from too great a disaster. Fundamentally, all are gambling, although there exist strategies to use these derivatives to offset risk against other share holdings. If you get it right, you make a bundle. If you get it wrong, you lose a bundle.

Futures
Mainly used by institutions to control risk. Obligation to buy shares at price agreed. The gain or loss is the difference between the buying and selling prices. Futures can be traded on any asset, so that most types are hard to trade (except for indices).

Universal Stock Futures (USF)
Like futures, but available only for certain large companies and therefore easier to trade through LIFFE.

Writing traded options
Mainly used by institutions to control risk. See Chapter 7.

Contracts for Difference (CFD)
Investor borrows money from broker to own shares (including their dividends), while paying interest (ca. three per cent over bank rate) to the broker. Dealing spreads are set by the broker, and can be painful since the investor cannot move to another broker.

Spread-betting
Betting whether shares or indices rise or fall. The sum won or lost is equal to the movement from the opening price. Dealing spreads are set by the broker. Betting gains are free from Capital Gains Tax.

In my view, all of the above are **totally unsuited** to the readers of this book, exposing investors to a very real risk of unlimited loss.

2. HIGH RISK RIGHT

The following instruments give the investor the **right**, but not the obligation, to buy or sell the underlying shares at the expiry date. Therefore the investor cannot lose more than the original investment. Some allow the investor to go short, none requires the investor to put up margin.

Buying traded options
The investor acquires the right to buy or sell the underlying shares at the predetermined price on a predetermined date. See Chapter 7.

Warrants
Issued by companies (especially investment trusts), they confer on the investor the right to buy shares at a fixed price some long time (usually years) into the future.

Covered warrants
Since few individual companies offer warrants, these are warrants where an investment bank has taken upon itself the duty to provide the shares on expiry of the warrant. The institution may have the right to issue cash instead of shares at the expiry date, which will trigger a capital gain to the investor (unlike receipt of the underlying shares). Although traded for years among institutions, when marketability was very poor, recent changes to the rules by the London Stock Exchange have greatly increased the size of the market. As well as granting the investor the right to buy shares at some distant date ('call warrant'), there are also covered 'put warrants' that confer the right on the investor to sell shares at a predetermined price at some distant date.

Covered certificates
These will be introduced shortly, and are effectively covered warrants for indices (such as the FTSE-100).

3. MEDIUM RISK – NEITHER OBLIGATION NOR RIGHT

Exchange Traded Funds (ETFs)
These are collective funds (such as for indices) backed by investment banks and other large institutions. They behave like the underlying index, entitle the investor to the dividends paid by the shares comprising the index, and can be held indefinitely. As derivatives they are not liable to stamp duty; however, the bank charges typically 0.5% commission. This compares very favourably with the average charge made by the manager of an index-tracking unit trust, but there remains the small chance that the issuing bank will not honour its guarantees. There will also be a dealing spread, currently around 0.4%. Many of these ETFs are run by Barclays Bank, such as the iFTSE100, which tracks the FTSE-100 index. ETFs have proved to be very popular in the USA.

American Depositary Receipts (ADRs)
Large foreign companies deposit some of their shares with a US

bank. These are used by the bank as security for new shares (ADRs) issued in the USA. The advantage to the foreign company is that difficulties of compliance with US law by the original shares are avoided. ADRs can be purchased in the UK even for British companies (such as Glaxo-SmithKine), and have the advantage of avoiding stamp duty. Dividends are paid on the ADRs.

Crest Depositary Receipts (CDRs)

These are the British equivalent of ADRs for foreign companies. The CDRs are priced in sterling, easily traded and constituted under British law. However, they often lack voting rights. CDRs are the most convenient way of holding individual foreign shares for a British investor.

Appendix 19
Alternative Investments

Dividends and wages are ultimately derived from company profits. Thus, when the economy is booming, company shares do well while collectors (very predominantly male) can follow their passion for collecting items such as paintings, fine wines, toy soldiers, postage stamps, vintage cars, bus tickets, *Beano* comics or the like.

When share prices fall, usually in anticipation of a fall in company profits, for a while the economy continues to boom, and genuine collectors are still willing to pay a good price to complete their collections. At this point, you can be sure that some journalist will observe that the prices of paintings, fine wines and other collectables are continuing to grow, and alert investors to the 'opportunity'. Immediately there is a sudden boom in the values of the collectable, as investors buy indiscriminately, thereby self-fuelling the original prophecy.

But at this point the genuine collectors decide either to stop updating their collections, or even to sell them to the new purchasers. With no new buyers the market collapses, and the herd of investors is left clutching worthless collectable items in which they have no interest.

Never be tempted to 'invest' in collectables, unless you have a genuine interest in the items being collected and a very long timescale.

Appendix 20
Inland Revenue Stamp Offices

If you carry out an off-market transaction, such as one friend buying shares off another, there will probably be a liability to stamp duty. The current rate is 0.5%, rounded upwards to the nearest £5. Payment must be made within 30 days of the transaction.

Send the appropriate documents to any address listed below, with a cheque made out to 'Inland Revenue – Stamp Duties', or call personally. It is probably wise first to call the office to confirm that stamp duty is payable and to confirm the amount.

Belfast, Ground Floor, Dorchester House, 52–58 Great Victoria Street, Belfast BT2 7QE. Tel: (01232) 314614.

Birmingham, 5th Floor, Norfolk House, Smallbrook Queensway, Birmingham B5 4LA. Tel: (0121) 633 3313.

Bristol, 1st Floor, The Pithay, All Saints Street, Bristol BS1 2NY. Tel: (0117) 927 2022.

Edinburgh, Mulberry House, 16 Picardy Place, Edinburgh EH1 3NF. Tel: (0131) 556 8998.

London – use Worthing office.

Manchester, Alexandra House, Parsonage, Manchester M60 9BT. Tel: (0161) 833 0413.

Newcastle, 15th Floor, Cale Cross House, 156 Pilgrim Street, Newcastle upon Tyne NE1 6TF. Tel: (0191) 245 0200.

Worthing (Post only), Room 57, East Block, Barrington Road, Worthing BN12 4SE. Tel: (01903) 508930.

Glossary

Account. Period of trading stocks and shares without need to settle for cash until the end of the account. Now replaced by Rolling System.

Account Day. Last day of the account (see above).

Advance Corporation Tax (ACT). Tax once paid by issuing company with its dividends. The tax could be offset against its company tax, and reclaimed by investors not liable to income tax on the dividends.

Advisory Service. Advice provided by a stockbroker to a client, normally more expensive than a 'dealing-only' service.

Allotment Letter. Temporary certificate of share ownership, received after shares from a new issue are allocated.

Alpha Risk. Variation of share price of an individual company due to changing perceptions of its value.

Alpha Stock. Highest classification of marketability of share; ie the most readily traded.

Alternative Investment Market (AIM). Market for smaller companies, regulated by the Stock Exchange.

Alternative Investments. Investments not traded on a recognised financial exchange. For example, houses, paintings, collectables.

American Depository Receipt (ADR). Shares traded in the USA that are backed by the shares of foreign (non-US) companies.

Amortisation. Spreading immediate costs over several years.

Annuity. Irrevocable payment of a large capital sum to an institution (usually a pension fund) in return for regular cash payments until an agreed final date (often the death of the recipient). Taxation is often an issue.

Apportionment. Dividing the indexed cost of an asset that was purchased in units on different dates by the number of units, so that each unit of the asset is considered to have the same cost.

Arbitrage. Exploitation of a minute difference between selling prices in different markets. Arbitrageurs buy assets in one market and sell at a fractionally higher price in another. These anomalies are due to market inefficiencies.

Assets. Possessions which can be sold. Includes shares, land, property, bonds, gilts, paintings and so on.

Asset Stripper. A company which takes over another, then sells off the victim's most profitable parts for cash.

Backwardisation. Profit made by buying from one market maker and selling to another. See **arbitrage**.

Bargain. Transaction between investor and his agent, such as a stockbroker.

Bear Market. Falling stock market. 'Bears' are those who sell shares today, expecting to be able to buy them back cheaper at a later date.

Bearer Certificate. Possession of these gives the present owner all rights to the underlying investment. Bearer certificates are as valuable as cash, and must be as well guarded. They are rare in the UK, quite common in Europe.

Bed and Breakfast. Selling shares and rebuying them on the following day in order to establish a capital gain, or loss, for tax purposes. No longer permitted in UK.

Beta Risk. Variation of the share price of a company relative to a general movement of all shares in the market.

Beta Stock. Formerly 'second division' stocks in terms of market-ability. Under the new 'NMS' system, stocks designated beta have only very limited marketability.

Bid Price. The price at which a broker will take assets from the investor, ie the price which he will pay if you sell the assets.

Big Bang. Wholesale changes in the regulations of the London Stock Exchange on one day in October 1986.

Blue Chip. Undefined term, usually taken to mean the most marketable, safest share investments. The name derives from the colour of the most valuable chip used in poker.

Bonds. Investments which pay interest (usually at a fixed rate) instead of dividends. Normally the investor will expect to get his initial investment back on a predetermined date.

Bond Stripping. Separate the coupons from a bond and sell them separately. See also **gilt strips**.

Bond Washing. Now obsolete procedure of buying bonds just after the interest was paid and selling just before the next interest payment was due. This avoided receipt of interest (subject to income tax), while making capital gains (subject to Capital Gains Tax) since the value of the bond was higher when interest was due for payment.

Book Value. Value of assets as stated in a company's books. This may or may not bear any relationship to their real, or market, value.

Bull Market. Rising stockmarket. A 'bull' is one who buys shares today, expecting to sell them at a higher price in the near future.

Bulletin Board. Stock Exchange system for matching bargains in little-traded stocks.

Bullion. Bars of precious metal, typically gold (can refer to silver, platinum or 'strategic' metals, such as cobalt or chromium).

Business Cycle. Process by which business confidence, or prosperity, ebbs and flows over a cycle of years. In the UK the cycle is typically around five years.

Business Expansion Scheme (BES). Tax favoured investment in the shares of small companies not yet listed on any stockmarket (Obsolete).

'C' shares. Shares issued for cash by an investment trust to avoid dilution of existing shares. When the cash has been invested, the 'C' shares will be converted into ordinary shares.

Capital Asset Price Model. Adjustment of portfolio risk by borrowing or lending cash and buying or selling the non-cash assets of the portfolio accordingly.

Capital Gain. Sale of an asset at a higher price than that at which it was bought (usually after adjustment for inflation).

Capital Gains Tax (CGT). Tax on capital gains (see above).

Capital Growth. Rise in the value of an asset over a period of time.

Capitalisation of Interest. Adding up all the interest on a loan, then adding this to the cost of the asset bought with the loan to give the true cost of the asset.

Capitalisation Issue. See **scrip issue**.

'Cash and Calls' strategy. Guaranteed performance from a share portfolio by holding mostly cash with exposure to the stockmarket through call options or warrants.

Cash and New. Sales of shares at the end of the account followed by repurchase at the beginning of the new account. (Obsolete.)

Cash Bonus. Extra cash paid out by a company to shareholders (as well as the normal dividend), usually after an unexpected windfall.

Cash Cow. Company which generates large profits from a well established business.

Chart Analysis. Plotting the price of a share against time (usually the logarithm of the share price is plotted). 'Chartists' claim to be able to predict future share price movements by examination of charts.

Chinese Walls. Insubstantial or token separation of activities which should not be influenced by each other.

Churning. Unnecessary trading in the shares of a discretionary client by a stockbroker in order to generate commission fees.

Close Company. Company with more than 65 per cent of the shares held by five or fewer shareholders. The company is frequently privately owned and run. Tax on investment income can no longer be avoided through use of a close company.

Commission. Charge made by a broker or other agent for transacting business for a client.

Commodities. Bulk-traded raw materials, such as wheat, oil, soya beans and metals.

Compliance Form. Written agreement by investor that he will abide by various regulations. The form is usually required by a stockbroker.

Composite Rate Tax (CRT). Tax once levied on most payments of interest or dividends at a rate slightly lower than the basic rate of income tax. It could not be reclaimed by those who were not liable to income tax. Now replaced by income tax levies, reclaimable (or not payable) by those not liable to income tax.

Conditional Bid. Provisional offer for the shares of a company, which will only go ahead provided that a majority of shareholders in the company being bid for accept the offer.

Conglomerate. Collection of diverse companies in different businesses, overseen by one head office.

Consolidation. Sending several share certificates, or temporary share certificates, to the company registrars and receiving one certificate back.

Contract Note. Note from broker or other agent saying that an investor's transaction has been carried out.

Contract for Difference. Means of borrowing money to invest in shares.

Convertible. A bond, paying interest, which can be converted into the shares of the issuing company before a fixed date.

Coppock Indicator. Index computed in a complex manner, whose changes are purported to show the beginnings of (especially) bull and also bear markets.

Core Business. The main, or principal, business of a company.

Coupon. Synonymous today with the interest paid on a bond. The term originally derived from the coupons on bearer bonds which had to be clipped out and sent to an agent in order to receive the interest. Bearer bonds are very rare in the UK, common in Europe.

Cover. The number of times that a company's profits exceed the amount which it pays out in dividends.

Crash. Sudden collapse in the value of an asset. A market crash occurs when the value of most of the assets in a market has suddenly plunged.

Crest. Electronic system for registering changes in ownership of shares.

Crest Depository Receipt (CDR). Shares traded in the UK that are backed by the shares of foreign (non-UK) companies.

Cum Dividend. (Latin: *cum* = with). Shares or bonds purchased cum dividend are entitled to receive the imminent, next dividend.

Dawn Raid. A rapid attempt by a company to purchase as many shares of another as it can, before its intention becomes clear. The intention is to launch a hostile bid for the second company, causing the latter's share price to rise steeply once the fact is known.

Daytrader. Investor who makes daily trades, usually via the Internet, to exploit small changes in price movements of shares.

Dead Cat Bounce. Short-lived revival in the share price of a company which has been rapidly declining in value.

Dealing. The process of buying or selling shares or other assets. Usually mediated by a broker, eg a stockbroker for share dealing.

Debenture. Interest-bearing stock, usually issued by private companies to raise money in return for a fixed rate of interest to the lender. The stock is secured against the assets of the company.

Deferred Shares. Shares that will pay a dividend only when certain conditions have been met. Many deferred shares passed their condition (eg date, profit level) years ago and are indistinguishable from ordinary shares.

Derivative. An asset which has, on or before a stated date, a claim on another asset. For example, a traded option has a claim on its underlying shares.

Dilution Levy. Charge levied on investors who sell unit trusts or OEICs, when too many shares are sold at once from the underlying fund.

Discount. Equal to the difference between the actual value of an asset and its lower market price. Seen mostly in connection with property and investment trusts.

Discretionary Service. Service offered by stockbrokers to handle an investor's share portfolio for him.

Disorderly Market. A market in a company's shares where information has leaked out unevenly, so that only some of the investors have full knowledge.

Distributor Bond. Insurance investment comprising underlying equities and bonds that distributes regular, tax-paid income with possibility of limited tax deferral.

Dividend. Payment made to shareholders by a company from its earnings (normally twice a year but may be more or less often).

Downside. Potential for an asset to decline in value.

Earnings. Profits made by a company averaged out over the number of shares in existence, to give earnings per share (EPS).

EBITDA. Earnings Before Interest, Tax, Depreciation and Amortisation. A fashionable and largely worthless measure of a company's ability to make money.

Efficient Market Hypothesis (EMH). Hypothesis which asserts that markets are efficient, so that prices of assets can never be cheap or dear in terms of investors' perceptions.

Emerging Markets. Stockmarkets in countries that are rapidly industrialising. Normally of high risk.

Enterprise Investment Scheme (EIS). Tax-favoured investment in the shares of small companies not yet listed on any stockmarket.

Equalisation. Repayment of part of price of a unit trust, to compensate for overpayment made for first dividend that was not received in full.

Equity. Another name for shares.

Ethical Fund. A fund which invests only in assets which do not break its stated rules of ethicality. For example, a fund which will not invest in any company involved in the manufacture of armaments.

Eurobond Market. Bond market for European governments and companies.

Exchange Traded Fund (ETF). Collective funds that track indices, guaranteed by institutions.

Ex-Dividend. (Latin: *ex* = out of). Shares sold without right to the next (imminent) dividend payment.

Exercise Price/Value. The price at which a derivative can be exchanged for the underlying asset.

Face Value. The stated value of an asset, frequently printed on it. Also referred to as 'nominal' or 'par' value.

Final Dividend. Dividend paid at the end of the company's financial year.

Fixed Interest Security. A bond paying a fixed rate of interest.

Flotation. Launch of a company onto the stockmarket, by the issue of shares.

Foreign Income Dividends (FIDs). Dividends paid out of income earned abroad, so that ACT could not be reclaimed by income tax-exempt investors. (Obsolete.)

Forward Contract. An arrangement to buy, or sell, assets at a future date. The contract normally has to be purchased.

Franked Income. Dividends or interest from which UK income tax has been deducted at the standard rate. The deduction was made at source and has been handed directly to the Inland Revenue.

Fund of Funds. A fund which invests its money in many other funds, the intention being to spread risk.

Futures. Contracts giving the purchaser the obligation to buy assets or commodities at a later date at an agreed price.

Gearing. Also known as leverage. Borrowing money in the expectation of investing it so as to provide a bigger profit than is needed to repay the interest on the debt.

Gilts. Bonds issued by the government to fund the National Debt. Widely believed to be the safest investment; ie the least likely to default on payment or go bankrupt.

Gilt Strips. Separation of capital values and income streams from selected gilts. The two parts may be purchased separately.

Gold. Yellow, heavy metal which does not rust or tarnish. Used since ancient times as a store of wealth, it can now only be bought in coin form by private investors in the UK.

Gold Standard. Paper money backed by conversion on demand into gold. Britain abandoned the gold standard in 1931. Its paper money is now backed only by government promises.

Gross. Income before tax is deducted.

Growth Stock. A company whose share price is expected to rise rapidly, in anticipation of a steep rise in profits.

Guaranteed Funds. Investment funds that guarantee to return most or all of an investment. The guarantee is only as valuable as the guarantor.

Hard Currency. Currency which does not fluctuate greatly in value.

Hedge. Investment made to have an opposite action to a previous investment. The hedge will make money if the original investment fails.

Hedge funds. Funds that usually hedge, but some have acquired notoriety for speculation with huge sums of borrowed money.

Hostile Bid. A bid by one company to take over another, which was made without the approval of the management of the second (target) company.

In-the-money. Options which can be exercised at once with profit on the striking value.

Independent Advisers. Advisers not tied to one specific financial institution, whose sole source of income is commissions on investments bought by customers, or fees paid by customers. They can recommend any type of investment.

Indices. Average values of the assets in a market, computed with a lesser or greater degree of complexity and/or sophistication.

Individual Savings Accounts (ISAs). New tax-free plan for shares, cash and life assurance, operated by a plan manager. Replaces the older PEPs and TESSAs.

Inflation. The rise in the value of prices of the same items over a period of time. Generally attributed to the circulation of too much money.

Insider Trading. Use of privileged (ie not publicly known) information to achieve an advantage in trading of assets. Now illegal in the UK.

Institutions. Large, well-respected and influential companies specialising in an area (in this case, finance). Financial institutions include banks, unit trusts and pension companies.

Interest. Money paid by a borrower to a lender in exchange for the use of the lender's money. Interest is usually paid once or twice a year at a rate which may be varied by the lender, and the lender will normally expect to get back at some future date all the money he lent.

Interim Dividend. Dividend paid on profits part-way through a company's financial year.

Introduction. Sale of privately held, existing shares in a company to the public, normally to institutions.

Investment. Purchase of an asset in the expectation that the asset will rise in value. (The colloquial expression, 'I invested in a new carpet' is incorrect, unless the carpet is expected to rise in value.)

Investment Company with Variable Capital (ICVC). Regulated UK collective investment scheme. See also OEIC.

Investment Trusts. Companies which invest principally in the shares of other companies.

Issue Price. Price at which new shares are issued.

Issued Share Capital. The nominal, or face value, sum of the shares issued by a company. *Cf*. **market price**.

Junior Debt. Borrowings which will be repaid by a bankrupt company after the more important borrowings (**senior debt**) have been repaid – but only if sufficient money remains. See **mezzanine finance**.

Junk Bonds. Junior debt which has been packaged into bundles and can be traded on a stockmarket.

Letter of Acceptance. Temporary certificate of ownership of newly issued shares.

Leverage. See **Gearing**.

Limits. Bounds between which a purchase or sale of securities is permitted by the investor.

Liquidation. Termination of a company by selling all its business or assets. Often described as 'winding-up'.

Liquidity. The ease with which an asset can be turned into cash.

Listing. See **Quote**.

Loan Notes. Interest-bearing bonds issued usually for the purpose of deferring CGT (shares are exchanged for loan notes).

Loan Stock. Fixed interest bonds, issued by companies. Unlike debentures, loan stock is not always secured on the assets of the company.

Long Position. Buying securities with borrowed money, in the expectation that their price will rise.

Longs. Gilts which will be repaid in more than 15 years' time.

Main Market. Companies which have met stringent financial criteria in order to be listed by the London Stock Exchange.

Margin. A proportion of the cost of the purchase of an asset put up by the investor as an advance payment.

Market (The). Place where assets are traded. The London Stock Exchange now trades shares and other securities over a complicated network of computer screens.

Market Makers. Professionals (mostly institutions) at the Stock Exchange who buy and sell shares, holding them on their own books in the interval between buying and selling.

Market Price. The current value of a freely traded commodity, such as shares. The market value of a company is obtained by multiplying the price of its shares by the number of shares in existence.

Marketability. The ease with which shares, or other assets, can be traded between buyers and sellers.

Matched Bargain. Agreement, usually mediated through stockbrokers or market makers, to bring together a buyer and a seller of poorly-marketable shares.

Mature Industry. Industry from which no further growth (in technology or number of customers) is expected.

Merger. Joining together of two companies, without a formal takeover.

Mezzanine Finance. Borrowings from a lender which carry a higher risk, and higher interest yield (to the lender) than other company debt. See **junior debt**.

Middle Price. Price half-way between the bid and offer prices of an asset.

Modern Portfolio Theory (MPT). Theoretical method of optimising the balance between risk and performance from an investor's assets to match his requirements.

Net. Income after tax has been deducted.

Net Asset Value (NAV). Value after adding together all assets and subtracting all liabilities.

New Issue. Shares sold for the first time by a company.

New Time. Late purchase of shares at the end of an account, to be paid for at the end of the next account. (Obsolete.)

Nil-paid. No money yet paid to buy an asset. The right to buy the asset is valuable, and can be sold as 'nil-paid'. The term is usually applied to rights issues.

Nominal Value. See **face value**.

Nominee Account. Assets held by an agent on behalf of the original investor. See also **Crest**.

Normal Market Size (NMS). Newly introduced measure of the marketability of shares.

OFEX. Market in very small companies made by brokers J. P. Jenkins. Now regulated by London Stock Exchange.

Off Market. Trades carried out without going through a recognised stockmarket. For example, a private deal to buy and sell shares between two friends.

Off-Shore. Refers to any base outside the mainland of the UK, and not subject to British tax laws.

Offer Price. Selling price offered by a broker. The price which an investor will pay to buy shares (or other assets).

Offer for Sale. New shares sold by a company at a fixed price to the general public.

Offer for Tender. New shares sold by a company to the highest bidders.

Open-Ended Investment Companies (OEICs). Pooled investment funds, intermediate between unit and investment trusts. Regulated by company law, often with several share types.

Options. Provide the opportunity to purchase or sell assets at an agreed price at a later date. Options normally have to be purchased.

Order-Driven Market. Stockmarket where buyers and sellers deal directly with one another (via computer), rather than through the agency of market makers.

Orderly Market. Market in which buyers and sellers trade in full possession of knowledge about the value of the underlying assets.

Out-of-the-Money. Options which cannot at present be exercised with profit at the striking price.

Over subscribed. More people applied for shares in a new issue than there were shares to meet the demand.

Over The Counter (OTC) Market. Limited market made by some dealers in shares of minor companies which do not match the requirements needed for a full listing on the AIM or London Stock Exchange. OTC stocks are now very rare in the UK, but are more common abroad for companies which do not qualify for a listing on their national stock exchange.

Par Value. See **face value**.

Pari Passu. Shares (or other assets) which rank equally with similar assets issued by the same company.

Penny Shares. Shares of undefined, low individual value. Typically the share price will be less than 40p.

Personal Equity Plan (PEP). Tax-free fund, operated by a plan manager, in which to hold a restricted range of investments in shares or bonds. New PEPs cannot be opened.

Physical Delivery. Hand over assets in settlement instead of their cash equivalent.

PIBS. Permanent Income-Bearing Shares. Actually un-dated bonds issued by a building society.

Placing. Non-public sale of new shares in a company to selected investors, typically the financial institutions.

Poison Pills. Measures taken by a company to make it less attractive target to be taken over by a raider.

Pooled Funds. Funds which invest in a range of assets, normally of a similar type (*eg* a unit trust investing in shares). This spreads the individual risk of owning each share, giving an averaged performance.

Portfolio. A collection of assets, not necessarily of the same type.

Pound-Cost Averaging. Buying assets at regular intervals, in order to even out ups and downs in the price of those assets.

Preference Shares. Shares which will receive dividends before the 'ordinary' shares (but after debentures and loan stocks), in the event of a shortfall in the ability of the company to pay dividends. Preference shares usually provide a higher (often fixed) yield than ordinary shares.

Premium. The extent to which the market price of an asset exceeds that of its real value. See **discount**.

Price Earnings (P/E) Ratio. Equal to the share price of a company divided by its EPS and providing a measure of how well the share price represents the ability of the company to generate earnings.

Prior Charges. The order in which payments are made by a company to the owners of its bonds and shares.

Privatisations. Sale of nationalised industries by the government to the public.

Program Trading. Use of automated (computer) programs set to initiate purchases or sales of assets when predetermined price limits are met.

Prospectus. Document which lists the financial and other details of a company which is seeking to issue new shares. The publication of a prospectus is now a legal requirement before issues of shares and company bonds.

Provisional Allotment. Temporary certificate of ownership of shares issued under a rights issue, pending payment of the purchase price of the shares.

PTM (Panel of Takeovers and Mergers). Oversees company takeovers, funded by £1 levy on large share purchases. See **Takeover Code**.

Quote/Quotations. A company is said to be 'quoted' (or 'listed') if it can be traded on one of the two London exchanges (the AIM or the Main Market of the London Stock Exchange). The Exchange provides a quotation for its current share price.

Raider. A company (or, rarely, a wealthy individual) which makes a hostile bid for another company.

Ramping. Artificially boosting the price of an asset. For an example, see **stabilisation**.

Rationalisation. Making a business more efficient (frequently a euphemism for closing down factories or stores).

Recovery Stock. A company whose share price is depressed as a result of poor profits, but which is expected to return to normal profitability.

Redemption Date. The date on which stocks are repaid, usually at par.

Redemption Yield. The overall yield which an investor will get if he holds a bond to the redemption date (inclusive of gains in the value of the bond).

Registration. Process by which changes in ownership of shares are recorded, normally by the registrars of the company concerned.

Renunciation. Giving up your right to own some shares, usually in connection with a temporary certificate of ownership.

Reverse Convertible Bond (RCB). Bond that can be repaid with a predetermined number of shares, instead of with cash.

Reverse Takeover. A company without a quotation buys up a company with a quotation.

Rights Issue. Issue of new shares for cash to existing investors by a company which has already issued shares.

Risk – Market. The risk that the whole stockmarket will fall steeply in value (see **crash**).

Risk – Specific. The risk that an individual company will go bankrupt, rendering its shares worthless.

Rolling System. System of settling share dealings soon after they occur, instead of at the end of the account. The current system allows 3 days.

Roll-up Fund. A fund which reinvests its income (dividends or interest) by buying more units of the same fund. This can result in rapid compound growth, especially if the income is received free of tax.

Rule 4.2/Rule 535. Now obsolete Stock Exchange rules that permitted matched bargains to be made in many poorly traded stocks and shares. Replaced by Rule 2.1.

Scrip Issue. Issue of new shares at no cost by a company to its shareholders (a capitalisation issue is similar). The share price of the company is adjusted to compensate for the increased number of shares in existence.

SEAQ. Computer screen-based Stock Exchange system showing quotations from market makers.

SEATS. Stock Exchange Alternative Trading System, for shares in little-traded companies.

Securities. Assets traded on an exchange (eg shares, bonds and gilts).

Securitisation. Conversion of a stream of cash receipts into a security that can be sold. See, eg, **gilt strips**.

Self-invested Pension Plan (SIPP). Pension fund administered by pensions provider for the investor, who makes the investment decisions.

Senior Debt. Loans made to a company which will be repaid first in the event that the company becomes bankrupt. See **junior debt**.

SETS (Stock Exchange Electronic Trading Service). A new market where buyers and sellers deal directly with one another (via computer), rather than through the agency of market makers. See also **Order-Driven Market**.

Settlement. The investor pays or receives cash in respect of his purchases or sales of assets.

Shaking the Tree. Process by which a market maker deliberately upsets the price of shares in a quietly-trading company in order to encourage investment activity.

Share Certificate. A certificate naming the investor as the owner of the shares. These certificates have no direct value. That is, they cannot be used as a substitute for cash (contrast bearer certificates). See also **Crest**.

Shell Stocks. Quoted companies whose main business has virtually ended, awaiting an injection of new ideas or a reverse takeover.

Short Position. Selling securities which are not owned, in the hope of buying them back at a cheaper price at a later date.

Shorts. Gilts which will be repaid in less than five years' time.

Splitting. Giving up part of your right to own some shares. See **Renunciation**.

Spread. Difference between bid and offer prices.

Spread-betting. Betting that the current share price of a company or index will rise or fall beyond the spread.

Stabilisation. Short-lived purchases by professional investors of the newly issued shares of a company in order to maintain an initial, artificially high price.

Stakeholder Pension. Tax-favoured pension scheme with maximum one per cent administration charge.

Stag. Investor who buys shares in a new issue with the intention of selling them at a profit as soon as they have been received.

'Stock and Put' strategy. Guaranteed performance from a share portfolio by holding mostly shares with protection against a market fall through the use of put options.

Stocks. Strictly speaking, securities paying a fixed rate of interest. Now often used as a synonym for the shares of a company.

Stop-loss/Stop-profit. Desist from holding a security when its value has fallen or risen to a preset limit.

Striking Price. Price at which an agreement between buyer and seller is made.

Striking Price (Traded Options). Price at which the underlying security can be bought or sold.

Suspension. The Stock Exchange will no longer trade the company's shares (private trades may still be possible).

Synthetics. That combination of borrowed (lent) money and shares which, after allowing for interest, is equal to the value of the call (put) option in the same stock.

Takeover. Purchase of one company by another.

Takeover Code/Panel. Government body which provides the regulations (the code) for one company to make a takeover bid for another.

Talisman. Computerised system for transferring ownership of most shares. Largely replaced by Crest.

Tap Stock. Government re-issue of gilts which were not fully taken up by investors on the day of issue.

Taurus. A former Stock Exchange system for registering purchases and sales of shares (abandoned in 1993). Taurus was a complex, electronic nominee account.

Tax Exempt Special Savings Accounts (TESSAs). Tax-free roll-up fund for investment of cash with a bank or building society. New

TESSAs cannot be opened.

Technical Analysis. See **chart analysis**.

Technology, Media, Telephone (TMT) Stocks. Shares in high-technology companies that were fashionable from 1999-2001.

Temporary Certificate. Certificate issued pending despatch of the 'definitive' (final) certificate. Usually encountered as a letter of acceptance (of a share offer) or as a provisional allotment of shares (rights issue).

Tender. Bid to buy stocks at an auction.

Tied Advisers. Advisers tied to one company or investment product. They cannot give advice on other investments.

Time Deposit. Deposit which cannot be withdrawn until the stated date.

Touch. Difference between the best and worst dealing prices quoted by different market makers. The term is often used synonymously for 'spread'.

Tracking Stock. Stock which tracks the performance of a subsidiary of a major listed company.

Traded Options. Options which can be traded on a recognised stockmarket. See **options**.

Tradepoint. Alternative order-driven market for virtually all shares. Used predominantly by institutions.

Transfer. Substitution of the old owner on a share register by the new. Form giving title to the new owner.

Treasury Bills. Bonds issued by Government for 1–3 months only.

Trustee. Independent supervisor of a fund.

Unbundling. Breaking up a conglomerate into its component parts, in the belief that the value of the parts is greater than the value of the whole.

Unconditional Bid. Offer to purchase the shares of a company which is made to the shareholders of the company regardless of how many accept.

Undertaking for Collective Investment in Transferable Securities (UCITS). European equivalent of an OEIC or ICVC.

Underwriter. Investor or institution who agrees to buy any unsold shares remaining after a new issue. The underwriter receives a fee for this service.

Unfranked Income. Dividend or interest income which is not taxed at source by the Inland Revenue. However, unfranked income frequently has tax deducted by its UK agent before being sent on to the investor.

Unit Trust. A fund which manages numerous assets, mostly of one type (eg shares), and whose overall value is divided into units which can be bought by investors. The fund is subject to the supervision of a trustee and government legislation.

Universal Stock Future. Tradeable futures for individual companies. See **futures**.

Unlisted Securities Market (USM). Former market for quoted companies which had less stringent financial requirements than those of the main market.

Unquoted. Stocks and shares not registered on any authorised stock exchange. See **quoted**.

Upside. Potential for an asset to increase in value.

Venture Capital. Money used to start up a new business.

Venture Capital Trusts (VCTs). Tax-favoured pooled-fund for investment in the shares of small companies not yet listed on any stockmarket.

Volume. Number of stocks traded in a single time span (normally one day).

Warrants. Derivatives providing the right to buy shares in the underlying company at a fixed price before a fixed, future expiry date. Not to be confused with options. 'Covered' warrants are backed by institutions instead of the underlying company.

White Knight. A friendly company that will counter-bid for a company which is the target of a hostile bid.

Wind-up. See **liquidation**.

Yield. The dividend of a share, expressed as a percentage of the share price.

Yield Gap. Difference between the average yield of gilts and the average yield of shares.

Yield Ratio. The average yield of gilts divided by the average yield of shares.

Further Reading

It takes years of experience to build up a good knowledge of share investment. Gaps in this knowledge can be filled by reading a number of indispensable publications.

The *Financial Times*, especially on Saturdays when there is good coverage of items of interest to personal investors.

Investors' Chronicle, published weekly and a mine of knowledge and factual information about companies. The information is very well indexed, both weekly and quarterly, so that the magazines form a major reference source. Subscription Department, PO Box 423, Sittingbourne, Kent ME9 8FA. (*www.investorschronicle.co.uk*).

The Complete Guide to Investment Trusts, the handbook of Investment Trusts from their official body, the Association of Investment Trust Companies (see Useful Addresses).

How to Make Money with Charts, T. H. Stewart, Woodhead-Faulkner, 1986. This gives an excellent account of technical analysis – for believers only.

Economist magazine, published weekly, and giving an excellent overview of the economic climate and academic theories.

Property and Money, M. Brett, Estates Gazette Publishers, 1990. This covers the basics of investment in property, and can be obtained directly from the publishers at 151 Wardour Street, London W1V 4BN.

Private Investors' Directory. A guide to stockbrokers prepared to act for private clients. Obtained from the Stock Exchange (see Useful Addresses).

The *Inland Revenue* publishes many pamphlets on tax and share/ bond dealing. Ask at your local branch. (Taxation changes so frequently that only the briefest overview can be given in this book.)

The Investor's Guide to Emerging Markets, M. Mobius, Pitman

Publishing. A book by one of the Templeton trust managers.

How to Make Money from Property: The best-selling and expert guide to property investment, Adam Walker, How To Books.

Making Money from Letting: How to buy and let residential property for profit, Moira Stewart, How To Books.

A Simple Guide to Pensions: Discover how to solve the pension puzzle and provide for a comfortable retirement, John Claxton, How To Books.

Useful Addresses

Association of Investment Trust Companies (AITC): Durrant House, 8–13 Chiswell Street, London EC1Y 4YY. Tel: (020) 7282 5555. Website: www.aitc.co.uk

Bank of England, Debt Management Office, Cheapside House, Cheapside, London EC2V 6BB. Tel: (020) 7862 6500. For information about gilts.

Barclays Capital Ltd, 5 The North Colonnade, Canary Wharf, London E14 4BB. Tel: (020) 7623 2323. Major London stockbrokers. Suppliers of the long-term comparative share-gilt-building society data used in this book.

Best Investment Publishing Co, 20 Masons Yard, London SW1Y 6BU. Tel: (020) 7321 0100. Website: bestInvest.co.uk Monitors BES and EIS investments.

Building Society Association (BSA), 3 Savile Row, London W1S 3PB. Tel: (020) 7437 0655. Website: www.bsa.org.uk.

Charles Schwab (Europe) Stockbrokers (formerly Sharelink), PO Box 1063, Birmingham B3 3ET. Tel: 0870 601 8888. Website: www.schwab-europe.com.

City Index Ltd, 4th Floor, Park House, 16 Finsbury Circus, London EC2M 7PQ. Tel: (020) 7550 8599. Website: www.cityindex.co.uk.

Companies House, 21 Bloomsbury Street, London WC1B 3XD. Tel: (020) 7253 9393. Also at Crown Way, Cardiff CF4 3UZ. Tel: (029) 2038 8588. For information about companies.

Debt Management Office. See Bank of England.

Financial Services Authority (FSA), 25 The North Colonnade, Canary Wharf, London E14 5HS. Tel: (020) 7676 1000. Website: www.fsa.gov.uk.

Flaxdale Printers Ltd, 5 Malvern Drive, Woodford Green, Essex IG8 0JR. Tel: (020) 8504 6862. Publishers of *Investment Trusts* magazine.

Halifax ShareDealing Ltd., Trinity Road, Halifax, HX1 2RG. Tel: (0870) 24 11114. Website: www.halifax.co.uk/share-dealing. Discount broker providing a very cheap, nominee service.

Hemscott, 2nd Floor, Finsbury Towers, 103–105 Burnhill Row, London EC1Y 8TY. Tel: (020) 7496 0055.

I. G. Index Ltd, Friars House, 157–168 Blackfriars Road, London SE1 8EZ. Tel: (0800) 195 3100. Website: www.igindex.co.uk.

Inland Revenue, Public Enquiry Room, West Wing, Room 62, Somerset House, London WC2R 1LB. Tel: (020) 7438 6622.

Investment Management Association (IMA), 65 Kingsway, London WC2B 6TD. Tel: (020) 7831 0898.

Investors' Compensation Scheme. See Financial Services Authority

LIFFE, Cannon Bridge House, 1 Cousin Lane, London EC4R 3XX. Tel: (020) 7623 0444. Website: www.liffe.com.

M&G Customer Services, M&G House, Victoria Road, Chelmsford CM1 1FB. Tel: (0800) 389 8601. Purveyors of the very first unit trusts and still one of the most highly regarded unit trust managers with a wide range of trusts. A free Yearbook of M&G unit trusts is published every year.

National Register of Fee-Based Advisers. A guide to local, independent fee-based advisers. c/o *Investors' Chronicle* (see Further Reading).

OyezForms Publishing, Oyez House, PO Box 55, 7 Spa Road, London SE16 3QQ.

Proshare, Library Chambers, 13–14 Basinghall Street, London EC2V 5BQ. Tel: (020) 7220 1750. Website: proshareclubs.co.uk

Securities and Futures Authority (SFA), See Financial Services Authority.

The Stock Exchange, Old Broad Street, London EC2N 1HP. Tel: (020) 7797 1000 (for general queries and lists of stockbrokers). (020) 7849 0000 (for CREST). Website: www.LondonStockExchange.-com

Index